D1104735

Virtual Orientalism

Virtual Orientalism

Asian Religions and American Popular Culture

JANE NAOMI IWAMURA

OXFORD
UNIVERSITY PRESS

2011

OXFORD
UNIVERSITY PRESS

Oxford University Press, Inc., publishes works that further
Oxford University's objective of excellence
in research, scholarship, and education.

Oxford   New York
Auckland   Cape Town   Dar es Salaam   Hong Kong   Karachi
Kuala Lumpur   Madrid   Melbourne   Mexico City   Nairobi
New Delhi   Shanghai   Taipei   Toronto

With offices in
Argentina   Austria   Brazil   Chile   Czech Republic   France   Greece
Guatemala   Hungary   Italy   Japan   Poland   Portugal   Singapore
South Korea   Switzerland   Thailand   Turkey   Ukraine   Vietnam

Copyright © 2011 by Oxford University Press, Inc.

Published by Oxford University Press, Inc.
198 Madison Avenue, New York, New York 10016

www.oup.com

Oxford is a registered trademark of Oxford University Press

All rights reserved. No part of this publication may be reproduced,
stored in a retrieval system, or transmitted, in any form or by any means,
electronic, mechanical, photocopying, recording, or otherwise,
without the prior permission of Oxford University Press.

Library of Congress Cataloging-in-Publication Data
Iwamura, Jane Naomi.
Virtual orientalism : Asian religions and American popular culture / Jane Naomi Iwamura.
    p.   cm.
ISBN 978-0-19-973860-1; 978-0-19-973861-8 (pbk.)
1. United States—Religion—20th century. 2. Monasticism and religious orders—Asia—Influence.
3. Suzuki, Daisetz Teitaro, 1870–1966—Influence. 4. Mahesh Yogi, Maharishi—Influence.
5. Kung fu (Television program)—Influence. 6. Orientalism—United States—History—20th
century. 7. Popular culture—United States—History—20th century. 8. Popular culture—Religious
aspects—History—20th century. I. Title.
BL2525.I92   2011
200.95'0973—dc22   2010017575

NOTE ON IMAGE USE
Though the images in this volume may be subject to copyright, their inclusion qualifies as
Fair Use under United States copyright laws, for the following reasons:
1. Images are only being used for informational purposes;
2. Their inclusion adds significantly to the argument because the photo and its historical
significance are the object of discussion in the volume;
3. The volume provides critical commentary on the images, film, or event; they are not solely
included for purposes of illustration.

Printed in the United States of America
on acid-free paper

For Dad, Des, Declan, and Siân

Contents

Acknowledgments

This book, like many others, has been a journey. From the start, I have been aided in that journey by the generosity and kindness of family, friends, and colleagues. Although I cannot possibly recount the many individuals who have sustained me along the way and to whom I am grateful, several bear mention. *Virtual Orientalism* emerged from my dissertation, written at the University of California at Berkeley. Judith Butler, Margaret R. Miles, Michael Mascuch, Sau-ling Wong, and Rudy Busto, as well as Elizabeth Goodstein, Young Mi Angela Pak, and Vivian Chin, were instrumental in giving the project its tenor and shape. The Pacific Asian North American and Asian Women in Theology and Ministry (PANAAWTM) and the UC Berkeley Townsend Center for the Humanities Working Group on Asian American Religions offered opportunities to present the work in its formative stages. Bruce Forbes and Jeffrey Mahan also believed in the project early on; their volume, *Religion and Popular Culture in America*, continues to offer my early work a wonderful home.

Major revisions of the project were undertaken at the University of Southern California and New York University. My colleagues in the School of Religion and the Department of American Studies & Ethnicity at USC have provided me a stimulating and supportive intellectual environment. Dorinne Kondo (and students in her graduate seminar), Lon Kurashige, and Viet Nguyen each read the entire manuscript and provided invaluable feedback. As a postdoctoral fellow at the NYU Center for Religion and Media, I also received generous support and assistance and would like to thank Angela Zito, Faye Ginsburg, Greg Grieve, and Heather Hendershot.

The editing prowess of Nick Street is evident in this book. The project has also been greatly enhanced by the skills of Myung Shin and Dianna Truong—two marvelous undergraduate research assistants.

I have been fortunate to present parts of the manuscript at the USC Literary, Visual and Material Culture Initiative, the Institute of Signifying Scriptures at the Claremont Graduate University, and the Asian American Studies Department at Cornell University, and I thank Richard Meyer, Vincent Wimbush and Shelly Sun-Wong for their interest.

The book would not have been possible without my colleagues and dearest friends—Janelle Wong, Macarena Gomez-Barris, Roberto Lint Sagarena and Anna Harlan, Cynthia Young, Sarita See, and Judith Jackson Fossett—who provided endless encouragement, a constant sounding board, laughter, and good cheer throughout. I am continually inspired by their example, both as scholars and as incredibly humane individuals. Luís León, David Kyuman Kim, Carolyn Chen, Russell Jeung, James Kyung-Jin Lee, Marie Lo, Sandra Oh, Jinny Huh, Crystal Parikh, Min Song, Paul Spickard, and my friends at APARRI—their abiding friendship has meant the world. Michael Masatsugu, Nithila Peter, Sylvia Chan-Malik, Mina Shin, and Sharon Suh generously shared their works in progress. I would also like to thank Lynn Schofield Clark, Ruth Wilson Gilmore, Pierrette Hondagneu-Sotelo, Nancy Lutkehaus, David Roman, Judith Weisenfeld, and Duncan Williams for their kindness and influential example. Rudy Busto merits special recognition for his keen intellect, mentorship, and friendship throughout the years. (And I also thank his many students, who have read my work in class.)

I am very grateful to Cynthia Read and Charlotte Steinhardt at Oxford University Press, and the production staff (Preetha Baskaran, Joy Matkowski, and Karen Kwak) for their expert hand, as well as Kimberly Connor for her enthusiastic encouragement. I also wish to thank Ken Wissoker, Leo Chavez, and Lynn Schwartz Dodd, whose generosity in terms of advice and equipment allowed the project to move forward. And to Tom Haar and Michael Goldberg for sharing their images and work.

My extended family—Malcolm Smith, Mick and Melanie Smith, and Sam, Tess, Jimmy, and Laurie, and especially Susan Broussard and Kieran Hannon—have kept me grounded throughout the process; their presence and love have been invaluable.

The journey I would take with the Oriental Monk began years before I began my research, and its impact on my personal life remains steady. I have memories of watching *Kung Fu* in the early 1970s with my father, a lover of

Westerns. Halfway around the world, my husband, Desmond, was watching as well. While I could recall only vague images, Des remembers the show's impact on him, growing up as a boy in England. Today, we watch our son, Declan, as he imitates kung fu moves and learns life lessons from television cartoons and movies, such as *Kung Fu Panda*, that continue Virtual Orientalism's work. His sister, Siân, too young to understand these things, will no doubt have her own encounter in the not-so-distant future. I thank my beautiful family (including my mother Mitsuko, and Des's mother, Mary, who would not see the publication of this book) for their love, support, and inspiration, as well as the incredible joy they bring. This book is written for them, especially Declan and Siân. While I can't help enjoying my children's delight in popular culture, I hope this book will one day disrupt their pleasure (at least for a moment) and encourage them to think critically about the representations they have come to love and embrace.

Virtual Orientalism

I

Introduction

In the spring of 1950, Daisetz Teitaro Suzuki arrived in the
continental United States for his third extended stay. Like his visits in
1897 and 1939, his arrival went largely unnoticed. Although the aged
scholar, at mid-century, was an author of international stature, his
work was primarily known to those in the West who held an esoteric
interest in Japanese religions and culture. All that would change
during his eight-year residency in the United States.

Through the new option of commercial air travel, Suzuki's status
as a global figure would be consolidated by side trips to Mexico,
Europe, and cities throughout the United States. The influence of this
small, unassuming Japanese man was spread not only by plane but
also by print; his image would be featured in the pages of *Time*,
Newsweek, and the *New Yorker*. By the time Suzuki left the United
States in 1958, he was no longer an obscure figure but someone whose
name and likeness would forever be associated with Zen in the West.

Two decades later, an American television audience viewed the
final episode of the popular television series *Kung Fu* on the evening
of June 28, 1975. Dubbed TV's first "Eastern Western," *Kung Fu*
chronicled the fugitive existence of a mixed-race Shaolin monk,
Kwai Chang Caine, on the nineteenth-century American frontier.
The series dealt with Caine's transpacific exile, his encounter with
European and Asian immigrants, and his flashbacks to his life in
China. The show was transnational in nature in terms of not only
the plot but also production. *Kung Fu* drew on the talent of Jewish

American writers, Chinese martial arts advisors, and Asian American actors. The success of the series was also buttressed by the growing popularity of martial arts films, both homegrown and internationally made. The show's run was brief—only three seasons—but it would remain vivid in the minds of American television viewers as a novel introduction to Chinese spirituality, and its characters would endure as pop culture icons.

The quarter century between Suzuki's arrival and *Kung Fu*'s departure was a time of change and ferment in U.S. religious history and in U.S. culture in general. This period marked an increase in popular awareness of Asian religions in the United States, as Americans had their first widespread introduction to Buddhism, Hinduism, and Asian spiritualities. The role of mass media was central to this process. Americans triumphed in the Dalai Lama's escape from Tibet in the pages of *Life* and despaired in Malcolm Browne's gut-wrenching image of Vietnamese monk Thich Quang Duc's self-immolation, circulated widely by the Associated Press. In lighter fare, aspects of Eastern spirituality seeped into weekly magazines, book reviews, and television programs. An American audience could follow along as the Beats sought enlightenment "on the road," and the Beatles pursued it in India. These pop culture moments broadened Americans' attitudes about Asian religions and both reflected and shaped the mind-set of a generation.

One could certainly view this period as the opening of the American religious mind or the latest in a series of American Great Awakenings. Will Herberg in *Protestant, Catholic, Jew*, the oft-cited classic published in 1955, chronicles the movement of Catholicism and Judaism into the American mainstream. While the ethnic consciousness of European immigrant groups slowly faded away, religious identity became more and more significant, according to Herberg, creating a place for Catholicism and Judaism as distinctly American religions. The growing acceptance of these once marginalized religious traditions was promoted by ecumenical activists and liberal scholars and also shepherded along by the popular press.[1] For instance, the lived religion of Jews and Catholics appeared in the pages of magazines such as *Life* for the first time in the 1950s, marking a newfound respect and recognition for these religious faiths. In similar fashion, Buddhism, Hinduism, and other Asian religious traditions gained more positive, widespread exposure in the 1950s, 1960s, and early 1970s. Popular media documented these traditions not only as they were practiced in Asia but also as they were transplanted, transformed, and taken up by Anglo practitioners in the United States. Images of college students "tuned in" to the practice of meditation or shots of Western celebrities pursuing their spiritual journeys abroad made for eye-catching copy and also served to foster a wider acceptance of Asian religions in the West.

If Herberg's book had been written two decades later, it might have been titled *Protestant, Catholic, Jew, Buddhist, Hindu*. But such a book has yet to be penned. While scholarly and popular accounts—with their focus on religious pluralism—gesture toward this viewpoint, their claims are not wholly convincing. Americans, for the most part, still rally under the monotheistic conception of "one nation under God." Hindus are mistaken for Muslims,[2] and Buddhism is taken as a Hollywood trend. At best, images and talk of Asian religions serve as exotica. The apparent openness, tolerance, and fascination that mark Americans' engagement with Asian spirituality have not yet translated into a full embrace of Asian religions. Why is this the case, especially given Americans' wider exposure to foreign cultures, the transformed religious landscape in the United States, and the sea change in Americans' attitudes toward Buddhism and Hinduism?[3]

What may seem like a paradox—or at the very least a diminished sense of progress—has to do with the ways in which an American audience came to know and, in many cases, embrace Asian religions. Growing tolerance toward Asian peoples and cultures was fostered in a mass-mediated environment in which the role of the visual image took on increasing importance. While this environment allowed a popular engagement with Asian religious traditions, it also relied on and reinforced certain racialized notions of Asianness and Asian religiosity. These notions form patterns of representation that, because they are linked to such positive images, go unchallenged and unseen.

The pages that follow offer close readings of the images of three key Oriental Monk figures that appeared in popular magazines, television, and film. In the quarter of a century from 1950 to 1975, D. T. Suzuki, the Maharishi Mahesh Yogi, and Kwai Chang Caine in the television series *Kung Fu* each made his appearance on the American scene and gave a mainstream American audience an unprecedented foray into the Asian religious world. While D. T. Suzuki would have a significant impact on a high-culture audience of intellectuals, university students, and cultured readers through his writings on Zen and Japanese culture, he enjoyed minor celebrity in the late 1950s as Beats and elites entertained a Buddhist worldview through his words and certainly his presence. With the Maharishi Mahesh Yogi, Americans would travel further into the world of "Oriental" mysticism and culture as the American press followed the Beatles and other well-known personalities on their trek to Rishikesh in pursuit of enlightenment and release in the 1960s. Popular media would make accessible in virtually sensuous form spiritual worlds that were once accessible in the mind's eye only through the literary word and imagination. The connection would be made even more immediate and widespread with the television series *Kung Fu* in the early 1970s, as the show's protagonist, Kwai

Chang Caine, and his monk teachers entered American living rooms each week. Here, the camera tracked the appearance of these fictional monk figures and imaginatively presented their religious perspective. Television producers and directors harnessed the full potential of the moving image and, through novel use of shots, flashback, and slow-motion edits, revealed what they understood as the inner world of the show's characters. *Kung Fu* would also concretize a narrative of cross-cultural encounter that powerfully defines Americans' relationship and views of Asian religions to the present day.

Americans' sense of Asian religions is figured by real-life personalities such as D. T. Suzuki and the Maharishi Mahesh and imaginatively represented in fictional offerings such as *Kung Fu*. We "know" each of these figures not only because we understand his views and admire his actions but also because we are deeply—even unconsciously—familiar with what he represents and the role that he plays. In U.S. popular culture, he is immediately transformed into a type of *icon*—the icon of the *Oriental Monk*—onto which we project our assumptions, fears, and hopes.[4] Although the Oriental Monk has appeared to us through the various media vehicles of American pop culture, we recognize him as the representative of an otherworldly (though perhaps not entirely alien) spirituality that draws from the ancient wellsprings of "Eastern" civilization and culture. And as Americans' current love affair with such figures as the Dalai Lama attests, the representation of this icon has only gained in popularity and impact. To get a sense of what makes these personalities so effective and affecting, we need to understand the history of this particular symbol and how it has been used both to express and transform our sense of Asian religions.

The term Oriental Monk is used as a critical concept and is meant to cover a wide range of religious figures (gurus, bhikkhus, sages, swamis, sifus, healers, masters) from a variety of ethnic backgrounds (Japanese, Chinese, Indian, Tibetan). Although the range of individual figures points to a heterogeneous field of encounter, all of them are subjected to a homogeneous representational effect as they are absorbed by popular consciousness through mediated culture. Racialization (more correctly, "orientalization") serves to blunt the distinctiveness of particular persons and figures. Indeed, the recognition of any Eastern spiritual guide, real or fictional, is predicated on his conformity to general features that are paradigmatically encapsulated in the icon of the Oriental Monk: his spiritual commitment, his calm demeanor, his Asian face, his manner of dress, and—most obviously—his peculiar gendered character. Although the figure is easily recognizable today, the Oriental Monk did not miraculously appear from out of nowhere. Rather, we have been primed for his appearance: trained to identify him from knowledge of his character, which can be traced to a series of historical encounters and imaginative engagements.

The critical perspective that I develop to investigate the icon of the Oriental Monk in American popular culture is informed by the work of Edward Said. In his book *Orientalism*, Said articulates a network of representations "framed by a whole set of forces that brought the Orient into Western learning, Western consciousness, and later, Western empire." As a "created body of theory and practice," Orientalism divides the world into "two unequal halves, Orient and Occident." Its "detailed logic [is] governed not simply by empirical reality but by a battery of desires, repressions, investments and projections," as well as a "whole series of 'interests.'" Hence, rather than offering perspicuous insight into its Oriental object, this system of representation reveals much about the Occidental subjectivity from which it emerges.[5]

Unlike its British and French predecessors, this new form of American Orientalism is more covert than its predecessors. Much of this has to do with the media through which it is now deployed: photography, film, television, and other electronic media. Gone are the days of direct colonial rule; the United States achieves hegemonic strength through channels that appear benign on their surface. This is not to say that the regime of knowledge these channels support is any less powerful. Indeed, in many ways it is more so, as images of the Orient become deeply embedded in a popular imagination that looks to the magazine page and to the big and small screens for products that are ready for immediate consumption. As Said points out, these new channels of communication rely on "more and more standardized molds," further reinforcing Orientalism's hold on Western imagination by limiting alternative possibilities.[6]

The prevalence of this type of cultural stereotyping by visual forms of media is an important element of what I will call *Virtual Orientalism*. The term *virtual* is often associated with computer-simulated environments, such as virtual reality. While the conventional use of virtual reality took root in the late 1980s as the potential of the digital became more fully realized and computers more accessible to the everyday consumer, the type of experiential engagement that such technology has fostered was already encouraged by mechanical forms of visual reproduction—most notably the camera. These forms train the consumer to prefer visual representations, and the visual nature of the image lends the representation an immediacy and ontological gravity that words cannot. Thus, the Asian sage is not simply someone we imagine, but his presence materializes in the photograph or moving picture before us. Buttressed by newsprint or a film's story line, the visual representation adds gravitas to the narrative and creates its own scene of virtual encounter.

The visual also serves as a sensory trigger that ultimately draws in all of the senses. By viewing an Oriental Monk figure in a magazine, we not only see his Asian face and manner of dress but also imagine the sound of his accent and the feel of his robes. Filmic portrayal implicates the senses even more, as we smell the wafting incense made visible in a temple shot. Prompting other sensory associations, our visually informed contact with Asian religious figures in news pictorials, television, and film generates its own simulated environment that brings to life our often unconscious notions about the spiritual East. In this way, Orientalist stereotypes become *embodied* and hence objectified in mediated form. Although their recognition still depends on our imagination, they achieve an existence all their own.

The fact that Americans, on a popular level, have come to know and experience Asian religions and Asian religious figures through mass-mediated representations that are primarily visual in nature has significant social effects. As we live out our lives in front of a screen, it becomes increasingly difficult to tell the difference between what is real and what is not (in the most conventional terms), to the point that these images *become* the real for us. Hence a postindustrial, mass-mediated age inaugurates the condition of the *hyperreal*, where images and reproductions (or in Baudrillardian terms, *simulacra*) become "more real than the real." For example, representations of the Dalai Lama—his image as part of an Apple ad or on the cover of a book, Richard Gere's description of him in a magazine interview—may be more real to an American audience than any personal encounter we might have with the actual person. Conversely, Americans who grew up watching *Kung Fu* and feel a special affinity with its protagonist, Kwai Chang Caine, often speak of the fictional character as if he were a real person. Mass media create new configurations of intimacy and attachment that have profoundly affected our epistemological sense. Within this hyperreal environment, orientalized stereotypes begin to take on their own reality and justify their own truths.[7]

As we will see, the change in Americans' perceptions of Asian religions from "heathen" cultures to romanticized traditions should not necessarily be taken as a sign of social progress. Rather, our contemporary attitudes emerge from historical circumstances and political concerns as much as they do from spiritual longing and religious ferment. These viewpoints are also shaped by how we have come to know the spiritual East—namely, through mass media representations and channels of consumption. There is much at work in our pursuit of Asian religions, far beyond the noble desire for universal understanding and world peace.

Preparing the Way

The Oriental Monk constitutes an American stereotype—one that must be placed alongside such easily recognizable figures as the inscrutable Oriental, evil Fu Manchus, Yellow Peril, heathen Chinee, and Dragon Ladies. Many of these negative portrayals of Asians emerged in American popular culture in the late-nineteenth and early-twentieth centuries, during the first wave of Asian immigration to the United States. These images reflected a widespread ambivalence toward Asia and Asian immigrants and served to embody a collective fear through representation. While many of these negative stereotypes persisted into the second half of the twentieth century, a definite shift occurred after the Second World War. Ominous caricatures were replaced with friendlier, more subservient models: the faithful caregiver, the warm-hearted prostitute, the docile Lotus Blossom, the humorous sidekick, and the model minority. It is during this postwar period that the Oriental Monk would most fully make his entrance on the American scene.

The Oriental Monk was not immaculately conceived however. America's more widespread engagement with Asian religions had begun more than a century before Suzuki's mid-century stay in the United States. As early as 1836, the influence of Hindu thought swept through the writings of Transcendentalists Ralph Waldo Emerson, Henry David Thoreau, and Walt Whitman, informing romantic visions of a transhistorical, transcultural spiritual essence. These writers drew on the "mysterious East" to pose an implicit critique of the effects of industrialization and technological change. (For Whitman, Asian culture is even figured as the source of America's "salvation.") Despite such valorization, Indian religion was still widely viewed as "overly spiritual and sensual,"[8] especially for Americans weaned on a Protestant work ethic and the bodily subjugation it required.

After these initially enthusiastic forays into Asian religion, Western discourse on Indian culture and religion did not remain so decidedly positive. British literature dedicated to India paints a more ambivalent portrait and deeply influenced American perceptions of the subcontinent. For many British writers, the "Jewel in the Crown" was regarded as "an exotic land of sadhus, snakes and suttee"[9]—a depiction that conveyed the fascination, fear, and feeling of moral superiority of its Anglo occupiers. All around him, the British colonialist found examples of social confusion and spiritual excess that it was his responsibility to contain—if only by literary means. This dynamic is nowhere more obvious than in *Kim*, Rudyard Kipling's "immortal story of a white boy in mysterious India."[10]

In Kipling's classic, young Kim O'Hara, the destitute offspring of an Irish color-sergeant in India, embarks on a spiritual journey with his self-appointed lama. The author's portrayal of the lama is for the most part quite sympathetic, but the fact that Kim's spiritual guide is Tibetan distinguishes him from the native "faqirs, Sadhus, Sunnyasis, byragis, nihangs, and mullahs, priests of all faiths and every degree of raggedness,"[11] who live off the goodwill of the people. The difference is significant. For the most part, Indian spiritual mendicants were primarily viewed with an air of suspicion and considered "mountebanks, clever hypocrites, 'fraud-men' rather than 'godmen,' who lead easy, lazy lives at the cost of the common, gullible, superstitious folk."[12] As part of the storehouse of Western cultural memory, Kipling's imperialist view[13] of Indian religion can be intimately linked to the critical assessments of Oriental Monk figures such as the Maharishi Mahesh in the late 1960s.

While literary works provided vivid portrayals of Oriental Monks to feed the imagination, popular periodicals and newspapers in the 1800s gave Americans their first actual glimpse of Asian religions and religious figures. As Laurie Maffly-Kipp documents, visual representation of Chinese religions in the form of engravings and photographs emerged in the mid- to late nineteenth century. Most of the images that appeared in magazines such as *Harper's Weekly* and *Collier's* focused on cultural scenes and "joss house" architecture. The Chinese themselves were almost always envisioned en masse—as yellow hordes wrapped in strange dress and strange customs. The rare scenes in which individual faces were highlighted were those in which children appeared. These visual choices reflected the prevailing attitudes of the time, which beheld the Chinese and their spiritual traditions with suspicion and disdain and thereby justified anti-immigrant sentiment and nativist fervor.

Still, not all the images of Asian religions that appeared[14] in the popular press were depersonalized and negatively cast. In the spring of 1893, a grand meeting was planned that would bring together clergy of various Christian denominations and emissaries from major religious traditions around the globe. The planning came to fruition in the Parliament of World's Religions, which officially began on September 11, 1893, in Chicago. The gathering featured 194 papers offered by representatives from the religious traditions of Protestant Christianity, Roman Catholicism, Judaism, Islam, Parsiism, Jainism, Shintoism, Confucianism, Taoism, Buddhism, and Hinduism. The two-week meeting was covered in varying degrees by the major newspapers across the United States and most thoroughly by the *Chicago Tribune*.

The 1893 Parliament has been rediscovered by religious studies scholars and journalists in recent times, touted as a significant event in U.S. religious history, and upheld as an early example of multifaith engagements, especially between the Christian West and the non-Christian East. In these accounts, Swami Vivekananda and Shaku Soyen are often highlighted as influential figures. Vivekananda is remembered for his resounding first lecture, or "Welcome Address," delivered on September 11, which many credit as the beginning of more widespread and serious interest in Hinduism. At the time, Soyen's contributions made less of an impression, but he is heralded as the forefather of Zen Buddhism in the United States through his training and dispatch of noteworthy figures such as Nyogen Senzaki and D. T. Suzuki.

Although history reserved a prominent place for these two men, other Asian religious emissaries also captured the imaginations of the *Chicago Tribune* and its readers in 1893. In its announcement and preview of the Parliament, the *Tribune* dedicated a full-page spread in its March 5 issue to the meeting's scheduled participants. The seemingly endless lists of names and titles were meant to demonstrate that the event would be "the most representative and remarkable religious gathering that history will ever have been called upon to chronicle."

The engraved likenesses of the representatives that accompanied these lists were perhaps the most fascinating aspect of the article. Many of these images were conventional headshots of Christian ministers in Western attire. Others were visually more arresting because of the person's robes or headgear. (Partenia, the Bishop of Sophia—a representative of the Greek Orthodox tradition—wore an impressive miter.) The two representatives from the "Orient" were depicted in wider perspective; Ashitsu Jitsuzen, with a monk's shaved scalp and in traditional Japanese robes, is seen from the waist up. It is unclear whether he is sitting in a chair or on the floor. (The lack of a visible chair seems to imply the latter.) Anagarika Dharmapala was the only figure to appear in full-length profile—a choice obviously meant to highlight the "loose flowing white robes of his office" (see fig. 1.1).[15]

Even though the exotic characteristics of these Asian religious figures were prominently featured, the engravings differed significantly from the more negative images that dominated the popular media of the time. Ashitsu, Dharmapala, and others appear as individuals—not as part of a large mass or horde of Asians. While their physiognomy differs from the other representatives, their "Asianness" is not exaggerated, and their expressions are natural and seemingly no different from those of their Western counterparts. The black-and-white engravings also disguised skin tone differences (even the African Methodist Bishop appears white). In powerful ways, the images included in the *Tribune* coverage reflected the "spirit of human fellowship" and "reasonably liberal thought" in ways that would prefigure media representations of the Oriental Monk in the century to come.

At the decade's end, on September 1, 1899, two Jodo Shin Buddhist priests—Shuye Sonoda and Kakuryo Nishijima—set foot on American soil. Their arrival did not escape the attention of the popular press, which quickly descended on the two men with notebooks and cameras in hand. The image of Sonoda and Nishijima that appeared in the September 13 issue of the

THE REV. ZITSUZEN ASHITSU, EDITOR OF "SHI-
MEIYOKA," OMI, JAPAN.

H. DHARMAPALA, SECRETARY OF THE MAHA-BODI
SOCIETY, CALCUTTA.

FIGURE 1.1. Images of Ashitsu Jitsuzen ("The Rev. Zitsuzen Ashitsu") and
Anagarika Dharmapala, ("H. Dharmapla"), *Chicago Tribune*, March 5, 1893.

San Francisco Chronicle was perhaps the average American's first sight of Asian religious missionaries (see fig. 1.2). The news caption reads:

> The two representatives of the ancient creed . . . have come to convert Japanese and later Americans to the ancient Buddhist faith. They will teach that God is not the creator, but the created; not a real existence; but a figment of the human imagination; and that pure Buddhism is a better moral guide than Christianity. Their priestly robes are as interesting as the lessons that they would present.

The spectacle of the two Buddhist ministers was highlighted by the black-and-white image of the men and the caption's attention to their exotic style of dress. And while the reporter endeavored to keep a journalist's distance, his words betray a religiously competitive attitude that reflects the time and place in which they were written. In truth, the reporter and other critics had little to fear. The two priests had come to minister specifically to Japanese immigrants at their request. Sonoda and Nishijima would help establish the first Japanese American Buddhist Church in San Francisco, which would come to serve as the spiritual, cultural, and social center of the community. After they adopted the usual Western attire of suit and tie, the priests disappeared into the undifferentiated mass of Japanese American migrants.

The moving image would do much to spark America's imaginings of Asian religions in the new century. The Oriental Monk made his on-screen debut in D. W. Griffith's classic *Broken Blossoms or The Yellow Man and the Girl*. The tale begins in an undesignated Chinese port town where we find the Yellow Man—a devout individual who becomes "convinced that the great nations across the sea need the lessons of the gentle Buddha." He journeys to the West to "take the glorious message of peace to the barbarous Anglo-Saxons, sons of turmoil and strife." The remainder of the movie chronicles his life in the Limehouse district of London and his encounter with Lucy, a gutter waif (played by Lillian Gish), whom he shelters from her brute of a father, Battlin' Burrows. The Yellow Man is portrayed as the only one who recognizes Lucy's "beauty which all Limehouse missed." But tragedy ensues: Battlin' Burrows discovers his daughter's whereabouts, beats her to death, and is then shot by the Yellow Man. The story ends with the Yellow Man, a knife between his ribs, slumped before Lucy and his Buddhist altar.

Griffith's masterpiece, produced in 1919, offers a tragic adaptation of Thomas Burke's short story "The Chink and the Girl." The changes that ensued in the translation of text into film are noteworthy. Most significant is the transformation of Burke's "Chink"—a "worthless drifter of an Oriental"— into Griffith's "Yellow Man," noble and pious in his sense of mission. Indeed,

MISSIONARIES OF
THE BUDDHIST FAITH.

Two Representatives of the Ancient Creed
Are in San Francisco to
Proselyte.

DR. SHUYE SONODA   REV. KAHURYO NISHIJIMA

D R. SHUYE SONODA and Rev. Kahuryo Nishijima, two Buddhist priests who are the sons of Buddhist priests of Japan, have come here to establish a Buddhist mission at 807 Polk street and to convert Japanese and later Americans to the ancient Buddhist faith. They will teach that God is not the creator, but the created; not a real existence, but a figment of the human imagination, and that pure Buddhism is a better moral guide than Christianity.

Their priestly robes are as interesting as the lessons that they would present. As they posed before the camera in a hallway near their rooms in the Occidental Hotel yesterday they were the wonderment of all the Japanese employes who could assemble for a glimpse of the sacred garb.

FIGURE 1.2. *San Francisco Chronicle*, September 13, 1899.

Griffith's main contribution to this early iteration of the Oriental Monk is the revised introduction of the story, where Griffith locates Cheng Huan, the Yellow Man, "in the Temple of Buddha, before his contemplated journey to a foreign land." Here, the Yellow Man gains inspiration and guidance not only from the environment of the temple but also from the Oriental Monks who reside there and provide "advice for a young man's conduct in the world—word for word such as a fond parent or guardian of our own land would give." Indeed, the motif of the temple—which begins and ends the story—lends a definite spiritual overtone to the tragic tale.

The fact that Griffith associates peace, gentleness, sensitivity, and altruism to the Buddha and his followers constitutes a significant moment in popular consciousness. At the very least, it assumes that a "heathen" religion stands on par with its "nonheathen" counterpart—although I believe much more is at work here. *Broken Blossoms* hints at a subtle but growing disillusionment with institutionalized Christianity and a budding fascination with alternative modes of moral and spiritual understanding. Griffith, as "cultural midwife," ushers this desire into popular consciousness through the Oriental Monk figures of the Yellow Man and his Buddhist teachers.

Although much of what the audience comes to know about the Yellow Man—his Buddhist faith and his mission in the West—is provided in the intertitles, Griffith's unique choice of visuals added a significant layer of meaning. It is here that Americans and other Western viewers caught their first glimpse of a Buddhist temple, best characterized by its smoky, mysterious opulence (see fig. 1.3). One sees the faces of the Chinese monks only briefly; it is their robes that are highlighted as they bow in mutual respect to the Yellow Man. These cues of clothing and gesture are enough to establish the religiosity of these figures. Portraying other aspects of the monks' "Asianness" would have jeopardized the film's potential to invoke in the audience a more tolerant stance toward the Chinese (a stated goal for Griffith).

Cheng Huan is played by American actor Richard Barthelmess in characteristic "yellow face." This version of the Yellow Man, however, differs from other portrayals of Asian men at the time. Except for the taped eyes and non-Western dress, Barthelmess's rendition lacks other outlandish features, such as Fu Manchu's menacing eyebrows and maniacal gaze. The actor's good looks remain fairly intact. As Laurie Maffly Kipp notes in her examination of visual representations of Chinese and Chinese religions at the turn of the century, this cast of whiteness was a way to confer goodness and moral character to its Asian subjects.[15]

Of course, *Blossoms* concludes in tragedy, not hope. This ending reassured the film's largely white and Christian audience and infused them with "a sense of mission" and justified their "paternalistic efforts" within their national borders and without. The film's moral lesson rests on a threat: If the Christianized West is unable to care for its children, the noble Buddhist East will. The tone and import of this message is conveyed by the dire consequences of the Yellow Man's intervention (the death of the three main characters); the message is to be taken as a warning for the Christian West to practice what it preaches.

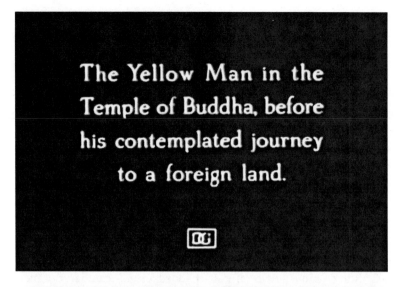

FIGURE 1.3. Intertitle and Chinese temple scenes from D. W. Griffith's *Broken Blossoms* (1919).

Although this is the intentional aim of Griffith's work, it does not preclude other, even contrary effects: Eastern spirituality has been representationally idealized and operates civilly in its new Western home. In this way, *Broken Blossoms* lays the groundwork for the West's further engagements and later

FIGURE 1.3. Continued

spiritual identification with the East. The message will be transformed from one of threat and consequence to one of desire and hope: *If the Christianized West is unable to care for its children, the noble Buddhist East will!*

While *Broken Blossoms'* more favorable representation of Asians and Asian religions was an anomaly at the time, this would steadily change over the ensuing decades. The most noteworthy transition came in the form of the popular Chinese detective, Charlie Chan. Chan was a creation of author Earl Derr Biggers, who became intrigued in 1919 with real-life Hawaiian police detective Chang Apana. The first of Biggers's novels appeared in 1925, and the Chan serial ran until 1932. The popular movie series commenced with *Charlie Chan Carries On* in 1931 and was followed by thirty-two more films over the next decade. A radio series, comic books, and other paraphernalia also served as vehicles for the unusually insightful Asian detective.

Charlie Chan's place in American popular culture cannot be overestimated. Audiences delighted in Chan's uncanny ability to discern the dishonesty, fraud, and sly maneuvers of his (usually Anglo) criminal subjects. Indeed, the Chinese inspector was able to perceive aspects of situation and character that others could not. Chan's skill appeared innate—or at the very least, inaccessible— which only added to his mystique. This inscrutability, however, was not of a threatening nature. Chan, dressed often in a white Western suit and white hat, was "trustworthy, benevolent, and philosophical" (see fig. 1.4).[17] His affable nature was further conveyed by his mannerisms: "He is a large man, but moves gracefully." While this grace certainly was meant to reflect Chan's intelligence and civility, it also made the character effeminate and ultimately nonmenacing for the American viewer. (Chan had fathered more than eleven children, and his sexual orientation was never in question however.)

Charlie Chan certainly embodied one of the first positive representations of Asian men. However, there is a further characteristic that makes him a direct precursor to the Oriental Monk: his unparalleled insight into a situation. Chan's approach to a case appeared methodical, but his method remained mysterious. His art of solving the crime seemed inextricably linked to a certain type of wisdom that was remote and inaccessible to even the cleverest of Westerners—Oriental wisdom.

This Oriental wisdom took special form in the convention of the aphorism, a concise saying phrased in such a way that it seemed to reflect an ancient truth: "If strength were all, tiger would not fear scorpion" (*Charlie Chan's Secret*); "Insignificant molehill sometimes more important than conspicuous mountain" (*Charlie Chan in Egypt*); "Confucius say, 'Luck happy chain of foolish accidents'" (*Charlie Chan at the Opera*). The pithiness of these Chanisms was further enhanced by the omission of key parts of speech, such as articles and verbs, highlighting the speaker's bilingual relationship with English and his nonnative status.

In other words, Chan's incorrect grammar served as a hallmark of difference and marked the detective as someone essentially foreign or alien. However, this difference is redeemed through the aphorism, in which the wisdom of the

FIGURE I.4. *Charlie Chan in Panama* (1940).

East and seemingly uncanny powers of discernment are translated for the insight (and delight) of his Western audience. Furthermore, in relation to other stereotypical characters, such as Sax Rohmer's Fu Manchu, whose British education made his speech indistinguishable from his Anglo counterparts, it is clear that Chan's English will never be as good as his Chinese. Racial difference is clearly marked, not only by the slant of the protagonist's eyes but also by the elisions in his speech. Yet, Chan's stereotypical accent, along with more visual cues, such as his rotund figure and well-pressed suit, make him a charming and likable figure. The pseudo-Asiatic linguistic form of the aphorism presents Oriental wisdom as mysterious yet unthreatening, easy to digest, and always entertaining.

Monk Story

The figure of the Oriental Monk, then, did not simply appear but was a figure that developed over time. The Cold War and the continuing involvement of the United States along the Pacific Rim demanded a different approach and new representations. By the second half of the twentieth century, the United States and the rest of the West had to confront a dramatically changing Asia. Major transformations included the push toward decolonization and the industrialization that occurred in many Asian nations, the Non-Aligned Movement and the Bandung conference in Indonesia, and the rise of Communist China. If Asians no longer fit a static portrait, the Oriental Monk provided a stable frame that encouraged an openness (if not a genuine appreciation) for Asian culture. This openness to spiritual alternatives reached full flower in the 1960s. Disillusioned with institutionalized religious practice, many Americans began to look beyond mainstream Christianity for new inspiration and direction. Sociologists Wade Clark Roof and Robert Wuthnow have documented the emergence of "seeker spirituality" during this period—a movement characterized by a yearning for personal experience and transformation and in which the sacred is less closely tied to religious institutions and communal practice, even as it is intimately linked to the individual psyche. Asian religions fit the bill, as did their enigmatic teachers, who seemed to provide the discipline and attention without the stifling structures of church or synagogue.

In the following cultural history of the Oriental Monk as American icon, we will see a complex dynamic unfold in which Orientalist notions of Asian spiritual heritages converge with Western disillusion and desire. These notions are configured in a formalized narrative with ritual aspects that demonstrate the distinctive character of America's engagement with "Eastern," non-Christian traditions. This narrative is quite simple and can be summarized as follows: A lone monk figure—often with no visible family or community—takes under his wing a fatherless, often parentless, child (usually a boy). This child embodies a tension—although he signifies the dominant culture in racial terms, he has an ambivalent relationship with that culture. This allows him to make a break with the Western tradition that is radical enough to allow him to embrace his marginalized self. The Oriental Monk figure discerns this yearning for difference, develops it, and nurtures it. As a result of this relationship, a transmission takes place: Oriental wisdom and spiritual insight is passed from the Oriental Monk figure to the West through the *bridge figure* of the child. Ultimately, the Oriental Monk and his apprentice(s) represent future salvation of the dominant culture—they embody a revitalized hope of saving the West from capitalist greed, brute force, totalitarian rule, and spiritless technology.

This distinctive narrative occurs time and again. Although the story of the Oriental Monk has the ability to function as a challenging counternarrative to the dominant culture in particular instances, this popular figuring also firmly establishes a strict religious and racial hierarchy. It also credentials the monk as an *ideological caregiver* who gains recognition by helping dominant white Americans gain spiritual insight and, often, political mission as they work out the meaning of their existence in modern life.[18] Indeed, the primary significance of the Oriental Monk is that the icon operates as an imaginative construction, circulating widely and subjectively reinforcing this new system of Western dominance, even in instances when the icon serves as a vehicle for social critique. In addition, the particular way in which Americans write themselves into the story is not a benign, nonideological act; rather, it constructs a *modernized cultural patriarchy*[19] in which Anglo-Americans reimagine themselves as the protectors, innovators, and guardians of Asian religions and culture and wrest the authority to define these traditions from others.

As Brian Massumi notes, the virtual "requires a multiplication of images." He goes on to note: "The virtual that cannot be felt also cannot but be felt, in its effects. When expressions of its effects are multiplied, the virtual fleetingly appears. Its fleeting is in the cracks between and the surfaces around the images." Orientalist notions of Asian religions in virtual form cannot simply be assigned to a particular image, although their force is palpable. In order to grasp this force, one must "take the images by their virtual centers [and] superimpose them." I follow Massumi's lead here. In the pages that follow, I track Virtual Orientalism's emergence in the American popular imagination through a study of three figures: D. T. Suzuki, the Maharishi Mahesh Yogi, and Kwai Chang Caine (*Kung Fu*). Although I discuss these figures chronologically, my method is not so much historical as it is genealogical. What I seek to capture is the "overimage of images of self-varying deformation" that allow Virtual Orientalism to appear.[20]

The 1950s mass media representations of D. T. Suzuki and the American "Zen Boom" are the focus of chapter 1. The popular narrative and image of the Oriental Monk begin to merge in this historical moment. Also, the specific way that Suzuki is portrayed (as a mysterious Oriental) and the medium in which these portrayals appear (the fashion magazine) also mark Eastern spirituality as a "stylized religion" and consumable object.

Chapter 2 examines the Maharishi Mahesh Yogi's colorful splash onto the 1960s countercultural scene. Celebrity defines a new authorial framework, as the Maharishi Mahesh and his Transcendental Meditation movement gain legitimacy through the guru's association with well-known entertainment stars in the 1960s. The spectacle of celebrity spiritual seekers lends a *hyperreal* dimension à la Baudrillard to Americans' understanding of Asian religions, as these media engagements surreptitiously offer the sense of a more direct encounter.

Kwai Chang Caine in the popular 1970s TV series *Kung Fu* is the focal point of chapter 3. At this cultural moment, a fictional monk takes his place alongside representations of historical figures, making the hyperreal effect complete. America's first "Eastern Western" also marks the rise of a new generation into cultural power—a generation that attempts to selectively blend their parents' ideals with their own countercultural values. With *Kung Fu*, Virtual Orientalism would make the Oriental Monk a recognizable icon and stock figure in U.S. popular culture.

The religious and philosophical views of these individuals—especially D. T. Suzuki and Maharishi Mahesh Yogi—have been widely discussed. My analysis instead focuses on the media representations that shape these figures' popular recognition and success. In the defining moments in the Oriental Monk's history, we will witness the different ways in which the icon appears and its formalized narrative is played out and further refined. Far from neutral representations, these figures offer social commentary on American culture and society, as well as a screen on which larger claims over cultural authority are projected, contested, and negotiated.

By examining the representation of particular Monk figures in sociohistorical context, the underlying nexus of Western interests, desires, and repressions that lend the icon its power are brought to light. Indeed, the icon of Oriental Monk reveals not only Americans' perceptions of the East but also their religious self-definition—a self-definition that in the second half of the twentieth century was informed by larger geopolitical power relations between the United States and Asia. Indeed, the figure of the Oriental Monk in its variegated forms serves as a measure of U.S. geopolitical relations with Asia; these forces are mapped onto the icon through aspects of race, class, national origin, and sexuality. Indeed, the monk as spiritual guide acts as a mirror as well as a screen for a wide range of ideological interests related to the posture of the United States in the global political economy.

This network of power relations is not only internationally informed but also configured according to interests within the national borders of the United States. Through the figure of the nonsexual, solitary Oriental Monk, Asian religiosity and spirituality are made palatable—psychologically, socially, and politically—for dominant culture consumption. Hence, the Monk as signifier serves as a way for Americans to manage Asian American religious communities by *re*-presenting Asian spiritual heritages in a specific way—that is, by reinforcing certain comforting assumptions and presenting the Other in a manner that is recognizable and acceptable. The role of the Oriental Monk as a popular representation and Virtual Orientalism as its milieu, therefore, has important implications for the American engagement with Asian religions and for Asian American self-understanding.

In these various ways, the genealogy that is recounted here is meant as an exposé of the life of the Oriental Monk and his journey through American popular culture. More specifically, I seek to reveal the ideological interests and processes at play in our popular encounters with him—so that we may no longer comfortably revel in our own fascination and reverence.

2

Zen's Personality

D. T. Suzuki

On October 1, 1997, the American reading public was greeted by a surreal sight. The cover of one of its most popular weeklies, *Time* magazine, featured the image of a bleached blond Brad Pitt, flanked by a group of Asians, emblazoned with the heading, "America's Fascination with BUDDHISM." For those who wondered what the Hollywood hunk had to do with the ancient Eastern religion, the subtitles provided the clue: "Up close with BRAD PITT, star of *Seven Years in Tibet*" and "Two new movies, celebrity converts and hundreds of books add zest to Zen."

In the cover article, *Time* reporters Jeanne McDowell and Richard N. Ostling contemplate whether a truly indigenized American Buddhism exists. Their overview cites not only established religious centers ("Dens of Dharma"), booming book sales on the subject, and "celebrity Buddha boosters" but also phenomena such as *Zen* blush makeup and the sitcom *Dharma and Greg*. In the late twentieth century, Buddhism's vocabulary and aura have become part of the American popular imagination. "Zen" and other terminology no longer stand as foreign concepts but carry their own unique meanings in their transplanted environment.

Americans' present "awareness" of this spiritual alternative is a far cry from earlier times. Up until the mid-twentieth century, Zen Buddhism was "a subject of considerable mystery to the relatively few people in [the United States] who ha[d] heard of it at all."[1] But it was during the 1950s that Zen took root in the United States—most notably due to an "unusually captivating, congenial, and enigmatic old man,"[2] named D. T. Suzuki.

Daisetz Teitaro Suzuki is known as one of the chief popularizers of Zen in the twentieth century and has been heralded as Zen's "missionary" to the West. He wrote prolifically, engaged in critical dialogue with intellectuals and engaged practitioners, and served as a general figurehead for the Zen Buddhist movement in the United States and Europe. He is known for his influence on famous Buddhist ideologues—from the Beats to Alan Watts—and remains a quintessential representation of Zen Buddhism for many Americans.

In the 1950s, Suzuki enjoyed his third stay in the United States. Unlike his previous journeys before the Second World War, Suzuki came into his own during this period as an independent thinker and recognized personality. There are several histories and accounts that document this stage of Suzuki's life and its significance to the establishment of American Zen Buddhism.[3] But these chronicles rarely address the question: What made Zen an integral dimension of the American religious landscape and Suzuki its most significant representative? How did this particular figure at this specific historical juncture allow Zen its unprecedented entrance into American culture?

Undoubtedly, Suzuki's large and influential corpus is an important factor. Suzuki effectively harnessed the power of the printed word. He wrote lucid introductions to Zen, Mahayana Buddhism, and Japanese culture and started the independent scholarly journal the *Eastern Buddhist* (with his wife, Beatrice Lane Suzuki). These publications lay the groundwork for an "imagined community"[4] of Zen scholars, practitioners, and general enthusiasts whose members inhabited both sides of the East-West divide. This intellectual foundation allowed ideas and information about Buddhism, in general, and Zen, in particular, to be easily disseminated in college classrooms, coffeehouses, and bookstores.

Suzuki's appeal and influence had much to do with the brand of Zen he presented in these texts. Zen offered its adherents the opportunity to go beyond logical thinking and the desire for moral certainty characteristic of Western religious traditions and philosophy and instead proposed a way to live with existential contradiction. Suzuki emphasized certain aspects of Zen, such as *satori*, which embraced within its realm of experience "irrationality, intuitive insight, authoritativeness, affirmation, exhilaration and momentariness."[5] Suzuki also unleashed Zen from its nativist roots and ritualistic moorings. According to his view, it professed a more universal understanding of humanity that was compatible with all of the great religions and philosophies of humankind. In addition to providing key introductions to Zen thought, Suzuki also wrote on Japanese culture, notably as a paradigmatic expression of Zen philosophy. His understanding presented an American audience with a positive glimpse into the "oriental mind" of their former World War II enemy. In these ways, Suzuki's writings served as a formidable bridge between East and West.

The contribution of Suzuki's writings to the establishment of Zen in the United States has long been recognized.[6] But this still does not explain why Westerners found Suzuki such a compelling presence. Hence, I would like to shift our attention away from his works and explore another dimension of Suzuki's status and peculiar influence: *his image*. Indeed, Suzuki served as a *figure* through which Zen Buddhism was made accessible to a wider English-speaking audience. Although the two—Zen Buddhism and D. T. Suzuki—are often taken as distinct forces, I would argue that they symbiotically worked together to shape an American conception of Zen. In this scenario, Suzuki is not viewed as simply a "cultural ambassador" or "translator" of the larger tradition, but the embodiment of that tradition—the *icon* through which Zen Buddhism achieved meaning for those in the West.

Although Suzuki's centrality to Americans' growing awareness of Zen was unmistakable, it relied on the contributions of other notable figures as well. In fact, much of Suzuki's intrigue rested on the fascination and influence his presence held for personalities, such as Jack Kerouac and Alan Watts, who were also part of the 1950s Zen bandwagon. This nexus of relationships between the different players would lay the foundation for one of the most popular twentieth-century spiritual narratives in the United States and would reflect Americans' attitudes toward Asia and its religious traditions for the next half-century. From D. T. Suzuki and the early "Zen boom" in the late 1950s, one can easily discern the shape of things to come.

Representing Suzuki

The propagation of public meanings through *images* and *image* was an important "seed" that took root in the 1950s, the decade that witnessed the advent of the television age. The rapid change in communications technology produced a new form of mass consciousness—one in which the surface of an object (its ready appearance) gained new stature in determining the object's worth. Television, with its constant flow of visual images, helped train its audience to quickly assess the subject at hand, relying more upon the body and bodily rhetorics than ever before.[7] This focus on the visual was reinforced by the multitude of popular magazines featuring glossy covers and photo-driven layouts (*Harper's Bazaar, Look, Time, Newsweek, Life*). Given this new communicative environment, D. T. Suzuki's accessible image and intriguing personality would allow Zen its foray into American popular life.

It was within this cultural context that Americans were first introduced to Suzuki. *Vogue*, in its regular column of cultural trends, revealed in January 1957:

> People are talking about . . . The Columbia University classes of the great Zen Buddhist teacher, Dr. Daisetz Suzuki, who sits in the centre of a mound of books, waving his spectacles with ceremonial elegance while mingling the philosophical abstract with the familiar concrete: "To discover one is a great achievement, to discover zero, a great leap"; or another time: "Have no ulterior purpose in work, then you are free."[8]

This brief, yet intriguing tidbit caught the eye of a *Time* reporter, who followed up with a more expanded introduction two weeks later:

> In the centuries since the death of its founder in 483 B.C., Buddhism has had little direct impact on the Christian West. Today, however, a Buddhist boomlet is under way in the U.S. Increasing numbers of intellectuals—both faddists and serious students—are becoming interested in a form of Japanese Buddhism called Zen.[9]

By the end of the year, the Zen boomlet or trend became so widespread that "lecturers on the subject attract[ed] enough attention to be photographed for popular weeklies."[10] D. T. Suzuki was by far the most popular of these lecturers to appear, his likeness gracing the pages of *Newsweek*, the *New Yorker*, the *Saturday Review*, and *Time*. A look at these images is significant, because it gives us an idea of Americans' first impressions of Suzuki, as well as of Zen. By all appearances, Suzuki seemed to fit the model of a venerable Eastern sage—wise, noble, aged, and mysteriously foreign. Popular press photographs accentuated Suzuki's physiognomy. His wrinkled features seemed to speak of an ancient wisdom that harked back to an age far beyond his considerable years. His not quite bald, yet closely shaven head added an otherworldly, ascetic quality to his appearance. And his "tiny eyes"[11] helped to racially distinguish him from Western personalities.

Perhaps most noteworthy is the fact that the *Saturday Review*, *Time*, and *Newsweek* all chose portraits highlighting Suzuki in more traditional Japanese attire.[12] This is particularly strange since Suzuki, during his public appearances, "almost invariably dressed in the neat American sports jacket and slacks that might be worn by any Columbia undergraduate."[13] Representing the Japanese scholar in this way was not without its particular intent. His robe romantically recalled a forever ancient and distant Japan, which added to the overall representation of Suzuki's authority and the authority of the philosophy he espoused. And in the case of the photo (taken by Cecil Beaton) that accompanied the November 1957 *Saturday Review* article on Suzuki, the image also evoked a somber sense of nostalgia and loss (figure 2.1).

Suzuki's image relied on more than just the visual texts readily at hand. It also relied on the reader's imagination. Almost every written popular account of Suzuki during this period describes his appearance, manner, and gesture. Especially admired and emphasized are his "ferocious eyebrows, which project from his forehead like the eyebrows of the angry demons who guard the entrances of Buddhist temples in Japan."

Winthrop Sargeant of the *New Yorker* continues:

These striking ornaments give him an added air of authority, perhaps, but the addition is unnecessary. Dr. Suzuki is obviously a man who thought every thing out long ago and has reached a state of certainty. The certainty appears, is so profound that it needs no emphasis, for it is expressed in quiet, cheerful phrases (marked here and there by the usual Japanese difficulty with the letter "l") and punctuated by smiles and absent-minded rubbings of his forehead. Now and then, he

FIGURE. 2.1. Image of Suzuki in the *Saturday Review*, November 1957 (Photographer: Cecil Beaton).

bounces up from his desk to make his certainties even more certain by drawing diagrams on a nearby blackboard, or chalking characters in Chinese or Sanskrit. To the uninitiated, these characters, and the talk that accompanies them, are likely to be enigmatic indeed.[14]

"Enigmatic" is a key feature that seemed to contribute to Suzuki's appeal. Although his texts are heralded as lucid introductions to Buddhism and Japanese culture, his persona attracted attention for quite the opposite reason. One of Suzuki's most notorious lectures took place at a symposium on Zen Buddhism and parapsychology. After lecturing for a while on the topic of Zen—virtually ignoring any discussion of parapsychology—he was asked by one of the audience members to expound on the connection between the two. He thought for a moment and replied (to the befuddlement of the crowd): "Absolutely nothing." Indeed, many of those who sat in on Suzuki's talks often could not follow his enthusiastic chalkboard scribblings or his line of thought. But just the chance to *experience* Suzuki was enough to draw "large and rabid" crowds.

Why were people so drawn to Suzuki if they did not fully understand what he was saying and often found his "message" fairly incomprehensible? Suzuki's enigmatic nature drew its power from a long-established Western notion of the mysteriousness of the East. In this way, Suzuki's incomprehensibility was wholly comprehensible to his 1950s American audience.[15] Popular accounts of Suzuki's persona—both visual and descriptive—met certain cultural protocols: that is, it fit into a particular heritage of viewing and understanding the East, allowing a more widespread recognition to take place.

What can account for such a visual portrayal? Suzuki's image, in order to be recognizable to its audience, drew its power from a particular "way of seeing" Japan (and the Japanese people) deeply ingrained in the American psyche. It is an image that speaks powerfully about Americans' attitudes toward their World War II enemy that had evolved in the 1950s. If one looks at the images of Japan and the Japanese in the previous decade, one finds a fairly unsympathetic portrayal. For instance, *Life* magazine often featured the uncompromising, seemingly hard-hearted Japanese soldier on its covers. During the war period, it was Japan as modern political threat that was popularly represented as disciplined, militaristic, and without humor (figure 2.2). In its August 16, 1943 cover story entitled, 'How Strong Is Japan?" the popular magazine pronounces in bold caption: "Japanese are Imitative and Traditional. . .but United by Emperor Worship and Hate." The report's characterization of Japanese spiritual traditions is no less inflammatory: "The asinine tea ceremony was evolved from the Chinese who have long since forgotten it. It derives from Zen Buddhism and represents a contemplative philosophy of relishing small things. The ceremony is fully as elaborate as a college fraternity initiation. Japanese life is full of similar nonsense."[16]

FIGURE. 2.2. *Life* cover featuring Japanese soldiers during the Second World War,
August 16, 1943 (Photographer: Paul Dorsey).

By 1951, after Japan's defeat and occupation by the U.S., *Life Magazine*
would return to Japan, but with a different eye. Its December 31st cover is graced
by a pretty Japanese girl in traditional dress, smiling amiably for the camera.
(figure 2.3a) Here the feature story proclaims, "The Example of Japan: The me-
dieval land that became Asia's most modern nation is exerting a new influence
today on the ways of the West." The color spread that accompanies the story
highlights Zen-inspired homes and serene gardens, as well as Japanese traditional
artwork ("a great, delicate art"). The photo of Suzuki that appeared in *Time* in
1957 (figure 2.3b) was part of a "friendlier" portrayal of Asia, and specifically
Japan. These Asian figures offered a nonthreatening re-presentation of the
Japanese in the 1950s that stood in stark contrast with earlier wartime images.
As Christina Klein notes, such cultural representations helped to "integrate"
Japan into the hearts and minds of Americans—a move that was politically
driven by Cold War politics.[17] This shift also was undoubtedly prompted (as the
1951 cover suggests) by United States interest in new global markets.

It is important to note the gendered context within which photos of Suzuki were viewed. Images of Japanese men rarely appeared during the postwar period; rather, their feminine counterparts were featured. Suzuki stood as the exception, his image tempered by age and pose. This context visually reinforced a hierarchical and Orientalist relationship between the dominant West and the submissive, now amiable East.

Suzuki seemed particularly "friendly" for several reasons. The first has to do with how he chose to define himself. Suzuki viewed himself as a scholar above all else. As the *New Yorker* article describes:

> Dr. Suzuki's status in all this is a peculiar one. He holds aloof from the doings at the First Zen Institute [in New York City]. Though he is deeply revered by everyone connected with the sect, he is neither a monk nor a practicing Zen master. His position is that of a lay theologian—a scholar of and a commentator on Zen principles.[18]

Indeed, Suzuki's role as scholar allowed a certain representational flexibility. On the one hand, it created a distance between him and the Japanese Zen Buddhist establishment that was portrayed as rigid and harsh. As commentator, he could speak about the shocking ways in which satori or enlightenment was achieved—for example, a master hitting his pupil with a staff—without advocating this seemingly cruel and rigid practice.[19] On the other hand, he maintained the authority of a teacher, which qualified him as a master of a different sort. Popular accounts chose to feature Suzuki as a living example of the Zen philosophy he espoused.[20] "There can be no doubt that the world look[ed] upon him as the foremost of the many venerable [Buddhist] sages."[21] Hence, his role as a scholar allowed the press to portray Suzuki as a living master sans the negative characteristics of more traditional Japanese monks.[22]

Suzuki seemed approachable in a second way. Although he was often described as a "missionary" of Zen, he appeared to wholly lack a missionary's coercive approach. Again, this impression was reinforced by his role as a scholar. His works were viewed as attempts to explicate, rather than convert; all that seemed to be at stake was the intellect and not the soul. Suzuki also exhibited a serious dedication to Zen, but a dedication devoid of the missionary's self-importance. (For instance, he often liked to joke that his Buddhist name, "Daisetsu," meant "Great Stupidity."[23])

FIGURE. 2.3. *Life* special issue on Asia, December 31, 1951 (Photographer: David Douglas Duncan) and image of D. T Suzuki accompanying the short *Time* article, "Zen," February 4, 1957 (Photographer: Ellen Auerbach).

Perhaps Suzuki seemed most friendly because of his demeanor. He was often described as "soft spoken," "humorous," "charming," and "earnest"— all characteristics shared by Japanese actresses, like Miyoshi Umeki, so popular at the time. As these women were portrayed, Suzuki similarly appeared attractively passive. He did not insist on his way and often was the one who was eagerly pursued by students, and to these religious suitors, he remained "invariably affable,"[24] turning no one away. It appeared that the only Japan with which Americans could amicably interact was a feminized one, even in Suzuki's case.[25]

Ultimately, Suzuki served as a "non-controversial, genial, reminder of Japan's own religious tradition"[26] not only to Japan but also to those in the United States. The 1950s were a time when America enjoyed great prosperity, as well as a heightened sense of national identity.[27] This attitude, along with the United States's new status as a world power, allowed Americans the psychological security, as well as the unprecedented means, to explore cultural alternatives in a way that they had never done before. Acknowledging the cultural and religious heritage of defeated Japan seemed like a magnanimous gesture.

Through press accounts and published reflections, an American popular audience encountered a figure that was strangely new, yet comfortably familiar. Suzuki appeared as an affable and idiosyncratic old sage eager to share the treasures of his ancient wisdom.[28] He had traveled great distances to do so, and his interest in cultivating a Western audience's understanding seemed selective and flattering. Furthermore, Suzuki's philosophy emphasized the religious universality of humankind that transcended boundaries of nation and race. This view was most appealing to postwar America and visually reinforced in popular representations. The timeless and engaging nature of Zen could be easily mapped onto the body of one who would become its most cherished propagator.

Image and Style

Although Suzuki worked tirelessly to cultivate a sophisticated understanding of Zen in the West, such understanding was not necessary for the philosophy to attain the status of a popular fad and for Suzuki to garner celebrity. That Suzuki was given media attention had much to do with the venue in which he was initially introduced—the fashion magazine. Indeed, Americans would get their first exposure to Suzuki in 1956. *Harper's Bazaar*, in its October issue, featured Suzuki (along with painter Geichiro Inokuma). The brief description of the Zen teacher, in the words of well-known fashion photographer Cecil Beaton, read: "He is curiously like both a saint and a dandy. His wide mouth has the inscrutable smile of the Buddha. The eye slits, as small as tadpoles, are sharply observant, and the eyebrows, like exotic butterflies in flight, flutter with comedy." Beaton also notes Suzuki's "stunning spiritual insights" and his ability to "see beyond the duality of thought and language to the heart of reality itself." These words on *Harper's Bazaar*'s oversized copy, however, were eclipsed by the full-page image that accompanied the text (figure 2.4). Here, Suzuki's serious expression adds authority and weight to the figure. The eyebrows are evident, but they do not "flutter with comedy," nor is the "inscrutable smile" apparent.

As mentioned earlier, *Vogue* was also one of the first periodicals to mention Suzuki and, indeed, the first to report Suzuki's presence on U.S. soil. With their cosmopolitan character and disposition, fashion magazines, such as *Harper's Bazaar* and *Vogue*, provided initial exposure to the Asian religious figure and served as a potent force for cultural integration. Indeed, Suzuki and Zen became objects of a particular *style*. Looking through issues of *Vogue* and other magazines of the period, it is evident that objects from Asia carried a certain cultural cachet: Oriental art, Japanese homes, Eastern clothing. Suzuki served not only as informant but also as object alongside others to which one could point in referencing "Japanese style."

This is not to say that there were not Americans who took Suzuki and Zen philosophy seriously. But this degree of engagement was never achieved on a

FIGURE. 2.4. *Harper's Bazaar*, October 1956 (Photographer: Cecil Beaton).

popular level. In a 1958 article for *Mademoiselle* magazine, "What Is Zen?" Nancy Wilson Ross recounts her conversation with a Zen enthusiast: "A young New Yorker telling a friend about a cocktail party she had attended described the conversation as uncommonly stimulating, even 'fascinating.' Everyone present, she said, had been 'talking about Zen.'"[29] When asked to explain what Zen really was, this New York woman began: "Zen is a kind of Japanese philosophy, vaguely Buddhist in origin." She goes on to cite noteworthy individuals who have been influenced by Zen: J. D. Salinger, John Cage, Dizzy Gillespie, Erich Fromm, painters Morris Graves and Mark Tobey. The young woman continued:

> She had an older friend who had faithfully attended for two years the learned Dr. Suzuki's seminars at Columbia, and she had just heard that Harvard was now giving a course in "Zen Meditation," in the Philosophy Department, under the tutelage of a bona fide Japanese master, with Dr. Suzuki standing by to help with the translating. She ended her reply with the abrupt admission that she honestly couldn't explain what Zen was and she feared, alas, it was "already too late to ask."[30]

Ross uses this humorous anecdote to characterize the understanding of Zen enthusiasts, "who may be heard loosely applying the word—in the form of an adjective—to everything from styles in painting to personality types and from forms of verse to states of consciousness."[31] Although it goes on to explain Zen in more substantial terms, Ross's article unwittingly serves to reinforce the philosophy as a cultural status marker by discussing the influence of Zen (and Suzuki) on Aldous Huxley's *Doors of Perception*. She also compares the Beat generation's eastward turn to the innovative techniques of the Dadaists and Surrealists a generation before. In addition to these references, images of objets d'art are intermingled with the introductory text (including a photograph of a famous wooden sculpture of the Buddha, whose reproduction "hangs on the wall of Dr. Daisetz Teitaro Suzuki's New York sanctum"[32]).

In these various ways, Ross's article helps situate Suzuki's inception into popular consciousness by squarely locating his influence in the realm of artistic culture. She does make an argument for Zen's contemporary relevance in everyday life: "Something has gotten badly out of balance: the 'flow of life' has been stopped. The emphasis on fulfilling the appetite for 'things' is at an all-time high. Zen invites one to another range of experience."[33] However, this appeal is justified by Zen's benign (if not productive) presence in the realm of high culture. Through this association, Suzuki and the philosophy he represents become stylized, and this stylization makes Zen approachable, if not chic.

Hence, referencing Suzuki and dabbling in Zen would take on an almost glamorous aura during the period. The 1950s was an era in which glamour flourished; in their postwar world of abundance, Americans indulged in a new frenzy of consumption based less on need and more on style. As Stuart Ewen notes in *All Consuming Image: The Politics of Style in Contemporary Culture*:

> The power of style, and its emergence as an increasingly important feature in people's lives, cannot be separated from the evolution and sensibility of modernity. Style is a visible reference point by which we have come to understand life *in progress*. People's devotion to the acceleration of varying styles allows them to be connected to the "reality" of a given moment. At the same time they understand that this given moment will give way to yet another, and another, and that as it does, styles will change, again and again.[34]

Zen's status as fad certainly provided another reason Americans were able to entertain Suzuki's presence. The realization that this fad "will give way to yet another, and another" made a foreign influence palatable. Even if one distinguishes style from fad—the former more enduring than the latter—style is traditionally seen as something that does not radically alter the substance of one's being. It simply adorns or enhances.

The style of the cosmopolitan rich as portrayed in such magazines as *Vogue* and *Mademoiselle* increasingly became sources of envy and delight for the 1950s middle classes who sought ways to escape the monotony of their everyday existence. "A vicarious feeling of superiority—[a] manifestation of class attitudes"[35] made this burgeoning group identify more readily with their upper-class cousins. Suzuki gained a peculiar sort of legitimacy by the mere fact that the New York elite were "talking about" the scholar and dropping his name at cocktail parties.

Americans' fascination with Zen during the late 1950s was fostered by the attention it drew in elite circles and by the way it was embraced in rowdier camps as well. The Beat Generation and its followers in their own unique interpretation adopted Buddhism as a way to distinguish themselves from "middle-class non-identity"[36] and to guide and justify their own pursuits. Unlike their elite counterparts interested in prestige and wealth, the Beats glorified a rootless, transitory lifestyle marked by menial odd jobs, poetic entrancements, endless travel, and carefree sex. In the face of stifling convention, the Beat movement presented an attitude of rebelliousness that resonated with the younger generation of the time. Part of their resistance was expressed in terms of Zen—a prominent source of their spiritual inspiration.

Because of the popular attention it received, the Beat movement generated its share of less committed followers. Eugene Burdick remarked:

Most of these people are not hipsters; they are fellow travelers. The Communist Party used to attract a thick fringe of people who were excited by the vision of violence and apocalypse but were utterly sure in their private minds that it would not occur in their time. With the hipsters, it is the same. There is a crowding around of people who are merely curious, who want to see the vision but not be in it, who have a contempt for Squaresville but live there, who dig jazz but don't live it.[37]

Real or not, these "fellow travelers" helped establish a widely recognized Beat style. Tim A. Ross, in an article critical of the Beat movement, describes this style:

I happened to be in San Francisco during the summer of 1958, and heard an elderly lady, noticing a bearded man passing on the sidewalk, say to her daughter, "Look, there's a beatnik." The beard, a readily seen outward sign of an inner dissent, had already become the badge. With it went sloppy clothes and dark glasses.[38]

Ross notes that the public image of the beatnik was so widespread that it was "instantly recognizable in *Saturday Evening Post* cartoons, on television, on the streets."[39] Along with the beard, sloppy clothes, and dark glasses came an association with those whose lives consisted mainly of "sex, vagabondage, and dabbling in Zen."[40]

By entering into popular consciousness through the artifice of style, Zen seized on a growing discontent in American society. It offered not only possible answers but also, more important, the sheen of glamor and hipness associated with the subcultures—Beat and elite—that embraced it. Introduced in this way, Zen became something to "try on" and "entertain," rather than something that directly challenged American values.

In fact, Zen as *stylized religion* covertly consolidated American national identity and its capitalist orientation. To understand this complex dynamic, one must examine the relationship between the United States and Japan in the postwar period. During the occupation of Japan (1945–1952), the United States set in place economic and political structures that would aid the war-torn country's recovery. U.S. forces vowed to minimize their presence and, beyond the nation's political structures, did not seek to transform Japanese culture. On an international level, this respect of cultural and religious differences served as a sign of American democratic principles. The United States was not interested in molding Japan wholly into its mirror image (as colonial forces of the past), but rather in capitalizing on the economic opportunity the defeated country held.[41]

It was Japan's cultural difference that made it such an attractive economic catch. The preservation of the island country's unique identity became highly marketable, influencing clothing and household fashions. Drawing from foreign sources, producers could expand the choices available to consumers. Conversely, Americans were given the means of self-expression that an individualist society demanded. Within this setting, Zen became a convenient import, unassuming and enchanting—supplemented by an interest in Oriental things and supplementing that interest. Suzuki's image played into this dynamic, adding a spiritual depth to this style and its products. The appearance of depth served as a convenient alibi for the mass consumer.[42]

In addition to economic benefits, America's increasing openness to foreign influence had two significant political and cultural payoffs. First of all, the aestheticization of Japan that took place in the 1950s not only assisted in rehabilitating the image of America's former enemy (and paved the way for economic exchange) but also neutralized it as political threat. Japan's cultural richness was something for Americans to admire, preserve, and appropriate. Second, an interest in Japanese style became an expression of the principle of freedom of choice, helping to distinguish American democracy from its Soviet counterpart. As Stuart Ewen astutely points out: "For decades, one of the most common ways that Americans compared communism and capitalist democracy was to say that communism encouraged sameness, denied individuality, and lacked style."[43] Americans employed style as a means to distinguish themselves and their tastes from other Americans and craft the uniqueness of their identities.

Hence, the appropriation of a Japanese aesthetic helped reinforce dimensions of individuality and freedom already strongly embedded in the American ethos. Furthermore, cultural options imported from around the world (and especially Japan) allowed Americans to disrupt the monotony of a potentially homogeneous identity. Whether these options were adopted by the cultural elite or the down-and-out Beat made little difference on a popular level. In fact, the fascination and interest Orientalia held for both factions only added to Zen's overall mystique and inaugurated it as a particular style.[44] As popularly conceived, Suzuki's image—affable, enigmatic, ancient, and deep—catered perfectly to these trends and offered an encounter with a "real live Oriental" to add to the mix.

Zen's Student

So far, we have examined the way in which Suzuki was first represented in the popular press and how his image participated in an overall stylistic interest in things Japanese during the late 1950s. Suzuki's image must be viewed within a symbolic nexus that places the image of the living thinker alongside objects of Japanese culture. His presence and philosophy endowed the superficiality of these objects (kimono robes, garden lanterns, Oriental furnishings) with a depth and significance that enhanced the appropriation and consumption of Japanese culture.

Unfurling Suzuki's image, as a symbol of stylized religion, reveals only half the story. The other half becomes apparent when we examine more broadly the story of Zen's popularization in late-1950s America. With Suzuki, Zen had certainly come West. But who would carry on his legacy? Concurrent with Suzuki's American stay, Buddhism was thriving in small centers and being brought to greater attention by individuals such as Alan Watts, Jack Kerouac, and Ruth Fuller Sasaki. Despite the range and depth of these engagements the popular press would seize on Watts and Kerouac as the most prominent of the set and stage the coexistence of their works as a competition. Would the Zen that emerged in America be "beat" (Kerouac) or would it be "square" (Watts)? Eventually, a figurative compromise would take place between two rivals and give birth to the sage's most promising pupil and rightful heir.

Jack Kerouac and the Zen Lunatics

Suzuki left Columbia in the summer of 1957 and, after a seven-month stay in Cambridge, Massachusetts, returned to Japan in 1958. But Zen remained alive and well after his departure. Much of this had to do with two seminal works that appeared in 1958: Jack Kerouac's *The Dharma Bums* and Alan Watts's "Beat Zen, Square Zen, and Zen."

Kerouac was certainly the more famous of the two. He had established a reputation for himself as the "patriarch and prophet" of the Beat generation through his *On the Road* (1957). *The Dharma Bums* hit the bookstores in the spring of 1958. Whereas *On the Road* chronicled "the cross-country adventures in cars, bars and beds of a bunch of fancy-talking young bums,"[45] *The Dharma Bums* followed its narrator, Ray Smith, on a journey through mountains and desert in search of a "rucksack revolution." In both books, the characters are modeled after Kerouac's own friends. In the case of *The Dharma Bums*, Kerouac took as his inspiration a fellow poet and Zen enthusiast, Gary Snyder, for the character Japhy Ryder.

Japhy Ryder is described as "the number one Dharma Bum of them all."[46] Ray is most impressed with Japhy's austere lifestyle as exhibited by his home:

> Japhy lived in his own shack which was infinitely smaller than ours, about twelve by twelve, with nothing in it but typical Japhy

appurtenances that showed his belief in the simple monastic life—no chairs at all, not even one sentimental rocking chair, but just straw mats. In the corner was his famous rucksack with cleaned-up pots and pans all fitting into one another in a compact unit and all tied and put away inside a knotted-up blue bandana. Then his Japanese wooden pata shoes, which he never used, and a pair of black inside-pata socks to pad around softly in over his pretty straw mats, just room for your four toes on one side and your big toe on the other. He had a slew of orange crates all filled with beautiful scholarly books, some of them in Oriental languages, all the great sutras, comments on sutras, the complete works of D. T. Suzuki and a fine quadruple-volume edition of Japanese haikus. He also had an immense collection of valuable general poetry.[47]

Japhy and Ray share an intense passion for Buddhism ("We had the same favorite Buddhist saint, too: Avalokitesvara, or, in Japanese, Kwannon the Eleven-Headed").[48] And it is Japhy who introduces Ray to the ninth-century poet and legendary Zen figure, Han Shan, "who got sick of the big city and the world and took off to hide in the mountains."[49] In Han Shan, modern-day Zen Lunatics, Ray and Japhy, would come to posit a spiritual ancestor.[50] Misunderstood by society and disillusioned with its practices, they find an outlet in poetry and travel. Kerouac draws an obvious connection between Han Shan and Japhy Ryder. In an informal yet significant way, Han Shan would serve as patriarch and model, and Japhy Ryder, his modern-day incarnation.

Creatively indiscriminate, the Dharma Bums confer the status of "Buddha" on any individual they see fit, including themselves. It does not matter whether the individuals they encounter are poor or rich, Buddhist or Christian, or otherwise. For the narrator (and Kerouac), spirituality exceeds the bounds of convention and can be realized by the least regarded in any given society. The Beat vision was marked by a high degree of anachronism and nonexclusivity; great wisdom could be found in a cook at a Chinese restaurant or a venerable teacher, such as Suzuki. Ray's question to one such unsuspecting cook in the *Dharma Bums* is one that Kerouac would later ask Suzuki during their first and only direct encounter.[51] According to Kerouac, he was summoned by the elder teacher; along with buddies, Lew Welch and Allen Ginsberg, he went to Suzuki's residence:

I rang Mr. Suzuki's door and he did not answer . . . —suddenly I decided to ring it three times, firmly and slowly, and then he came—he was a small man coming slowly through an old house with panelled wood walls and many books—he had long eyelashes, as everyone knows, which put me in the mind of the saying in the Sutras that the Dharma, like a bush, is slow to take root but once it has taken root it grows huge and firm and can't be hauled up from the ground except by a golden giant whose name is not Tathagata—anyway, Doctor Suzuki made us some green tea, very thick and soupy—he had precisely what idea of what place I should sit, and where my two other friends should sit, the chairs already arranged—he himself sat behind a table and looked at us, nodding—I said in a loud voice (because he had told us he was a little deaf) "Why did Bodhidharma come from the West?"—He made no reply—He said, "You three young men sit here quietly & write haikus while I go make some green tea"—He brought us the green tea in cracked old soupbowls of some sort—He told us not to forget about the tea—when we left, he pushed us out the door but once we were out on the sidewalk he began giggling at us and pointing his finger and saying "Don't forget the tea!"—I said "I would like to spend the rest of my life with you"—He held up his finger and said "Sometime."[52]

In this reminiscence, Suzuki's mystical aura is further cultivated. Suzuki's physical features, as in popular accounts, are taken as obvious signs of the old man's wisdom. His gestures are captivating, friendly, and open, yet his words elusive. Although Suzuki never directly responds to the Zen Lunatic's pointed question, Kerouac still leaves with an impression that seems to provide its own answer. He reads intention into Suzuki's every gesture and word.

Perhaps more significant is the way Suzuki came to symbolize for Kerouac—even for a brief moment—a living Asian sage. His impulsive devotion ("I would like to spend the rest of my life with you") attests to a nonrational, immediate recognition of Suzuki's measured response as sprouting from the same Eastern spiritual wellspring from which the Dharma Bum drew. Accounts such as Kerouac's would help transform Suzuki beyond simply an expounder of Zen—into an Oriental Monk.

From this account, one is given the impression that Suzuki is not personally put off by Kerouac's brand of Buddhism and is at the very least intrigued by the young writer. But the scholar was philosophically wary of "Beat Zen." He wrote in the *Japan Quarterly*:

Zen is at present evoking unexpected echoes in various fields of Western culture: music, painting, literature, semantics, religious philosophy, and psychoanalysis. But as it is in many cases grossly misrepresented and misinterpreted, I undertake here to explain most briefly, as far as language permits, what Zen aims at and what significance it has in the modern world, hoping that Zen will be saved from being too absurdly caricatured.[53]

In the article, Suzuki points out: "Spontaneity is not everything, it must be 'rooted'"[54]—a critical comment aimed at Kerouac's model. Despite these objections, it is Kerouac's dynamic account that becomes popularly available during the late 1950s.[55] As Gary Snyder would later comment: "We took Dr. Suzuki as our own."[56] The connection between Suzuki and the Beats would be further strengthened, as Kerouac's encounter with the Buddhist sage would be recounted time and time again.

Alan Watts

Alan Watts was drawn to the East at an early age. Surrounded by his mother's "Oriental treasures"[57] and imaginatively fed on a diet of Kipling, Watts developed a fascination with Asia. He would later tell *Life* magazine that he first fell in love with the East at age twelve, "when he ran across the sinister and inscrutable *Dr. Fu Manchu* and fellow orientals in the literary works of Sax Rohmer."[58] Another childhood turning point came when he visited:

> a small, ruined, and ancient church in which I most earnestly sought the Christian God and didn't find him, and at which point I bought, from a curio shop in Weston-super-Mare, a small image of the Buddha—of the Daibutsu in Makakura. I liked the expression on his face. It wasn't judgmental or frantic, but stately and serene, and the title "Buddha" went along in my mind with buds.[59]

As he grew into adolescence, the young Watts gained a more formal entrée into Buddhism through several books on Buddhism lent to him by Francis Croshaw (Edwards Holmes's *The Creed of the Buddha* and Lafcadio Hearn's *Gleanings in Buddha Fields*). Duly impressed, he became an active member in the Buddhist Lodge in London, where he had the opportunity to sit in on the lectures of such luminary figures as T'ai-hsü, Krishnamurti, Annie Bessant, and D. T. Suzuki. Of his first impressions of Suzuki, Watts wrote: "He was versed in Japanese, English, Chinese, Sanskrit, Tibetan, French, Pali, and German, but while attending a meeting of the Buddhist Lodge he would play with a kitten, looking right into its Buddha-nature."[60] Watts went on to voraciously read the scholar's works. So inspired, he would attempt to "clarify and popularize" Suzuki's thought in a book called *The Spirit of Zen*, written at the age of twenty. Watts would finally meet the "unofficial master of Zen Buddhism"[61] a year later in 1936 at the World Congress of Faiths. Suzuki "stole the scene,"[62] and Watts "attended every lecture and seminar that Suzuki gave" at the Congress.[63]

As captivated with Eastern religions as he appeared to be in his formative years, Watts embarked on a decidedly more Christian-leaning path in the 1940s and eventually became an Anglican minister. But he left the church six years later and resumed his prodigious writing career in which he attempted to articulate his unique spiritual vision. In 1956, one of his most popular books, *The Way of Zen*, would be published. It contributed significantly to the heightened interest in Zen exhibited in the late 1950s.[64] During this time, Watts met with Suzuki on several occasions. The elder scholar continued to serve as the inspiration and the touchstone for Watts's views on Zen.[65] Of Suzuki, he would later say: "I have never had a formal teacher (guru or *roshi*) in the spiritual life—only an exemplar, whose example I have not really followed because no sensitive person likes to be mimicked. That exemplar was Suzuki Daisetz."[66] For Watts, this "exemplar" would become "the most gentle and enlightened person [he] had] ever known."[67]

"Beat Zen, Square Zen, and Zen"

In the summer of 1958, the *Chicago Review* dedicated its issue to the burgeoning phenomenon known as Zen. The respected journal featured writings and translations from all the notable players: D. T. Suzuki, Jack Kerouac, Shinichi Hisamatsu, Philip Whalen, Ruth Fuller Sasaki, Nyogen Senzaki, Gary Snyder, Harold E. McCarthy, Akihisa Kondo, and Paul Wienpahl. Perhaps none was quite as widely read or as influential as the essay by Alan W. Watts, "Beat Zen, Square Zen, and Zen." In his overview (which also served as the lead-in article), Watts attempted to make sense of "the extraordinary growth of western interest in Zen," which he attributed to "our vague disquiet with the artificiality or anti-naturalness of both Christianity, with its politically ordered cosmology, and technology, with its imperialistic mechanization of a natural world from which man himself feels strangely alien."[68] Although such commentary was insightful, the piece gained its main significance by the way it captured the current dialogue about Zen in the United States and the different constituencies involved.

Watts succinctly delineated the unique problem that confronted the Western Zen enthusiast as follows:

> The Westerner who is attracted by Zen and who would understand it
> deeply must have one indispensable qualification; he must understand

his own culture so thoroughly that he is no longer swayed by its premises unconsciously. He must really have come to terms with the Lord God Jehovah and with his Hebrew-Christian conscience so that he can take it or leave it without fear or rebellion. He must be free of the itch to justify himself. Lacking this, his Zen will be either "beat" or "square," either a revolt from the culture and social order or a new form of stuffiness and respectability. For Zen is above all the liberation of the mind from conventional thought, and this is something utterly different from rebellion against convention, on the one hand, or adopting foreign conventions, on the other.[69]

It is clear which type of individuals Watts associates with both Zen "extremes"— beat and square. The word *beat* is meant to bring to mind the much-talked-about literary movement that included illuminati such as Clellon Holmes, Allen Ginsberg, and Jack Kerouac. Watts seems to want to apply the term more broadly to refer to "a younger generation's nonparticipation in 'the American Way of Life,' a revolt which does not seek to change the existing order but simply turns away from it to find the significance of life in subjective experience rather than objective achievement."[70] Those who engage in "the hipster life of New York and San Francisco" are a convenient figure for his criticisms. The Beat interested in Zen is in fact a "displaced or unconscious Christian"[71] who is less concerned with a spiritual practice than with justifying his or her own self-centeredness and "underlying Protestant lawlessness."[72]

On the other extreme of the Zen continuum was the "square" practitioner. Watts describes this type of seeker as one who "imagine[s] that the only proper way to find it is to run off to a monastery in Japan or to do special exercises in the lotus posture for five hours a day."[73] More specifically, he notes:

Square Zen is the Zen of established tradition in Japan with its clearly defined hierarchy, its rigid discipline, and its specific tests of *satori* . . . a question for the *right* spiritual experience, for a *satori* which will receive the stamp (*inka*) of approved and established authority. There will even be certificates to hang on the wall.[74]

Here, Watts most likely had in mind his former mother-in-law, the formidable Ruth Fuller Everett Sasaki.[75] In an interview with *Time* magazine in the spring of 1958, she notes: "It's not easy to become a Zen Buddhist. I can sit in a monks' hall for seven days, sitting cross-legged, sleeping only one hour a night."[76] Sasaki was a woman from the American upper class who went to study for an extended period of time at Kyoto's Nanzenji Temple in the 1930s. She returned to the States and began working at the Manhattan Zen Institute of America alongside Sokei-an (Shigetsu Sasaki), and after the death of her husband in 1944, she married the Zen roshi. Sasaki later returned to Japan and was ordained by Zuigan Goto, head roshi at Daitokuji Temple, and installed as the head priest of the subtemple, which catered to Americans and Europeans who traveled to Japan in pursuit of Zen.[77]

One wonders how much of Watts's criticism of Zen's square proponents is rooted in his personal experience with Ruth Sasaki. Although there is obviously a feeling of indebtedness to his former mother-in-law,[78] he nevertheless writes in his autobiography: "Until her marriage with Sokei-an Sasaki, Ruth was something of a social climber—not too offensively—but for a woman of spiritual and aesthetic resources such as hers, she seemed unduly impressed with the industrial captains and kings of Chicago and their especially feather-headed wives."[79] Watts apparently drew a correlation between Sasaki's early preoccupations and her immersion into the hierarchy of the Japanese Zen establishment. In his eyes, the matriarch's view of formal, uninterrupted training in Japan as a prerequisite of bringing back "true" Rinzai Zen to the West did not escape the dichotomous tendency of Protestant thinking (true/untrue, proper/improper) and fell into the same trap of self-justification as Beat Zen.

There was, of course, a third possibility for the Zen enthusiast in the West besides the beat and square extremes. As the title of Watts's essay implies, there is "Zen" in its truest form, unadulterated by the cultural weaknesses of "sheer caprice" or "rigid discipline." Here, it is helpful to reiterate his definition of a genuine Zen practitioner:

> He must understand his own culture so thoroughly that he is no
> longer swayed by its premises unconsciously. He must really have
> come to terms with the Lord God Jehovah and with his Hebrew-
> Christian conscience so that he can take it or leave it without fear or
> rebellion. He must be free of the itch to justify himself.[80]

In many ways, Watts fulfilled the qualifications of his own definition.[81] In the 1940s, Watts struggled with the relationship between Christianity and Buddhism. In search of a vocation, he enrolled in the Seabury-Western Theological Seminary in Chicago. Watts's education was impressive, and his course of study included early Christianity, Patristics, Russian theology, mystical and ascetic theology, and modern interpreters of the tradition.[82] The accomplished student was ordained an Episcopal priest in 1945 and went on to become the chaplain at Northwestern University.

During his ministry, Watts became increasingly disillusioned with Christian practice and never fully resolved his tense relationship with the religion's theology and dogma. In 1950, he offered his letter of resignation, in which he wrote: "My departure from the Church is not a moral protest; it is simply that, seeing what I see, I cannot do otherwise. I take no credit for it. My viewpoint is not one of moral judgment and condemnation, but of simply inability to conform to a rule of life based on what I see to be illusions."[83] In his ten-year encounter with Christianity, Watts would attempt to "come to terms with the Lord God Jehovah." And in his mind, his struggle proved that an unconscious attachment to Christianity no longer informed his spiritual belief. Thus, he felt an able representative of Zen in its most genuine form.

To a large extent, Watts's commentary on the Zen clears a path or "middle way" for his own definition of Zen. Employing popular lingo, he isolates and labels the different factions for easy consumption ("beat" and "square"). Already implied in such terminology is that these two alternatives represent two extremes that do not accurately reflect Zen in its truest form. He is careful to qualify his criticisms ("I see no real quarrel with either extreme")[84] but still bolsters his attack by calling into question the motivations behind his competitors' views (fear, rebellion). For a middle-class American audience who had little interest in "hitting the road" (i.e., wandering around aimlessly) or traveling to a monastery in Japan, Watts's conception could not help but come as somewhat of a relief.

Aftermath

It is interesting to trace the ways in which the popular press re-presents Watts's delineation after its publication. *Time* magazine featured a brief article—"Zen: Beat & Square" (July 21, 1958)—on its religion page that summarized and condensed Watts's essay. The most noteworthy dimension of the article is its clear condemnation of Beat Zen: "The Beat Generation have Zen wrong."[85] On the level of the popular, commentators appeared quite wary of Beat Zen (especially as it was portrayed in Jack Kerouac's *The Dharma Bums*) and harnessed Watts's criticism to bash the authority of its expression.

All in all, the popular press transformed Watts into a figure that could easily be played off the Beats and the unruliness of the subculture. Soon after the *Chicago Review* issue appeared, J. Donald Adams, noted columnist for the *New York Times Book Review*, harshly criticized *The Dharma Bums* and its spiritual underpinnings (October 26, 1958). Not only did he tag the Beats' religiosity as "brief flights into the Buddhist stratosphere" but also added: "And I remain skeptical as to what can be salvaged from the mystics of the Far East that can be adapted to the emotional and rational needs of a people as different as ourselves."[86] Obviously, Watts's essay had resonated with the critic. In a later offering (November

16, 1958), Adams would admit to a secondhand knowledge of Zen. But in justification of his initial view, he cites Watts's analysis. A column-long excerpt from
"Beat Zen, Square Zen, and Zen" appeared alongside the editorial.

An interesting misconception takes place in Stephen Mahoney's article for the
Nation titled "The Prevalence of Zen" (November 1, 1958). Even though Watts
carefully attempts to disassociate himself from either Beat or Square versions
of Zen, he becomes associated with the latter. Mahoney writes: "Beat Zen and
Square Zen, the factions have been designated by Watts, whom observers take
for the captive spokesman of the latter."[87]

> The Beat book is the Zen novel *The Dharma Bums* by Jack Kerouac,
> author of *On the Road* and other Beat scripture. . . .. The Square book,
> *Nature, Man, and Woman*, is the prolific Watts's 1958 directory of Zen
> wisdom. It is a masterful, lucid popularization of Zen that does not
> distort its difficult subject.[88]

Throughout the article, Mahoney seems sensitive to Watts's original delineation; he is careful not to label Watts as an outright Square Zenist and keeps
intact the exponent's claim of authenticity (i.e., Watts's book "does not distort
its difficult subject"). The link between Watts and Square Zen has more to do
with those who affiliate themselves with Watts:

> Clearly, Beat Zen does not score at the ol' deliberative level. . . .. But
> Square Zen now. It does *very* well on the delib'rative level. Last April
> in New York Watts held a weekend-long seminar. It went over much
> of the ground Watts covers in *Nature, Man, and Woman*. Previously
> he had given Zen seminars in Illinois, where he used to be an
> Anglican priest and a chaplain at Northwestern University, and in
> California, where until recently he was Dean of the American
> Academy of Asian Studies, near San Francisco. Forty people were
> allowed to attend this one at $25 a head. There were architects,
> engineers, writers, housewives, professors, an Episcopalian priest, a
> publisher—a group of people one might come upon at a cocktail
> party in Westport. Nobody removed his clothes.[89]

The point that Mahoney is attempting to highlight is the way in which Square
Zenists have adopted Watts as their representative. This constituency of "clever,
bored novelty-seekers"[90] may not feel compelled to travel to Japan and study
with bona fide monks, but they do seek channels (e.g., Watts's seminars)
through which to not only expand but also legitimate their interest. Watts may
have distinguished himself from "the Zen of established tradition in Japan,"[91]
but he did not foresee the ways in which he would play a significant role in the

hegemonic creation of American Zen Buddhism. Many years later, he would also depart from his own definitions and admit to the squareness of his 1950s façade.

In 1959, Zen continued to make appearances in the popular press. Watts furthered his excursions into Asian culture; *Vogue* reported, "People are talking about . . . the voice of Alan Watts, on a recording, reading and discussing *Haiku*, the Japanese seventeen-syllable verse."[92] Suzuki's book, *Zen and Japanese Culture*, was reissued and reviewed in the *New York Times*.[93] In the *Christian Century*, Peter Fingesten critically questioned Buddhism's viability for Americans in "Beat and Buddhist.[94] And Alfred G. Aronowitz presented a sympathetic ten-part series on the Beat Generation for the *New York Post* (including an article dedicated to their Zen spirituality).[95] Post–*Dharma Bums*, Zen was becoming a convenient buzzword. Barnaby Conrad's review of Kerouac's new book, *Doctor Sax: Faust Part Three*, was titled, "Barefoot Boy with Dreams of Zen."[96] The title was obviously chosen solely for its exotic appeal, since the piece makes no mention of anything remotely related to Zen or Kerouac's unique interpretation of it.

But by 1960, the Zen boomlet had receded from popular attention and, along with it, Suzuki's role as Zen's personality. Although he remained active until his death in 1965, his name vanishes from the news weeklies and magazine articles. His role in the transplantation of Zen into American popular consciousness had become obsolete by this time—his duties and mission passed on to a much more "accessible" exponent. Indeed, by the early 1960s, the American popular press had selected Alan Watts as Suzuki's heir apparent and focused the attention of their pens and cameras on him.

The selection of Watts as the new representative figure of Zen was not without its own peculiar logic. Despite the integral role his book played in bringing Zen to popular attention, Jack Kerouac could not stave off the harsh reviews of his critics and, by the early 1960s, was no longer taken seriously in press accounts. Kerouac's work remained in the public eye during this period. But instead of articulating a clear vision of the "religious movement"[97] that the Beats had professed to embody, he (along with his protagonists) seemed to continue on their meandering path.

In a review of Kerouac's *Big Sur*, the critic for *Time* magazine commented: "What can a beat do when he is too old to go on the road? He can go on the sauce. . . .. In the end, [the narrator] settles for a howling emotional crisis—which on a grown-up would look very much like the DTs."[98] Although the cultural legacy of the Beats eventually made its way into American life and letters, its initial promise had greatly diminished by the turn of the decade. Beat Zen, after much brouhaha, was dismissed as a fad, a youthful preoccupation, something that had been dabbled with but not seriously entertained.[99] Until later rearticulation in the mid-1960s (most notably by Gary Snyder), Beat Zen was dismissed. Watts's *Chicago Review* article had achieved its obvious intent.

Watts, during the early 1960s, continued to offer seminars on Zen and write prolifically on the subject. He fit the conventionalized model of a religious enthusiast with which Americans felt more comfortable.

> Watts is a crewcut, cleancut, and has a shy, boyish, scholar's grin. He is 43, looks 30; he lived in England until he was in his twenties and speaks with an accent that is U. Watts sprawled out awkwardly in an armchair, clutched at his ankle, and the words flowed in an unending, shiningly lucid stream. He never looked at a note.[100]

Not only did Watts differ from the Beats in appearance and temperament but also distinguished himself in terms of pedigree. He enjoyed a gentrified upbringing attending King's School, Canterbury—one of the oldest boarding schools in England. Although his family could not afford to send him to Oxford, he embarked on his own course of study ("my own university"). As previously mentioned, Watts also had extensive theological training under his belt. (This fact was often noted in articles about Watts.) Hence, unlike his Beat counterparts, Watts seemed to lend legitimacy to Zen via his British upbringing, class background and religious training.

As the 1950s drew to a close and a new decade emerged, Watts appeared to prevail over his Beat competitors. In a 1960 *Life* magazine pictorial of Watts, he is heralded as the "chief exponent of the burgeoning Zen movement in America" and "its most lucid interpreter."[101] Unlike the Beats, Watts's main goal centered on the development and propagation of Zen in a Western environment. He made a concerted effort to introduce Zen on a popular level through the use of a variety of media—"a radio program in five cities, taped TV shows, a nonstop lecture program and a book a year."[102] Compared with Suzuki, who made himself accessible only according to the demand and invitation of his Western audience, Watts actively sought to create such a demand.

The *Life* photographic essay is most interesting to study in relation to understanding Watts's appeal. These glimpses into his world show Watts in a number of different poses and settings: contemplating a dew-covered spider web, sorting mail for a haiku contest, lecturing to students at Brandeis and Big Sur, taking part in experimental movement with a bamboo pole, writing Chinese calligraphy, and at work in his study (figure 2.5). The pictorial gives one the impression that Watts achieves the seamless incorporation of ancient Asian traditions into a modernized Western way of life.

Whereas Suzuki generated popular interest because of his enigmatic nature and exotic appeal, Watts seemed to achieve his for exactly the opposite

FIGURE. 2.5. Alan Watts in the photo essay, "Eager Exponent of Zen," *Life*, April 21, 1961 (Photographer: Joern Gerdts).

reasons. In the photos, his clothing is Western conservative. In work settings, he is wearing a suit and tie and appears no different from any other middle-America, white-collar worker of the time, but even in casual short-sleeve gear, his shirt is buttoned to the top (also, a marked contrast to the Beats' disheveled look). The only distinguishing marks of an alternative lifestyle are the serious, focused expression he exhibits throughout the photo spread and the Asian paraphernalia he employs in his pursuits. With his Western dress and Anglo-Saxon looks, he appeared wholly familiar—someone with whom his audience could easily identify.

Watts was also portrayed as a family man. Even though on his third marriage, he is pictured in *Life* with his three children. The caption reads: "In library of his Mill Valley home in California Watts works oblivious to presence of three of his four children."[103] This alone might imply an attitude of distance from his family. But Watts's own words, which immediately follow the caption, serve to qualify this impression and demonstrate his devotion as a father: "*They ask the usual children's questions like 'Who made the world and who made me?' I ask them, 'Why use the word* made, *like a machine—why not use another word:* grew?'"[104] Squarely placed within the constellation of the family, Watts is distinguished from both Suzuki and Kerouac—both of whom could boast no progeny.[105]

Throughout the *Life* photographic essay, Watts is portrayed as a highly intelligent as well as intelligible individual. Unlike Kerouac and the Beats, whose brand of Zen was viewed as jazzy and nondeliberative,[106] Watts is taken as an articulate source. The momentariness of Kerouac's prose, as well as the mysteriousness of Suzuki's esoteric speech, is abandoned for Watts's clear commentary on Zen. The magazine's editors allow his words to stand alone, as if sufficient in and of themselves—their translation unnecessary and their meaning direct.

In the early 1960s, the publication of Watts's book reviews and articles in prominent magazines and journals would attest to the reputation he had developed. His appeal is not surprising. Watts fit the conventional standards of the time in terms of educational background, class standing, lifestyle, and image. Unlike the Beats, he posed no offense to a popular audience. Studied, nonsensationalistic, yet provocative, Watts seemed to emerge as Suzuki's most perfect pupil, his most appropriate heir.

The discursive interplay between Watts and the Beats, as enacted by the mainstream accounts, demonstrates the final vestiges of a strategy of containment so prevalent in the 1950s. Kerouac and the Beats represented an unruly set whose lifestyles seemed to pose a direct challenge to American society at the time,[107] and their attitudes were viewed as infecting the minds of a younger generation. It was hoped that Watts—his clean-cut image and precise words—would serve as an alternative example. But the Beats would have a momentous effect and pave the way for the counterculture to come. Although Kerouac suffered slow decline until his death in 1969, others (among them, Allen Ginsberg and Gary Snyder) carried on the movement's spirit and would later be lauded for their literary and spiritual independence.

Ultimately, Watts did come to accept the Beats and their brand of Zen. He would later say that he had been "somewhat severe" in his 1958 essay and that he now considered Jack Kerouac, Lawrence Ferlinghetti, Allen Ginsberg, and Gary Snyder among his friends.[108] More than simply acknowledge his earlier asperity, Watts would go on to defend the Beats against enduring misunderstanding.[109] And he would eventually forge a special relationship with Gary Snyder, about whom he would respectfully say: "When I am dead I would like to be able to say that he is carrying on everything I hold most dearly."[110]

A little more than decade later, Beat and Square Zen, as first popularly portrayed in the late 1950s, would merge into a unified cultural force. Both Snyder and Watts would share a similar sensibility and direction. Watts's biographer, Monica Furlong, comments: "The vision that Watts, Snyder and Kerouac shared was the renunciation of the values of bourgeois and suburban life."[111] This vision was undergirded by a spirituality grounded in a new American configuration of Zen equally indebted to both Beat and Square factions. Although those who carried on Suzuki's legacy saw themselves in direct contradistinction to the rest of American society, they still held a special allegiance to America, and their efforts would help secure the United States (and more specifically, California) as Zen's hegemonic center.[112]

The Western pupil of Zen would become an important figure. He would come to represent the protagonist of the story that would make Eastern spirituality attractive to a popular audience. Without him, the labor of the Eastern sage or Oriental Monk, whose express mission it is to transmit his ancient spiritual heritage, would bear no fruit. The pupil's function in the narrative would come to depend not so much on his capacity to teach, but rather his ethos. It is the pupil's ability to challenge convention and embody the promise of a new cultural synthesis that transforms him into a hero.

Unlike the popular narrative that would later emerge, the lineage of master and pupil was less discrete in real terms. Even in the early days of American Zen, there were a number of teachers and a multitude of pupils. Some students never studied with a master but creatively drew their knowledge and inspiration from a wide variety of influences (this was true of Watts and especially the case with the Beats). However, it is often difficult to capture such complexity and relay it to a popular audience. We have seen that even in journalistic accounts, these real-life individuals were often molded into accessible person-alities that a mainstream audience could readily recognize and identify—their interactions dramatized for intriguing effect.

It is not a far stretch to see how these personalities contributed to the Ori-ental Monk narrative's stock character of the pupil. From the Beats, this figure would inherit bravado, spunk, and independence; he would feel like a misfit as they once had. From Watts, he would receive his seriousness, focus, and under-stated demeanor. And from both, he would garner a passion for the East,[113] as well as the brave individuality so attractive in the characters Americans have come to love. In this way, a character and role began to take shape that would reflect and draw cumulatively from the pages of "real life." And we are left with a most heroic pupil for the venerable sage.

The Decline of the East: Figuring Japan

As we have seen, the media's "narration" of the transmission of Zen to the West depended on at least two significant characters: the Oriental Monk and his des-ignated pupil. Suzuki—the "wisely foolish, gently disciplined, and simply pro-found"[114] individual whose life had been dedicated to cultivating an understanding of Zen in the West—was well suited for the role of the Monk. And the Beats and especially Alan Watts contributed to the figure of the student who would passionately continue the teacher's work. But the narrative in which these two figures played a prominent part helped emplot Zen's movement West within a teleological framework. In the 1950s, one begins to see the outline of what would become the raison d'être of American Buddhism: the United States would be the site of Zen's future development. Within the founding narrative, Suzuki's "mission" was imbued with a more transcendental purpose.

The justification for this mission began to emerge as soon as Zen's popu-larity was firmly established in 1959. Two articles appeared that are especially worthy of note. In its February 23 issue, Time magazine reported a current "Zensation" in Japan. A scandal had erupted at the "great temple of Shofukuji [sic]" in Kobe, where photographer Mikio Tsuchiya[115] witnessed:

> loinclothed priests playing mah-jongg instead of sitting in immobile
> meditation, a priest drinking with a bar hostess, two novices
> staggering along a Kobe street late at night with a barmaid between
> them. Tsuchiya quoted one priest as saying: "By listening to good
> music and gazing on *ikibosatu* [the living Buddha]. I feel I can
> understand the teachings." This wisdom was Tsuchiya's caption for a

photograph of the same priest happily gaping at pictures of virtually naked women.[116]

Other indiscretions are further noted. Mumon Yamada, the temple's head priest, "blamed it all on an influx of university-trained novices who lack moral fiber." As a result of Tsuchiya's revelations, *Time* reported that the temple council not only expelled the boys but also compelled the photographer to apologize and destroy all her negatives.

The status of Zen in Japan was further brought into question in a *Newsweek* article, "The Real Spirit of Zen?" (September 21, 1959). The weekly publication was surprised to find that "although nearly 5 million Japanese still profess to be Zen followers, few know anything about the discipline."[117] For the piece, Suzuki was cited:

> "Buddhism . . . in Japan is passé," adds Dr. Daisetz T. Suzuki, Zen's leading missionary to the West. Suzuki, who returned to Japan last year to write the definitive encyclopedia of Zen, says that his colleagues are constantly asking him why Americans are "so interested in what is so old and worn out as Buddhism."[118]

This is the last time Suzuki would appear in American press accounts until his death in 1966. The article is accompanied by photograph of Suzuki looking even older and wiser than before. The caption underneath the photograph reiterates and reinforces the philosopher's comment: "Buddhism in Japan is passé."

Unruly monks more concerned with women and drink, Japanese who lacked appreciation for their Zen heritage: It is through press portrayals such as these that Americans began to perceive Japan in spiritual retrograde. At the time, there were two prominent explanations for this: (1) Japanese Zen Buddhists had lapsed into establishment thinking, and (2) the Japanese had been corrupted by Western influence.[119]

Suzuki, as well as Alan Watts, had certainly helped to promulgate the first view. For Suzuki, the critique was less direct but still could be intimated in his vital hope of a revitalized Japanese Zen. Watts was much more outspoken. As we have already seen in his essay "Beat Zen, Square Zen, and Zen," he considered the Zen practiced in Japanese monasteries as formal and spiritually rigid (i.e., square). In both cases, it was thought that Zen in Japan had gone the way of most established religions and lost its spiritual direction and inspirational power.

The second explanation, which attributed Japan's spiritual decline to the corruptive forces of Western mass culture and capitalist greed, was more expansive. The occupation of Japan by American forces under General MacArthur was seen as a successful project. In some ways, it was perhaps too successful—as an ancient culture seemed to be in the process of becoming a modernized industrial nation with all its trappings. Americans may have helped lead Japan into the twentieth century, but it also felt partially responsible for the demise of its native traditional culture. The victory over the Japanese triggered an imperialist nostalgia that would become a defining feature of Americans' views of the East.

In 1961, Arthur Koestler published a controversial book that would explore this residual guilt. *The Lotus and the Robot* was previewed in *Esquire* (December 1960, under the title "The Decline of the East").[120] Koestler put the issue in this way:

> Asians have a tendency to lay the blame for this decline on the
> soul-destroying influence of the West, and Western intellectuals are
> inclined to accept the blame. "As pupils we were not bad, but
> hopeless as teachers"—Auden's *mea culpa*, though addressed to Italy,
> might serve as a motto for the Western guilt complex towards Asia.[121]

Koestler proceeds from the premise that such guilt leads liberal intellectuals to engage in the view that "material poverty of Asia is a sign of its spiritual superiority."[122] Such a view in his opinion is ill informed. The material "progress" brought to Asian countries may have negative effects on native culture, but such effects are inevitable (they are part of the package deal). If rampant consumerism is adopted by a native people, it is their own fault: "Uneducated Asiatic masses are bound to be attracted by the trashiest influences and wares."[123] But this does not take away from the benefits introduced by Western political intervention: "literacy, culture hunger and leisure time." The real culprit is the lack of "creative talents" to engage and steer this newly privileged state of affairs.

For Koestler, the search for such "talents" was misdirected. In his own travels to India and Japan in the late 1950s, he had hoped to find an "answer to offer to our perplexities and deadlocked problems."[124] But instead, he was led to the following conclusion: "Lilies that fester smell far worse than weeds: both India and Japan seem to be spiritually sicker, more estranged from a living faith than the West."[125] According to Koestler, the West should not be looking toward Asia for inspiration but rather draw from its own cultural resources. For the remainder of the epilogue, Koestler goes on to make an argument for European culture and its superior evolution. Compared with Asia, whose philosophical systems remain stunted with concerns of "essential Being" and detachment toward human suffering, Europe has developed a form of rationality and conceptual knowledge that is best able to cope with contemporary problems. In addition, European culture has evolved through a process marked by "continuity-though-change and unity-in-diversity."[126] Asian cultures, in comparison, represented "continuity without change" and unity without diversity—civilizations that have remained relatively stagnant since the dates of their origin.[127]

The argument behind Koestler's defensive account here is not new. His view takes part in a long tradition of European intellectual thought that denigrated Asian religions and cultures in order to boost its own worth.[128] But it did spark an explosive reaction. Koestler's damning critique of Asian religions obviously did not sit well with Zen enthusiasts such as Alan Watts.[129] Four months later, Watts's response made its way into *Esquire* ("Aftermath: The Decline of the East"). In it, Watts is quick to comment: "Comparisons of this kind between East and West have no constructive results whatsoever. They are merely self-satisfying to those who share Mr. Koestler's cultural provincialism, and to any educated Japanese or Hindu, simply insulting."[130] In response to Koestler's charge that guilt has led intellectuals to entertain the connection between Asia's material poverty and its spiritual superiority, Watts argues that Koestler has committed his own sort of fallacious reasoning. The "backwardness" of Asian countries in terms of technological and material progress does not "by any means imply either that there is a historical tradition of Western culture necessarily superior to the Eastern,"[131] as Koestler would like to have it.

Watts then goes on to demonstrate the ways in which Asian philosophies do have something to contribute to the urgent problems of the modern world. Zen meditation (as well as Yoga), for example, overcomes the dangerous tendencies of Western rational thinking, which encourages a distinction between consciousness and its objects; it allows one to see the world as one and work toward the restoration of ecological balance.

Taken together, Koestler's book and Watts's response can be viewed as a debate regarding the value of Asian religions to the West that was taking place at the turn of the decade. Read on a superficial level, Koestler and Watts seem to present opposing viewpoints on the matter. But examined more closely, there appears to be a common thread that unites the two. As we have seen, Koestler portrays Asian religions as stagnant systems of thought based on his own experiences in Japan and India. Although Watts admirably counters the Koestler's major presumption—that Eastern religions have little to offer the West—he does not challenge the view that these religions have become impotent in their context of origin. This is most clear when the Zen advocate pronounces: "Considering [Eastern wisdom's] *sophisticated following in the West*, no old-fashioned denunciation of heathen doctrine will do"[132] (my emphasis).

As an example of this "sophisticated following," Watts cites biologist Joseph Needham, who he declares is "as eminent in Western science as in

Far-Eastern history."[133] According to Needham, when European thinking moved ahead of Chinese scientific theories in the seventeenth century, "Europe (or rather, by then, the world) was able to draw upon a mode of thinking very old, very wise, and not characteristically *European* at all."[134] Here, Watts (via Needham) attempts to establish the indebtedness of Western thought to the Asian theories.

In Watts's account, no mention is made of spiritual developments *in the East*. Asian systems of thought are rather portrayed as "very old, very wise," which unwittingly seems to support Koestler's view of their "continuity without change." It is true that, unlike Koestler, Watts had never traveled to Asia. However, he did have the opportunity to meet with Asian religious luminaries (such as Suzuki), and even these individuals are not ones to which he refers. Instead, Joseph Needham is represented as a contemporary innovator of Eastern thought. It requires historical skills such as Needham's to excavate the ancient source and defend its value. In this way, Watts and Koestler seem in strange agreement: Asian religions appear barren in their context of origin. What they disagree on is whether these religions are worth regeneration. According to Watts, they are. But such regeneration only seems possible in a new environment.

These various portrayals and accounts we have examined are all striking in their common assumptions. In each case, Zen in Japan is characterized by its decline—a decline caused by the spiritual stasis of the Japanese people. Americans could perhaps accept the view that Suzuki helped propagate—namely, the extremely intimate relationship that exists between Zen and the Japanese people: "Zen is the expression of the Japanese character."[135] But this did not mean that they would remain Zen's primary cultivators; indeed, there were signs that its productivity was beginning to wane. Whether one believed that the vine has reached maturity and fails to bear fruit or that its stalk has become irreversibly corrupt by the disease of Western influence, the results were the same—Japan's claim to Zen was falling away. The spiritual species could only be saved if transplanted into new soil and cross-fertilized in just the right way. Such opinions would provide the justification for the transmission of Zen from the Orient to the Occident, from Asia to America, from Oriental Monks such as Suzuki to pupils such as Watts.[136]

Mihoko Okamura: Figuring Japanese Americans

If the Japanese were figured as a people neglectful of their spiritual heritage, how were Japanese Americans portrayed? Was there any difference between the two in the minds of a popular audience? If a generalized American consciousness did indeed distinguish between the two, what part would Japanese Americans come to play in the transplantation of Zen and in the Virtual Orientalist scene?

Logically considered, Japanese Americans seemed to embody the prerequisite features of a people that would carry forth Suzuki's legacy. Culturally, Japanese Americans had inherited a predisposition to Zen that Suzuki argued (and a Western popular audience believed) was deeply ingrained in the Japanese psyche. However, because of immigration to the United States, they no longer lived under the formal strictures of Japanese society and culture. It appeared that Japanese Americans could enjoy a new freedom of cultural expression unavailable to those in Japan. Their immersion in American culture would stimulate that expression. All in all, it would seem as if Japanese Americans represented a group who could integrate the characteristics of Japanese spiritual depth and American initiative that was thought to be needed for Zen's healthy survival.

Indeed, Japanese Americans played an important role in Suzuki's 1950s sojourn to the West. In 1950, Suzuki had been given a temporary appointment at the Claremont Graduate School in southern California. When the school could not come up with Suzuki's living expenses, it turned to Bishop Takahashi of the Los Angeles Shingon Temple for help. Because of his successful appeal to the Japanese American community, the funds were secured for Suzuki's visit.[137]

The Berkeley Buddhist Church in the Bay Area—a temple that served local Japanese American Buddhists—was the site of Zen's early ferment. There, an "Advanced Study Class" that met on Friday nights included:

> the Reverend Imamura and his wife Jane, Bob and Beverly Jackson, a
> high school teacher and his wife who had both studied with Senzaki
> in L.A. Alex Wayman, a graduate student in Tibetan at Berkeley, and
> Will Peterson, the printmaker and editor of the group's magazine,
> the *Berkeley Bussei*, and, as Gary Snyder remembers, "a number of
> really sharp Japanese-American Nisei and Sansei."[138]

At one meeting, Alan Watts was asked to give a talk.[139] It was there that Watts would make Snyder's acquaintance.

But perhaps the Japanese American who would play the largest role in Zen's movement West would be Mihoko Okamura. In figure 2.6, she peeks out on the far-left side of the photo.[140] I have purposely chosen this photo to introduce Okamura because it is telling of her representational role in the narrative we are discussing. She is a figure by which one can read the predicament of Japanese Americans in the larger scheme of American Buddhism.

FIGURE. 2.6. D. T. Suzuki at Koko An Zendo, Hawaii, 1964 (Photographer: Francis
Haar ©Francis Haar).

From 1953 until Suzuki's death in 1965, Okamura served as the scholar's
secretary and constant companion. Personal reflections offered by those who
met with the Zen patriarch make note of her presence. She is often referred to
as his "lovely assistant," characterized by an unparalleled patience and grace.
By all accounts, Okamura is recognized as Suzuki's primary caretaker in his
later years, looking after his administrative and personal needs and freeing the
preoccupied scholar from these everyday concerns.

Okamura makes her most prominent appearance in William Sargeant's
1957 *New Yorker* article on Suzuki. In an extensive section dedicated to her and
her family, he describes Okamura in the following way:

> Miss Okamura—who was born in California, speaks English as glibly
> as any American college girl, and in a very feminine way, is quite a
> shrewd thinker herself—dedicates her time to acting as [Suzuki's]
> secretary, editorial assistant, social hostess, and traveling companion,
> as well as his most devoted disciple. . ... Her ministrations might
> occasionally bring to mind those of a cultivated and lovely geisha
> attending a grizzled patriarch in the pages of Lady Murasaki, but any
> such resemblance is purely romantic. Miss Okamura, for all her
> almond eyes and porcelain complexion, is an American girl with
> ideas of her own, as well as a sound knowledge of typing and
> shorthand.[141]

Sargeant's account is useful in understanding the dimensions of gender and race at play in her representation. It is obvious that Sargeant has a difficult time placing Okamura; she does not conform to the racial script. There certainly is a recognized desire to view her in Orientalist guise as the "cultivated and lovely geisha." This is what her appearance immediately brings to the author's mind. But Okamura's unaccented English throws him off, and Sargeant feels compelled to cite her national allegiance and identity. She is no subservient geisha, but "an American girl with ideas of her own." All in all, his declaration of Okamura as truly American feels somewhat forced and apologetic.[142]

Sargeant's reference to Okamura's "sound knowledge of typing and short-hand" is also telling. That these skills are meant to demonstrate her initiative also attests to the limited role she is allowed to play as a woman[143] and as a Japanese American. She is allowed to serve as helpmate but can never be considered as Suzuki's intellectual partner and peer. These conditions extend to the role of her family as well:

> Dr. Suzuki, who often remarks somewhat ruefully that he is so old he has vastly outlived nearly all his close friends, finds in the companionship of the family a warmth that relieves the austerity of his studies. Miss Okamura's father, Frank Okamura, is a landscape gardener at the Brooklyn Botanic Garden, and her mother is a capable housekeeper and cook who is well up to making Dr. Suzuki's favorite Japanese dishes, including specially prepared turnips, *yu-dofu* (a cake made of bean curd), and *azuki* (red rice with beans).[144]

Sargeant's inclusion of the Okamura family is meant to provide a humanizing touch to his portrayal of the dedicated scholar. But again, the part they play falls within the domestic realm. Together, the attentive Okamura, and her gardener father and culinary mother compose a background of sustenance in which Suzuki's scholarly role stands in relief. Japanese Americans (including men, such as Okamura's father) are permitted only a feminized role in the Zen scheme.

For Sargeant, the distinction between different sects of Buddhism[145] delineates the Okamuras from Suzuki ("The Okamuras are *not* Zen Buddhists") and is one way Sargeant precludes the Japanese American family from truly sharing in Suzuki's scholarly and spiritual interests. Rather, the author attributes the Okamuras' concern for the aged scholar to "the traditional Japanese reverence for age" and "the honor of being hosts to Japan's most noted philosophical thinker."[146] Any religious commitment the Okamuras might have is downgraded to motivations of shared racial and national origins. Although they may live in the United States, their lives still conform to traditional sensibilities and the hierarchical conventions of Japan. Despite their experiences in the United States, they cannot help but remain a racial throwback. This throwback strategy served as one of two ways in which Japanese Americans were precluded from being recognized as making any significant contribution to the emerging discourse of American Zen in particular and American Buddhism in general. The second method portrayed Japanese Americans in the entirely opposite light—as an ethnic people who had become "too Americanized." In an article titled "Buddhism in America," *Time* reported on October 26, 1962:

> Buddhism owed part of its current health to some shrewd borrowing
> from U.S. Christianity. To hold their largely Japanese-American
> membership—which yearly becomes more American and less
> Japanese—most congregations are turning from Japanese to English
> to their services, call themselves churches rather than temples to
> avoid identification with the occult. Services are held on Sunday,
> although all days are holy to Buddhists. The Buddhist Church of
> Seattle sponsors a Boy Scout troop, a day nursery, a Sunday school
> and a drum and bugle corps.[147]

Here the reporter recognizes Japanese American Buddhists for their efforts to assimilate into mainstream American religious life. But the reporter also notes in the same article that "the most active members of a [Buddhist] congregation" are a "small group of Occidents [who] continue to find a unique serenity in Buddhism."[148] The implication here is clear: Japanese American members seem more concerned with "fitting in," while Euro-Americans are the ones who express a genuine religious commitment.[149] The larger social forces that prompt this dynamic are never explored.

In the representational scheme, Japanese American Buddhists were either portrayed as hopelessly tied to their Japanese roots or comically estranged from them.[150] The most prominent role they are allowed to play in the history of Buddhism's development in the United States is a minor one. Like Mihoko Okamura, Japanese Americans are allowed to serve as able caretakers providing a comfortable environment for more authentic Buddhist representatives from Asia. Indeed, Okamura helps figure the marginal (often invisible), yet necessary role that Asian Americans have come to play in shaping the discourse on Asian religions in the United States. If recognized in popular discourse, they are never seen as major contributors and are often exoticized. In the narrative of the Oriental Monk, the character of the Japanese American will always be relegated to the supporting cast *if* she appears at all.[151]

The Recursive Mold

Now it happens that in this country (Japan) . . . [t]o make a date (by gestures,
drawings on paper, proper names) may take an hour, but during that hour,
for a message which would be abolished in an instant if it were to be spoken
(simultaneously quite essential and quite insignificant), it is the other's entire
body which has been known, savored, received, and which has displayed (to
no real purpose) its own narrative, its own text.

Roland Barthes, Empire of Signs

In his dedication to Suzuki, "The 'Mind-less' Scholar," Alan Watts remarks:
"Perhaps the real spirit of Suzuki could never be caught from his writings
alone, one had to know the man."[152] Watts seems to suggest that experiencing
Suzuki in his full personhood communicated as much as, if not more than, his
writings ever could. In many ways, Suzuki's body—his demeanor, gestures,
personality, and appearance—would comprise his most definitive text. In the
eyes of those who came to know him, as well as of those who never did, Suzuki's image would serve as a precious icon in Zen Buddhism's Western pantheon. Hagiographically, it would help recall the great sage who in his firm
devotion traveled beyond his native land to share openly the wisdom of his
faith.

Outside that pantheon—in the American religious and cultural world at
large—the icon would be stripped of its individuality; that is, Suzuki's name
would be known less and less in this realm. What would remain are the icon-
ographic remnants: his shaved head, his small eyes and jutting eyebrows, the
unassuming repose of his expression, his ancient ware, his Orientalness.
Suzuki's image would replenish and reconstitute the more generalized icon
of the Oriental Monk—the harsh austerity replaced by a new openness and
approachability.

As Barthes reminds us, icons and myths often go hand in hand. The icon
is often "at the disposal" of the myth, although the icon itself can take on mythic
proportions. In the case of the icon of the Oriental Monk, both are the case. The
Oriental Monk participates in the myth of the spiritual East; the figure embodies that spirituality, acts as its most cherished sign. It is mythic in the sense
that is "is decorated, adapted to a certain type of consumption, laden with literary self-indulgence, revolt, images, in short with a type of social *usage* which
is added to pure matter."[153]

The "social usage" of the myth of the East on the surface is quite evident.
As in the case of Alan Watts and Jack Kerouac, its use lay in its power to entice
and inspire. For Arthur Koestler, it served as derisive object. Myth, by its very

name, allows such exposure. But to go deeper and examine the conditions of its possibility—the political valence of its elements—reveals its more significant operation.

By examining Suzuki and Zen in the popular context of the late 1950s, I have tried to do just that. The myth of the East, as I argue throughout, has taken on a particular narratological form in the last half century. In many ways, the myth has become so condensed that it no longer needs to be told; the icon of the Oriental Monk is sufficient. Examining its semiological form, the narrative the icon encapsulates depends on several figures to consolidate its meaning: the wise Asian sage, his Anglo pupil, and the Asian masses that fail to appreciate the value of their inherited tradition. From the racial and gender specificity of these "characters," one is able to discern the ideological impetus or the underlying "social usage" of the myth.

Put more concretely, the tale of the Oriental Monk—who travels West in search of someone to carry on his spiritual legacy and finds that student in a feisty, yet committed white (male) pupil—helped legitimate a new ideological center for Zen. This center was not only racially but also geopolitically informed. Racially, it authorized the transfer of Zen spirituality from Asian master to white pupil. Geopolitically, it specified the United States as its new spiritual center. The narrative also served to fortify a "modernized American cultural patriarchy" as it aestheticized Japan, then commodified and stylistically appropriated its religious and racial difference in the name of democratic choice and freedom.

It is ironic that Suzuki's image would become the most powerful of signs—pleasurably compelling in its continual recollection. Barthes once likened "Japan" to an "empire of signs," but of signs that were empty.[154] In the Westerner's play with the "irreducible differences" (that Suzuki's foreignness provides), Americans cannot help but fill this empty figure with meaning, to claim ownership over its contents, and ultimately to diffuse much of its productive challenge.

3

Hyperreal Samadhi

Maharishi Mahesh Yogi

In December 2003, director David Lynch—known for his dark and quirky portrayals of American life—vowed to raise $1 billion to build a hundred "peace palaces" around the world. These palaces would be dedicated to the "life-supporting programs" of the Maharishi Mahesh Yogi and his Transcendental Meditation (TM) movement and serve as centers of education and meditation and a place where *siddhas* or yogic flyers are able to congregate in their energetic pursuit of world peace. Raised as a Presbyterian, Lynch was introduced to TM in 1973 and has been a practitioner ever since. In 2000, Lynch became a *siddha* himself. He explains to reporters that the regimen not only gives his life "coherence" but also nurtures his creativity. Since his initial announcement, the filmmaker has upped his fund-raising commitment to $7 billion and officially launched the David Lynch Foundation for Consciousness-Based Education and World Peace.

While a younger generation of Americans is familiar with Lynch through his oeuvre (which includes *Blue Velvet, Mulholland Drive*, and the television series *Twin Peaks*), it is their parents who recognize his spiritual leader, the Maharishi Mahesh Yogi. Mahesh is best known as the personal guru to the Beatles. The world-famous pop group, especially member George Harrison, found spiritual inspiration from the unconventional yogi, whose simple meditative technique and hopeful outlook appealed to the busy singers. Transcendental Meditation, a practice derived from the Hindu tradition, which

Mahesh refined through thirteen years of ascetic practice, refocuses the practitioner's mind on "pure being" and taps into his or her wellspring of "creative intelligence."[1] Perhaps most attractive is the fact that TM requires only forty minutes of one's day and can be practiced in any location.

The pop singers first met the Maharishi Mahesh Yogi in London in 1966. By that time, Mahesh had already made seven trips around the globe, established thirty-eight centers, and amassed more than 100,000 followers since his announcement about bringing peace to the world in 1957.[2] Despite these impressive achievements, he and his Spiritual Regeneration Movement did not capture widespread American interest until the late 1960s, when his name became associated with famous musicians and film personalities. By the end of 1967, the *New York Times Magazine* declared him "The Chief Guru of the Western World," and in 1968, *Life* magazine announced "The Year of the Guru." Transcendental Meditation, as an alternative to a drug-induced high, had become a full-fledged phenomenon in the United States, especially among the nation's youth.

In the late 1960s, the Maharishi's philosophy seemed to appeal to a generation that had become increasingly disillusioned with traditional forms of religious belief and practice. Henry Idema III self-reflects in *Before Our Time: A Theory of the Sixties*:

> In reaction to dry dogmatism, the Sixties Generation cried out, "The inner world is worth nurturing!" Indeed, many of us became fascinated with the inner world and immersed ourselves in emotionality and spirituality. For some, psychology became the rage; for others, Eastern religions (e.g., Transcendental Meditation or the Hare Krishna and Vendantist movements); for yet others, drugs and sex filled the bill. All those trends became popular in the Sixties because they focused on the inner world, the inner self that was home to spirit and feeling, the world of mystery and fantasy, the world of symbol, myth, and perhaps even magic.[3]

As Americans faced rapidly changing times and increasing turmoil brought on by mounting racial tensions, urban uprisings, and the Vietnam War, the Maharishi offered a solution to problems that, to some, seemed insurmountable. With unfettered ease and joyful confidence, he publicly asserted that "world peace would come if he could spread his teachings."[4] These teachings, the Science of Creative Intelligence, along with its practical component, Transcendental Meditation, focused on the inner world of the individual. The "bliss consciousness" and "illuminating expansion of the mind" the Maharishi promised made his spiritual alternative extremely compelling, if not magical.

Mahesh enjoyed spectacular attention by the American media from the autumn of 1967 to the spring of 1968. Whereas the popular audiences became familiar with D. T. Suzuki only through black-and-white images, their encounters with the Maharishi took place through a colorful lens reflective of the psychedelic style of the time. This vibrancy made for eye-catching copy and reinforced long-embedded notions of a spiritual, exoticized, and extravagant India.

However, Mahesh's endeavor and image fell prey to an ambivalent press. Perhaps the guru was a genuine spiritual revolutionary, or perhaps he was simply a clever con man. In this chapter, I discuss the two distinct attitudes toward the Maharishi expressed in the popular press reports of the late 1960s. Although a few pieces expressed a sincere interest in the Maharishi and his movement and reverently imbued the leader with spiritual import, the majority of articles often maintained, through means of irony and satire, a more critical stance.

Despite these varying views, media portrayals had one thing in common. Both types of commentators—critical and reverent—subscribed to Orientalist notions to argue their case. The icon of the Oriental Monk seemed stubbornly fixed within the American imagination and continued to serve as measure and model. Within its racialized scheme, Mahesh was viewed as either woefully lacking or in utter conformity to the icon or, put more plainly, popular expectations of an Asian religious figure. In either instance, the yogi's image as conceived by late-1960s American mass media could not escape these stereotypical restraints and would serve as a convenient screen on which to project larger debates over cultural authority.

First Impressions

A small news item appeared in the Sunday edition of the *New York Times* on December 12, 1966: "Beatle Tells Preference for Religions of India." The obscure column reported that George Harrison "believed much more in religions of India than in anything he ever learned from Christianity." Although undeveloped at the time, this interest would lead Harrison and his fellow Beatles to seek out the Maharishi Mahesh Yogi, Indian founder of the Spiritual Regeneration Movement and the proponent of Transcendental Meditation, whom they would eventually meet in the winter of 1967.

The meeting took place in London, and the singing group then joined Mahesh on a five-day retreat in Bangor, Wales (a scheduled stop on the Maharishi's eighth tour around the world). The encounter was auspicious for both parties. The Beatles apparently found a new spiritual guide, who offered consolation during a very difficult period of their lives. (During the retreat, the guru broke the news to the group that their long-time manager, Brian Epstein, had died.) As for Mahesh, the pop group represented not only new adherents but also unprecedented public exposure for his movement's mission to spiritually regenerate the world.

As the Beatles made plans to join the Maharishi in Rishikesh, India, the news media covered the spiritual alliance with increasing fervor. *Time* magazine featured the first image of Mahesh to appear in the popular press. In the "Religion" pages of its October 20, 1967, issue, the American public caught a glimpse of the guru who had so enthralled the Beatles. The photo offers a humble portrait of the Maharishi, in both gesture (with one hand rested gently on his forehead and another clasping a bouquet of flowers) and presentation (the photo's black-and-white medium) (See figure 3.1.). Like the press images of Suzuki, the unassuming representation seemed befitting of a spiritual luminary from the East in all his ascetic and mystical promise. However, any mystique the image itself might evoke is offset by the article's caption: "How to succeed spiritually without really trying." The simple legend, paradoxically phrased, calls into question the Maharishi's authority by drawing attention to his potentially unscrupulous practice. The piece further dismisses Mahesh by generically identifying him as "The Guru."

The Maharishi would be featured in four full-length articles, visually supplemented with countless photos. Despite the representational abundance, the tone of

FIGURE 3.1. The Maharishi featured in the Religion section of *Newsweek*, October 20, 1967 (Photo credit: Gilloon).

most of these reports (e.g., the *New York Times Magazine, Saturday Evening Post*) would be similarly posed, as they offered skeptical, if not critical assessments of Mahesh and his Spiritual Regeneration Movement.[5] (Only one, *Look's* cover feature, would be notably deferential.) The suspicion of Mahesh was undoubtedly a residual from Cold War diplomatic relations between the United States and an independent India. India's position of nonalignment with not only Communist China but also the democratic United States fostered Americans' ambivalent feelings toward the Asian nation. With the India–Pakistan war of 1965, American policy makers gave up much hope "of ever creating any durable anti-Communist partnerships with countries as durably hostile to each other as India and Pakistan."[6]

While television was certainly an important medium on which Mahesh appeared (most notably on the *Tonight Show*),[7] magazine articles provided information that this broadcast representation of him did not.[8] Telecasts allowed a national viewing audience to experience Mahesh "firsthand"—his gestures, voice, and overall presentation—but only within the limited environment of the interview setting. Magazine copy rounded out Mahesh's image by capturing his behavior in a wide variety of settings (e.g., in Germany or at his ashram in Rishikesh). In addition, print media offerings were also able to develop and present a specific stance toward Mahesh and his movement in a way that television commentators could do only in a limited fashion. A TV interviewer such as Johnny Carson occupies the same space as Mahesh at the time of broadcast and therefore does not offer extensive commentary on his guest. However, magazine reporters enjoy the opportunity to critically reflect on their experience and share these impressions with their audience. Although this was largely accomplished within the written account, such impressions were visually transmitted through the selective use and placement of the images that accompanied the piece. These photographs, far from neutral representations, enacted their own visually condensed commentary that was most accessible to a popular audience, as well as reflective of their views. This is not to say that photo layouts of Mahesh offered a singular portrait of the religious figure uncomplicated by multifarious intent or varied response. The following "readings" of magazine articles that feature Mahesh are meant to highlight the ways in which image and text conspire to create culturally specific messages not only about the guru but also about the worldview he purportedly represents.

"Chief Guru of the Western World"

On December 17, 1967, the first feature-length article on the Maharishi would appear. A larger-than-life, color head shot of the Maharishi graced the cover of the *New York Times Magazine*, with the accompanying headline "Chief Guru of the West: The secret of life is the basis of life" (figure 3.2). Although this photo enveloped Mahesh in a mystical aura, the images that accompanied the article cast him in a much more mundane light. Three images command the opening pages of the article. The main full-length shot of Mahesh features him speaking on the phone and represents a study in contrasts. This photo alone might seem benign, almost amusing, as the anciently garbed guru interacts with modern communications technology. But the photos that flank this image give it another spin. On the left of the guru's picture is a shot of Mahesh and followers strolling through an exhibition hall filled with posters bearing his image and words (figure 3.3a). On the right, a half-page photo features a group of the Maharishi's German followers meditating in Bremen (figure 3.3b).

Taken together, the images depict Mahesh, not as a humble religious figure struggling in isolation to articulate an underappreciated Asian spiritual tradition, but as a spiritual powerbroker with whom to be reckoned. The exhibition hall shot demonstrates the movement's proactive strategy to attract new members. Although American readers most likely cannot

FIGURE 3.2. *New York Times Magazine* cover from December 17, 1967 (Photographer: Raghubir Singh/Nancy Palmer Agency).

read the poster board slogans written in German, they get the impression that Mahesh is not merely interested in expounding his spiritual outlook to a Western audience, but in propagating his views. The words—in a Western language but one that is foreign to American English speakers—also lend a cosmopolitan dimension to the movement. Mahesh seems to rely heavily on publicity (with its focus on slogans and image), rather than on the extended argument of the published text to disseminate his spiritual knowledge.[9] By deploying such methods, he appears as a master of marketing, that is, one who illegitimately circumvents the acceptable ways religious movements gain recognition in the West. In these various ways, the exhibition hall shot offers a profane impression of a supposedly sacred figure and ultimately works to degrade Mahesh's spiritual image.

The exhibition hall shot is discomforting for another reason. In a straightforward portrait of Mahesh as Oriental Monk figure, the viewer-reader remains anonymous and invisible as she or he gazes at the image. The exhibition hall highlights the act of viewing, as objects, artifacts, and images are laid out for visual consideration. This voyeuristic dimension is made present in the photo, and a source of power revealed. Perhaps most disturbing, is the viewer-reader's realization that Mahesh is aware of this source of power, which he effectively exploits. He capitalizes on a hidden privilege and private indulgence. Mahesh, as Oriental Monk, is no longer at the representational beck and call of a Western audience; they are not the ones who visually and spiritually "take in" his image at will, but rather are the ones who are meant to be "taken in."

The photo of the German meditators, which flanks the right side of Mahesh's image, reinforces this sense. Although the contemplative group displays the Maharishi's technique at work, it also attests to the power of the movement's attraction. To the magazine's audience, the four "followers" in the photo's foreground look like any Westerner neatly garbed in professional attire. The image creates a mood of both fascination and threat. On the one hand, it evokes curiosity in the viewer-reader who identifies with the meditators through appearance and dress. ("If these individuals practice the technique, there must be something to the Maharishi and his movement.") On the other hand, the image constitutes a threat for the viewer-reader, who may already be wary not only of foreign spiritual influence but also of the seemingly shrewd way in which it is marketed. ("If these individuals are so easily duped, how many others will also be spiritually swindled?")

I would argue that the exhibition hall shot primes the *New York Times* audience for this latter interpretation. If the photos are "read" from left to right in a conventional manner, the publicity image serves as the lens through

Maharishi Mahesh Yogi, who numbers the likes of Shirley MacLaine, Mia Farrow and the Beatles among his followers, is an apostle of the contemplative life but makes waves like any celebrity when he goes on tour.

FALSTERBO, Sweden.

THE dinky railroad that runs down the east coast of Sweden, linking Malmö and Falsterbo, is going out of business. Falsterbo, explained the taxi driver, is the last stop on the line and within walking distance of the southern tip of Sweden. And everybody drives to-day. The only time within memory when the railroad carried a full load of passengers, he said, was last Oct. 15. That was the day two of the

BARNEY LEFFERTS, formerly with The New York Times Magazine, is assistant editor of The Scandinavian Times, published in Copenhagen.

Beatles (Harrison and McCartney) came to Falsterbo. A local news-paper suggested afterward that if the Beatles visited there once a year the railroad could be saved. "You see," said the taxi man, "the people would not be told when they were coming, so the train would be full every day."

The Beatles came to Falsterbo to see Maharishi Mahesh Yogi, guru of the Hindu order of Shankaracharya, life-celibate, spiritual and active leader of the International Meditation Society (headquarters in Rishikesh, Uttar Pradesh, India), which is some-times called the Spiritual Regenera-tion Movement and is thought to embrace a following approaching

Chief Guru

of the

Western World

By BARNEY LEFFERTS

44

FIGURE 3.3a. Page spread from the *New York Times Magazine* article, "Chief Guru of the West," December 17, 1967 (Photographer: Der Stern/Black Star).

which the rest of the article's images are viewed. This includes the primary image of the Maharishi on the phone. Revisiting the photo, one now sees it in a different rhetorical light. As previously mentioned, the image is a study in contrasts, but it can no longer be viewed in such a pleasantly amusing fashion. Mahesh is portrayed as an Eastern religious figure who is suspiciously adept in the ways of the modern West. The manner in which Mahesh presents him-self—ancient, modest, and mysteriously foreign—helps to establish his au-thenticity as a spiritual figure in the eyes of a Western audience. However, the slogans, publicity images, and, indeed, the exhibition hall itself symbolically

115,000 persons in 35 countries. The guru was in Falsterbo to establish a new Academy of Meditation.

The Beatles first met the Maharishi (the accent is on the "har" and the "i" is slurred so that it almost becomes "Maharshee") late last summer at the Hilton Hotel in London. If the Hilton seems an unlikely meeting place for a Great Sage (which is what "Maharishi" means) and the world's best-known pop combo, it should be said that the hotel was chosen by the Maharishi's followers only because it has a ballroom large enough (3,000 seats) to make a public lecture worthwhile. The Beatles requested, and were granted, an audience with the Maharishi after his address and

talked with him for an hour behind the drawn curtains of the stage.

The next day they accompanied him to Bangor, Wales (the places become more unlikely), where the Maharishi was to conduct a 10-day course in meditation. Pulling out of Euston Station became a scrimmage. The photographers had been stirring up a good bit of fuss photographing the Maharishi. When the Beatles arrived, their mooing knew no bounds. Cynthia Lennon (John's wife) was left on the platform, telling the battling bobbies that she really was Mrs. Lennon, as the train rolled out.

DO NOT FORGET THE NEEDIEST!

full of flowers, Beatles, the Great Sage and a number of citizens who had suddenly changed their minds. "Quantities of people jumped on the train," said a lady who was there, "who had not had any previous intention of visiting Bangor at all."

In September in Los Angeles, 3,000 students met the guru's plane.

. . . Incidents in the Maharishi's eighth world tour since he began to teach Transcendental Meditation beyond the borders of India eight years ago. This time around, the itinerary was Britain, Canada, the United States (California only), Scandinavia, Italy and Germany. The Maharishi lectured, exchanged flowers at railway stations, spoke to artists in a

loft in Berlin ("The success of an artist will be great if his conscious mind is in tune with the source of thought"). Everywhere it was standing room only. The little man with the hairy face and big brown eyes, who studied for 13 years with a great swami in the Himalayas and then, he says, imbued what he had learned with "the light of modern understanding," was clearly chief guru of the Western world.

TRANSCENDENTAL Meditation is always described by those who practice it as a very simple, very practical technique through which a person is enabled to reach his innermost *(Continued on Page 48)*

CRUSADER—Maharishi Mahesh Yogi (left), leader of the Transcendental Meditation movement, arrives in Cologne, Germany (far left), during his just completed eighth world tour; he paused long enough to make a phone call. "When you travel with him," says a disciple, "you don't have time to meditate."

"THOUGHT BEYOND THOUGHT"—Some of Maharishi's followers meditate transcendentally in Bremen. "Just sitting quiet is not meditation," says the guru. "It keeps the mind on the surface of the conscious-thinking level, as if exploring the lake on the surface. The meditation I talk of is getting to the depth of the ocean."

FIGURE 3.3b. Continued

undermine this authenticity. The *New York Times Magazine* effectively corrupts (or at least calls into question) Mahesh's image by visually portraying him as at once too profane (exhibition hall) and too powerful (white Western followers).

The final image of the article appears several pages later (figure 3.4). In it, the Maharishi poses with George Harrison and Paul McCartney in Falsterbo, Sweden. The two Beatles carry large white mums. Several onlookers also crowd the photo. Amid celebrity, Mahesh not only appears at ease but also seems to enjoy the media attention. He is comfortable with his own image (as his stroll through the exhibition hall confirms) and not afraid to deploy its power. Again, the magazine calls into question the guru's motivations and methods through a selective use of images. These images enact

FIGURE 3.4. Beatles George Harrison and Paul McCartney with Mahesh
(Photo credit: Svenskt Pressfoto).

their own argument, their own rhetorical commentary, which the viewer-reader can instantaneously process, with far greater economy than words.

Look's Reverential Portrait

In January 1968, less than a month after the *New York Times Magazine* article appeared, the Maharishi packed the Felt Forum in the newly built Madison Square Garden in New York City.[10] During his visit, he also met with United Nations Secretary-General U Thant to discuss ways of aiding "permanent peace."[11] Shortly after, on February 6, 1968, *Look* magazine featured the guru on their cover, with the headline "AND NOW—MEDITATION HITS THE CAMPUS; How Hindu monk Maharishi turns the students on without drugs" (figure 3.5). The magazine features two articles on the Maharishi phenomenon. The first piece, "A Visit with India's High-Powered New Prophet" by Paul Horn, is accompanied by an elaborate photo spread—eleven images of Mahesh and his ashram in Rishikesh, India. In the second feature, "The Non-Drug Turn-On Hits Campus," William Hedgepeth reports on student meditators at the University of California at Berkeley and at UCLA with seven photos throughout.

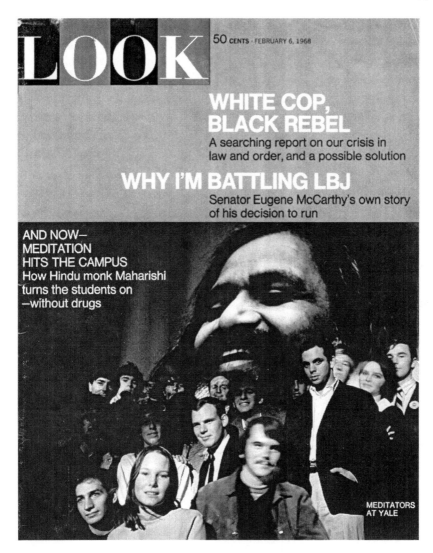

FIGURE 3.5. *Look* cover image of Mahesh (Photographer: Michael Alexander) superimposed with "Meditators at Yale" (Photographer: Paul Fusco), February 6, 1968.

While the *New York Times Magazine* article adopts a critical posture toward Mahesh, *Look* resacralized his image. In "India's High-Powered New Prophet," American jazz musician Paul Horn traces the development of Transcendental Meditation and explains the philosophy behind it. The photos and their captions provide a separate text, in which Horn narrates his visit with Mahesh "on the Ganges." The primary photo of the yogi is minimalist in nature and features a windswept, contemplative Maharishi stoically posed. On the two-page opening spread, this image is supplemented by a host of other photos, mostly of Mahesh among the Indian people. If one looks carefully, a Westerner or two— distinguishable by either hairstyle or dress —can be seen. However, it is the South Asians who provide the main backdrop for the guru's activities (figure 3.6). These images portray Mahesh as intimately connected with the Indian people.[12] Viewing the Maharishi ministering to the native population caters to a paternalistic vision shared by *Look*'s Western audience: a spiritual leader in tune with the needs of the "most oppressed," India's third world population. Hence, these photos lend a human dimension and spiritual legitimacy to Mahesh's mission.

Such legitimacy is also supplied by another image in the photo spread: a portrait of the Maharishi's own spiritual teacher, Brahmanda Saraswati or Guru Dev (as he was called by his disciples). In the article, Guru Dev is described as "a spiritual leader of the Hindus,"[13] who "revived the meditation technique Maharishi is now spreading."[14] The image is not simply of the portrait, but of Dr. R. C. Verma painting the likeness of Dev (figure 3.7). According to Horn, Verma "supplies portraits of Dev to meditation centers in 50 countries."[15] This complex image is significant for two reasons. First of all, it places Mahesh within a spiritual lineage of a recognized religious tradition (Hinduism). Second, the fact that the paintings are made for meditation centers relativizes the Maharishi's own image, that is, takes the focus away from his image. This may seem contrary to the development of Mahesh's own iconic status as an Oriental

FIGURE 3.6. "Maharishi teaches meditation, not religion. This is a private ceremony for the Hindu God Shiva" (Photographer: Paul Horn). The caption serves to simultaneously dissociate Mahesh and the TM movement from religion, while at the same time place him within the religious tradition of Hinduism.

FIGURE 3.7. Dr. R. C. Verma paints a portrait of the Maharishi's teacher, Guru Dev (Photographer: Paul Horn).

Monk. But given the "bad press" of previous articles, this referential nod toward Guru Dev, in fact, rehabilitates Mahesh's image.

This favorable view is also evident elsewhere. In yet another image, the Maharishi is shown with camera in hand, taking snapshots (figure 3.8). This picture depicts the guru once again engaged with modern technology, but unlike the *New York Times Magazine*'s portrayal, this representation commands a lighter interpretation. Amid the photos of Mahesh in his "natural surroundings" in India, the camera appears as an anomaly, an amusement. And if there is any doubt to this read, the caption[16] confirms it. Mahesh's use of the camera is framed as a moment of unadulterated enjoyment. He seems to approach the device as an amusing novelty. Unlike the image of him on the phone, where modern technology is shrewdly employed for the purposes of self-promotion, this photo re-creates a disjunction between the Indian sage and Western invention that is more comfortable for a Western audience. Image and text also lend the Maharishi's image a childlike simplicity: The guru is enthralled with a "new toy," in which he seems to delight.

The opening spread, for the most part, achieves the solemnity befitting a spiritual leader. The somber nature of its images demands the viewer-reader to take seriously the Maharishi and his movement. The photo of

FIGURE 3.8. Article image caption: "Maharishi's message is that men are born to enjoy. He's a superb host, and loved to escort us on tours around India so we could take pictures. Sometimes, he borrowed cameras to take pictures himself"(Photographer: Paul Horn).

Mahesh with camera is perhaps the exception. But even this somewhat amusing shot is clearly situated within the realm of the yogi's philosophy: *Men are born to enjoy.* Likewise, the three photos (figures 3.9a, 3.9b, and 3.9c) on the following page are meant to capture the essence of this philosophy. In each of these images, Mahesh's pleasant expression is the focus. Indeed, the spiritual leader becomes the embodiment of his teachings. Surrounded by Indians in his native setting, the Maharishi's smile does not represent an indulgent decadence (as it will come to symbolize in later articles), but rather the nonattachment of a wise man.

In the second article of the same issue, "The Non-Drug Turn-On Hits Campus: Student meditators tune in to Maharishi," Mahesh's joyful face is superimposed on a group of meditators at Yale (figure 3.10). His larger-than-life image looks down on a group of well-scrubbed youth with what can be read as almost

FIGURE 3.9. Paul Horn's photographs, which accompany his story, "A Visit with India's High-Powered New Prophet," give the reader a sense of Mahesh within the Indian environment (Photographer: Paul Horn).

a look of approval. The visual montage offers a study in contrasts. Although the piece does feature a photo of Maharishi spokesperson, Jerry Jarvis (who, dressed in coat and tie, looks like a college professor), the majority of images depict student meditators (figures 3.11a and 3.11b). Like the article's main photo, each student is fairly clean-cut and seemingly happy and at ease. These images reflect the reporter's generally positive stance toward the Student International

FIGURE 3.9. Continued

Meditation Society (SIMS) and favorably portray Mahesh's influence. The image
of the student followers as respectful, drug-free individuals persuasively makes
a case for Mahesh, as a general audience contrasts these with the stereotypical
image of the disobedient, disheveled, and drugged-out youth of their time.[17]

   Look magazine's coverage of both the Maharishi in Rishikesh and the SIMS
in California cast Mahesh in a favorable light. The images selected contribute to
a positive stance toward the Spiritual Regeneration Movement and imbue its
chief mystic with authority and grace. I would argue that the persuasive force of
the visuals is achieved not only by the way they are arranged within the separate
articles but also by the manner in which they are collectively divided. Images of
Mahesh are sequestered to Paul Horn's visit to Rishikesh, which locates the spiritual figurehead squarely in India. Images of Western adherents occupy a separate textual and geographic domain. Even the one image that connects the two
(the Maharishi and meditators at Yale) relies on two distinct images that are
superimposed.

   When one compares this visual separation of spheres (East and West) with
the images from the *New York Times Magazine* article, in which Mahesh min-
gles effortlessly in a Western setting, the implication is subtle, yet clear. The
Maharishi is awarded spiritual clout when he can be squarely located within
certain bounds—geographic and racialized. Under *Look*'s surveilling eye, he
conforms to this Virtual Orientalist contract. And any breach of this contract
results in a negative assessment. Transcendental Meditation, as an Eastern

FIGURE 3.10. Visual iteration of the cover image of Mahesh (Photographer: Michael Alexander) superimposed with "Meditators at Yale" (Photographer: Paul Fusco) for the *Look* article "The Non-Drug Turn-on Hits Campus."

spiritual alternative, is allowed legitimate consideration only when it can be properly managed.

Indeed, a certain degree of foreignness and a strict divide between East and West emerge as significant prerequisites for recognition of an individual as an Oriental Monk figure.[18] When an Asian spiritual leader crosses that divide, like Mahesh, his behavior becomes suspect, and his image subsequently tainted. Likewise, when Westerners engage in such traipsing, the spell is similarly broken, as the next set of articles reveals.

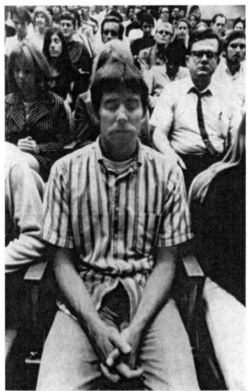

FIGURE 3.11. Students in meditative poses at Harvard (Photographer: Paul Fusco) and UCLA(Photographer: Ron Thai/Globe).

"There Once Was a Guru from Rishikesh"

The cover image of the May 4, 1968, issue the *Saturday Evening Post* would offer the most direct visual link between the Maharishi and his Western celebrity following (figure 3.12). Similar to *Look*, the *Post* cover offers a montage of images—this time a large side profile of Mahesh juxtaposed with smaller images of Mia Farrow and the Beatle entourage. The magazine positions these celebrities as the main audience draw, even as the Maharishi visually dominates the frame. It also characterizes "the scene" as one in which

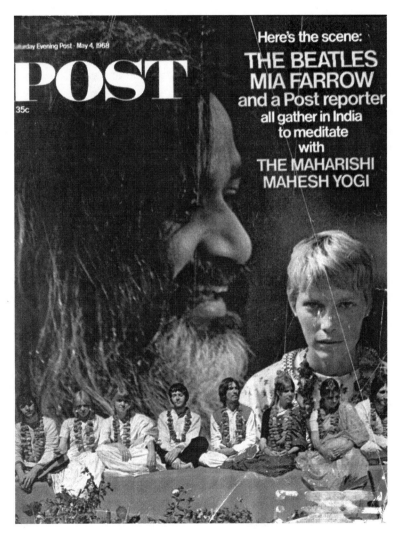

FIGURE 3.12. *Saturday Evening Post* cover, May 4, 1968 (Photographer: Marvin Lichtner/Lee Gross Agency and Larry Kurland).

Mahesh has considerable influence over youth and youth culture. Again, his presence is cast as menacing, especially as the guru seems to gaze directly at a seemingly young and innocent Farrow.

The *Saturday Evening Post* included a two-part report on the Maharishi and his Rishikesh settlement included in this volume and the following issue. The series, in which correspondent Lewis H. Lapham offers an account of his visit to Mahesh's compound in India, was whimsically titled "There Once Was a Guru from Rishikesh." The images chronicle Lapham's trip and accurately reflect the narrative development of his account. Unlike previous articles, the photos are scattered throughout the piece, but if one scans these images, one is able to get a sense of the story's progression.

Part 1 of "There Once Was a Guru from Rishikesh" (May 4, 1968) begins with an image of Mahesh meditating calmly on a sofa, microphone poised in front of the contemplative figure (figure 3.13). The darkened auditorium in which the picture is set also serves as a textual backdrop against which the article's white print is highlighted, and the viewer-reader is visually drawn into the story. The Maharishi is obviously photographed at a public event, but his meditative pose—eyes closed and hands folded—sets him apart from the mundane setting. Indeed, it is the microphone that appears as a curious and imposing probe. It beckons the yogi to speak. An instrument of undiscriminating amplification, it accentuates Mahesh's every sound, even his silence.

In the article, the image of the Maharishi's noninteraction with what is, at once, a Western technological device and an instrument of publicity establishes him as a serious spiritual figure—one who appears impervious to the microphone's corrupting presence. The sacred dimension of Mahesh's movement is further captured in the next photo, which depicts a group of student followers in California meditating peacefully in a grassy field. They are well dressed, well coiffed, and well behaved. Similar to the images in *Look*, these first two photos seem to make a distinction between the Indian leader (and the Eastern mystical realm he embodies) and his students (and their world in the West). Although the next photo includes both Mahesh and members of his Western audience, the initial setup allows the viewer-reader to interpret the interaction with requisite seriousness. The audience members, on which the camera is focused, seem intent on the Maharishi's every word (figures 3.14a and 3.14b).

These opening photos reflect Lapham's initial stance toward Mahesh and his Spiritual Regeneration Movement, developed through interviews with the spiritual leader's most avid followers. Indeed, the images capture the Maharishi's movement through the eyes of American adherents, who view him as a spiritual icon and themselves as serious seekers. In the article, Lapham does not wholly adopt a convert's perspective but is heavily intrigued. The

THE **POST**

THERE ONCE WAS A GURU FROM RISHIKESH

PART I

In which our reporter learns about
Transcendental Meditation, makes a
voyage to India and meets the Maharishi,
the Beatles, a Beach Boy and other
notables in search of something.

By Lewis H. Lapham

Now when I try to remember what it was like, or when people stop me and demand a reasonable explanation, I think first of the sweet madness that was as much a part of the place as the incessant squalling of the crows. Nearly always there was bright sun, but now when I remember, I think of the one afternoon when there was mist rising from the Ganges, and it is through that mist that I still see them, moving serenely among the sheshum trees with flowers in their hands. I see them smiling at me, as if from an immense distance, and it is their gentleness and the Maharishi's laughter that make nonsense of all the reasonable explanations.

Geoffrey, of course, foresaw the difficulties, just as he foresaw everything else, and so did Anneliese, who told fortunes and liked to listen to the Beatles playing music on the roof of their bungalow. That last morning they gave me oranges and a necklace of marigolds, also a coin for the ferryman who would transfer me to the other side of the Ganges.

"They won't believe you," Geoffrey said. "Surely you must understand that?"

I said I did, and Anneliese smiled and pressed my hands, as if I'd said something especially wise. Whatever anybody said there seemed especially wise, and nobody could make any serious mistakes. Even Mia Farrow's abrupt departure from the ashram could be explained, as could her wanderings in the south of India.

They wanted me to stay, partly because they thought I'd begun to attain God-consciousness and partly because, later that afternoon on the shore of the river, Donovan had promised to sing. At the time both reasons seemed entirely plausible. I can remember thinking how pleasant it would have been to follow the others into the garden, where the Maharishi sometimes would speak to us in a voice that was both high and musical, like the piping of a flute.

A month earlier, in New York, my reluctance would have seemed absurd. The Maharishi Mahesh Yogi I then knew only as a name in the newspapers, presumably another in the succession of Indian magi who have promised the riches of the spirit to generations grown bored with the clumsier profits of the dehumanized West.

The first news of his message had reached me a year before, through the witness of a disillusioned theatrical agent named Leon Auerbach. We had been smoking cigarettes in his office on the West Side, exchanging the customary polite clichés about the low-grade sensibilities of all producers, the hollow opportunism of most politicians and the suffocating anxiety so prevalent upon the local scene.

"The façade," Leon had said. "The sickness and despair."

Every few minutes he interrupted the conversation to take calls from big-time show-business personalities on both coasts, smiling wanly across

FIGURE 3.13. Opening page of the *Saturday Evening Post* two-part story, "There Once Was a Guru from Rishikesh"(Photographer: Larry Fink/Nancy Palmer Agency).

commentator's ensuing visit to India serves as the critical event, and he seems to reserve final judgment until then.

Lapham eventually arrives at Rishikesh, where the fourth photo is taken (figure 3.15). This visual moment foreshadows the perspective the reporter will eventually take. The image depicts a sentry stationed outside the Maharishi's compound, and its caption ironically reads: "A banner said WELCOME, but the

FIGURE 3.14. Meditative poses featured in "There Once Was a Guru from Rishikesh, Part 2"(Photographer: Larry Fink/Nancy Palmer Agency and Don Ornitz/Globe).

FIGURE 3.15. Hindu guard at the entrance of the Mahesh's compound (Photographer: Marvin Lichtner/Lee Gross Agency).

way to the ashram was barred by a Hindu guard, a gate and a barbed wire fence."[19] For the author, these physical barriers symbolize an exclusionary attitude on Mahesh's part and seem to contradict his universally conceived message. Inevitably, it provokes suspicion in the mind of both author and viewer-reader.

The final two photos in part 1 of "Guru from Rishikesh" visually illustrate those who are allowed to enter Mahesh's compound and those who remain outside its gates. The first of these photos shows the Beatles and their companions, along with Beach Boy Mike Love, engaging in conversation with the Maharishi (figure 3.16). Within the circle, Mahesh sits cross-legged as before, but his celebrity guests appear nonchalant about the special meeting. Unlike the student meditators in California, the Beatles do not adopt a reverent attitude toward the guru. In fact, they appear rather bored; John Lennon looks idly at his fingernails, while George Harrison snaps a photo of another guest.

The flip attitude of the famous visitors stands in sharp contrast to the final image of the Lapham's first installment. This picture depicts two Westerners (John O'Shea and an anonymous man) meditating solemnly outside the walls of the Maharishi's settlement (figure 3.17). According to the caption, these two individuals are among "a group of Americans living near the ashram, searching for a guru of their own."[20] Compared with the Beatles, O'Shea and the

FIGURE 3.16. Celebrity visitors unwind with Mahesh (Photographer: Larry Kurland).

FIGURE 3.17. A group of Americans outside the ashram (Photographer: Marvin Lichtner/Lee Gross Agency).

anonymous meditator represent serious spiritual seekers, unimpressed with Mahesh.[21] Together, the three photos taken on and around the premises of Rishikesh (guard, Beatles, O'Shea) help the viewer-reader distinguish the different types of adherents who journey to India in search of spiritual insight. They also reflect Lapham's budding disillusionment with the Maharishi, whose fascination with Western fame and success seem to contradict his sagely status.

This interpretation is confirmed in the set of images that accompany part 2 of "Their Once Was a Guru from Rishikesh" (May 18, 1968). The article opens with shots that emphasize the worldly nature of the guru's spiritual retreat. The first is of Mahesh, sitting cross-legged in the passenger seat of a helicopter (figure 3.18a). Once again, he appears overly enthusiastic about the West (its technologies and personalities).

The other photo, on the facing page, shows Beatle Ringo Starr fiddling with an 8mm movie camera (figure 3.19a). The famous guests appear to approach their spiritual instruction with all the seriousness of a holiday. In addition to Starr, Lennon and McCartney are also caught filming their visit (figure 3.19b).[22] Mia Farrow, in another image, is seen dining at the compound. According to the report, she "called her pilgrimage 'a romp,' but had left the ashram for a few weeks to go tiger hunting."[23] As the article progresses, the captions that frame the images take on an increasingly ironic tone.

The penultimate image shows two individuals meditating near the Ganges (figure 3.20). Despite the irreverent activity that accompanies the celebrity visits, at least two adherents appear to seriously engage the Maharishi's technique. The caption acknowledges the pair as "Nancy Jackson and Beach Boy Mike Love." Jackson's dress and posture reflect her social status, which Lapham elaborates in the article: "A chic, blond woman in her 40's, Nancy always dressed as if for a late lunch around one of her neighbors' pool in Beverly Hills. She had a brisk way of talking that suggested she was accustomed to managing things and her conversation invariably contained references to the important people she knew."[24] Mike Love, in comparison with the maven's formal pose, sits cross-legged on the ground. At a glance, the image captures two very different individuals engaged in meditation, which lends the photo a peaceful and alluring tone. However, the caption once again calls into question the sincerity of the followers: "[Jackson] and [Love], two of the Maharishi's disciples from California, *meditate for the camera*" (my emphasis).[25] The textual commentary highlights the superficiality of the captured moment; the photograph's aura is shattered, and the meditators become little more than spiritual "posers."

Given the reporter's mounting skepticism, the final image of the article comes as little surprise. It captures Mahesh on the phone in his office (figure 3.21). Although the room appears modest, the few articles captured within the frame of

FIGURE 3.18. Mahesh takes a ride on a helicopter. One of the opening images for the *Saturday Evening Post* article "There Once Was a Guru from Rishikesh, Part 2," May 18, 1968 (Photographer: Larry Kurland).

the photo are telling: a copy of the *Indian Express*, a notebook, and, of course, the phone. The way the Maharishi sits—upright in a cloth-covered chair, legs firmly planted on the ground as he leans forward to take the call—signifies the guru in a moment much more mundane. Indeed, a comparison of the first and final images

FIGURE 3.19. Celebrity candids of Ringo Starr and John Lennon in "There Once Was a Guru from Rishikesh, Part 2"(Photographer: Larry Kurland).

FIGURE 3.20. Nancy Jackson and Mike Love as they "meditate for the camera"(Photographer: Marvin Lichtner/Lee Gross).

of the two-part report encapsulates and reveals the persuasive flow of the article, as it works to disrupt any "illusion" the viewer-reader may have about Mahesh and his Spiritual Regeneration Movement (see figures 3.13 and 3.21). Like the *New York Times Magazine* (with its image of Mahesh on the phone), *Look* ultimately presents the Indian guru as an individual more interested in image than soul. The article does not necessarily place the entire onus for this situation on the Maharishi; his celebrity guests are partly to blame. The allure of the West provides a serious temptation (helicopters, phones, cameras), which the company of famous guests only seems to heighten. Celebrity presence, especially the Beatles, overwhelms and disrupts the sanctity of the compound. The Maharishi's ashram turns into "a scene"— one in which an American popular audience is critically distanced, yet phantasmically involved.

Through these first impressions of Mahesh and his followers, one immediately senses not only the two different attitudes—critical and reverent—that prevailed during the period but also the way in which they were constructed and communicated through the visual image. One also begins to see how their meaning depends on certain preconceived notions, most significantly the Orientalist divide between East and West. However, many questions remain: What accounts for these two divergent views? What exactly was at stake? And how did they each specifically deploy the icon of the Oriental Monk in their representations of Mahesh?

FIGURE 3.21. Mahesh on the phone in his office. The final image of the article series "There Once Was a Guru from Rishikesh" (Photographer: Larry Kurland).

Life *Magazine's Psychedelic Encounter*

Let us first take a look at the fourth article. The most visually extravagant of the four full-length features, *Life's* "The Year of the Guru" (February 9, 1968), perhaps offered the greatest insight into the Maharishi phenomenon. The relatively brief, four-page piece consisted overwhelmingly of color images (the text itself takes up less than half a page) and gave its audience one of the most spectacular photos of the Maharishi (figure 3.22). The reproduction here cannot fully capture the vibrant nature of the magazine copy, which takes up an entire 11 x 14 page and shows the Maharishi floating peacefully in some heavenly realm. Despite its metaphysical overtones, this fanciful portrayal and lead-in image was not meant as an expression of the guru's spirituality, but rather to capture his "aura" as a pop cultural phenomenon. The article's two other photos of Mahesh (figures 3.23a and 3.23b) attest to growing public interest. Both a capacity-filled

FIGURE 3.22. Spectacular opening image of Mahesh for the *Life* magazine article "Year of the Guru"(Photographer: Phillippe Halsman).

auditorium (at Harvard) and press microphones (at Boston's Logan airport) symbolically capture the Maharishi's newfound recognition in the United States.

Except for a photo of Mahesh with Mia Farrow, lusciously draped in marigolds, these are the only images of Mahesh to appear in *Life*'s visual feast. The spread on the following pages, instead, measures the concurrent shift toward

FIGURE 3.23. Mahesh at Boston's Logan Airport meeting the press; and in front of an audience at Harvard (Photographer: Grey Villet).

"Indian style" in music and dress to hit the West. Like Zen in the late 1950s, Americans approached Transcendental Meditation as *stylized religion* that signified a way of life, that is, an identity, more than something that transformed one's consciousness. One could sample this alternative perspective and subscribe to its outlook simply by wearing Indian attire and listening to the inspired sitar of Ravi Shankar. Inversely, by adopting this particular style of clothing and/or music, one demonstrated openness to such spiritual alternatives.

Whereas Zen as stylized religion was more sparsely developed (with Japanese clothing, architecture, and philosophy separately portrayed and promoted), TM's role in the symbolic nexus was clearly defined as *Life*'s photo spread so succinctly portrays. Again, such mundane connections downgraded its spiritual, philosophical, and cultural import to the status of fad and, more specifically, a fad associated with youth. Ultimately, "The Year of the Guru" reduces Mahesh and Transcendental Meditation to a set of crude signs made to represent a generational preoccupation. No image makes this more obvious than the article's final photo (figure 3.24). Here, Marlon Brando appears as the Maharishi's twin figure, levitating effortlessly against a spectacular background. The image is from the comedy film *Candy*, adapted from Terry Southern's satirical novel about contemporary pop culture. Brando plays Grindl, a caricature of Mahesh, who travels around in his "gurumobile." As parody, *Candy* critically portrays both yogi and follower, treating the popular embrace of Eastern spiritual alternatives as symptom. Again, the larger dis-ease, which this symptom betrays, is widespread, but only among the nation's youth. (As the large caption which ends the article reads: "His *young* followers take the Maharishi at his word: Enjoy! Enjoy!" [my emphasis].)

The battle between youth and adults—their divergent views on cultural authority—seemed to fuel the popular interest in Mahesh and his Spiritual Regeneration Movement. The way in which popular press reports generally conformed to the Oriental Monk narrative is particularly illuminating in this instance. As laid out in the previous chapter, this conventionalized narrative depends on two primary figures: the Oriental Monk teacher and his dedicated Anglo pupil. The character of the Monk, mysterious and foreign, operates as the embodiment and transmitter of Eastern spirituality. His Western pupil functions as the figure with which the audience most identifies or, at the very least, serves as an entry point into the Monk's mystical realm.

In representations of the Maharishi in the late 1960s, this narrative is maintained. Mahesh is portrayed as a spiritual sage whose mission it is to spread his teachings beyond his native homeland, specifically with an eye toward the West. As the guru reportedly commented, he "admired the American mind and compared it to the flower of the tree, while the other peoples of the earth were bark

FIGURE 3.24. Real life satirized on the big screen: Marlon Brando in the adaptation of Terry Sothern's *Candy* (Photo credit: Selmur Productions).

and branches."[26] Whether Mahesh's comment, metaphorically posed, is taken as genuine compliment or sycophantic gesture, it signals a particular type of recognition of the West (and specifically the United States) as a significant site of regeneration and reinforces American's own sense of self-importance.

Within the representative mix, the Beatles paradigmatically serve as the Monk's Western pupils, who, disillusioned with their inherited spiritual heritage, are drawn to Mahesh's philosophy and practice. It is important to examine the complex layers of this figuration. First of all, the Beatles primarily function as a synecdoche for Western youth. In press reports, the two are almost interchangeable, as the popular rock group is referred to as "the blessed leaders of the world's youth,"[27] and young people are seen as increasingly defining themselves in relation to their musical heroes. The Beatles reflect both the exuberance and excess of their young audience. Given this metaphorical fluidity, American youth occupy a primary place in the Maharishi/Monk narrative. It is members of this generation who are seen as the ones most attracted to his wisdom.

As discussed in the previous chapter, the relationship between Oriental Monk teacher and Western pupil is usually romanticized in order to legitimate the transfer of Eastern spiritual knowledge from one to the other and, more broadly, from the cryptic East to the white Western world. The more reverent accounts of the Maharishi phenomenon reinscribe this romantic account, akin to *Look*'s positive portrayal. Not only is Mahesh's image appropriately sacralized but also his American followers are represented as serious spiritual seekers. In addition, the clear distinction between East and West, maintained in the magazine's coverage, allows the transmission of mystical wisdom to serve as a dramatic event. Overall, positive reports adopt a tone that is fairly straightforward and respectful toward Mahesh and his philosophy. The audience is meant to identify (or at least sympathize) with the pupils—portrayed as earnest and reliable in their spiritual endeavors, as well as in the high regard they hold for the yogi.

In comparison with these reverent offerings, critical accounts are structured in a more complicated manner. Although the same elements of the conventional narrative are maintained, a strong element of irony pervades the discourse. In media reports on the Maharishi, examples of verbal irony[28] are plentiful. Loudon Wainwright, in his commentary "Invitation to Instant Bliss," surmises:

> When I excused myself so that the Maharishi could get a brief rest before his lecture, he had still resisted my tacit invitation to tell me my sound. But he had given me his rose, a gift I had never received before and one I accepted with real pleasure. As for the sound [mantra], perhaps he didn't feel he knew me well enough to make such a vital judgment. If I were guessing, I would guess it lay somewhere between a *h-m-m-m-m* and an *o-o-o-o-h*.[29]

Here, it is difficult to get a sense of Wainwright's stance toward the Maharishi. But one gets the impression that, despite the seemingly warm interaction between reporter and guru, Wainwright maintains a critical distance between himself and Mahesh ("somewhere between a *h-m-m-m-m* and an *o-o-o-o-h*"). In comparison with more reverent accounts, he does not approach the phenomenon with requisite seriousness, but rather "entertains" the spiritual option:

> On the first occasion I saw him he was describing the joys of family meditation to members of the Stockholm press. "What a happy thing the family becomes through meditation," he said in his high voice,

"for just a few moments night and morning." I tried to imagine such sessions in my own house and was in trouble right away.[30]

In Wainwright's account, the Maharishi appears as a comical figure. He is characterized by "a hearty cackle that was an irresistible invitation to join him in a huge joke—even if one was not at all sure what that joke was."[31] Mahesh's bliss is not necessarily linked to his spiritual insight, but ironically to famous converts and the "boost" they have given his movement around the world. News magazine reports that featured the yogi often relied on a similar twist. This is evident in *Time*'s photo caption—"How to succeed spiritually without really trying"[32]— as well as the quote with which *Newsweek* selectively ends its piece: "On the question of the cost of his ashram, the otherwise candid guru is circumspect. 'I deal in wisdom,' he says, 'not money.'"[33] Mahesh's response is not necessarily coy, but the way in which it is framed ("the otherwise candid guru is circumspect") draws into question the truth of his statement. Although the reporter does not "flatly condemn"[34] Mahesh, he does not take the guru at his word.

The writers for *Look*, *Life*, and other newsweeklies were usually viewed as reliable sources of information; at the very least, they were taken as commentators whose perspective provides unusual insight into a phenomenon. Perhaps most significant is the set of shared assumptions between author and audience that truly lend these instances of verbal irony their force.[35] Media reports critical of the Maharishi invoked deeply embedded notions of Christian asceticism to shape the public's opinion and encourage a skeptical view. For instance, a religious leader should be "in the world, not of it"—that is, not overly taken by celebrity, as Mahesh seems to be. Spiritual worth cannot be assigned a material value; in other words, the guru is not justified in charging the nominal fee for instruction. Spiritual insight requires dedicated commitment and practice; namely, there is no "Peace without Penance,"[36] as TM is portrayed to achieve. Assumptions of religious asceticism were evident in commentaries, such as Harriet Van Horne's for the *New York Post*: The Beatles "seem to have learned that salvation comes hard. This could be the beginning of Wisdom. For we are delivered out of our miseries only to the degree that we labor, repent and accept ourselves. No creed, no inspired conversion ever guaranteed an Instant New You. We have had precious few Pauls traveling the road to Damascus."[37] In these underlying ways, Christianity provided the frame of reference for understanding the emergent TM movement, as well as for the media commentator's critical rhetoric.

Despite examples too numerous to recount, verbal irony was not the only rhetorical mechanism at work in such critical assessments. Certainly more revealing is the dimension of dramatic irony in these presentations. Dramatic irony occurs when "there is a tension in a literary work between what a character knows and what the audience knows."[38] Ironist and audience usually foresee consequences unbeknownst to the characters involved. There are at least three ways dramatic irony is achieved in the various accounts of Mahesh, each predicting the eventual disillusionment of all the characters involved (guru and youth) or one in particular (guru or youth).

Dramatic irony, in the first instance, occurs in accounts that portray Transcendental Meditation as a passing fashion and Mahesh as its celebrity spokesperson. *Life*'s "Year of the Guru" can be squarely located in this vein, with its focus on TM as part of a larger cultural trend.

> The Maharishi's un-Hindu-like concern with the here and now, his concentration of self-interest and a philosophy of "Enjoy, enjoy" square beautifully with his show business followers, and with the hedonist bent of the swinging young who are making a fad of Indian clothes, Indian music and Indian culture in general.[39]

Indeed, *Life*'s reporter squarely locates TM as just another current in line with "previous waves of interest in Eastern mysticism." Although intense at the moment, interest is bound to wane. But this insight is something that both Mahesh and his followers do not currently comprehend, simply choose to ignore, or perhaps accept. The audience is to approach the phenomenon with little seriousness, if not benign amusement. Supposedly, they (along with *Life*'s reporter) see the fad for what it is, and what the actors involved most likely cannot.

In the second instance, dramatic irony is cast by highlighting the guilelessness of one of the characters. Arnold M. Auerbach, in his satirical piece "When West Goes East," presents the diary of fictional character Maharishi Khoto Ghilbrani. The Maharishi muses on the curious preoccupations and practices of his Western converts, who are primarily celebrity singers and New York theatrical folk. On their stay at his ashram, the daily entry of the fictional guru reads:

> *November 15*: Catastrophe, alas, has struck. What, I ask Vishnu, have I done to be so scourged by the Marutas? I have endured the formation of the ricepaddy Players and their all-goatherd production of "Waiting for Godot." I have survived the ghastly moment when I found my Pagoda of Contemplation piled high with corned beef sandwiches flown up from the Stage Delicatessen by the infamous Kornreich.
>   But now a crueler blow has befallen me: the "Spoons" have scheduled a "remote telecast" with an American guru—one Ed Sullivan. This person—evidently a revered man of learning in his own

land—is to broadcast on my very grounds. Worse still he has invited all
my seminar pupils to participate. The halls resound with quarrels over
"billing" and "residuals."[40]

The "Maharishi" is portrayed as the unwitting victim of his celebrity followers—
their excesses and eccentricities. With the yogi as unsuspecting figure,
Auerbach's column highlights the lack of seriousness with which these converts approach their adopted Oriental sage—the self-indulgent and superficial
nature of their commitment. The overall effect of the piece is comic yet offers
critical commentary on booming interest in this latest wave of Eastern spirituality. Although Auerbach mimics the Maharishi, in particular, and Eastern religions, in general, through the use of Orientalized lingo and overformalized
speech ("What, I ask Vishnu, have I done to be so scourged by the Marutas?"),
the guru is ultimately represented as the casualty of Western spiritual whim.[41]

In most press reports, however, it is the pupil who is defined as the fateful
victim of faddish circumstance. Although such reports are careful to acknowledge the promise the Maharishi's Spiritual Regeneration Movement holds
for young people in the United States, they ironically cast American youth
(via the Beatles) as enthusiastic, yet naive individuals who fall prey to their
own romanticized hopes, as well as Mahesh's clever tactics. Both the *New
York Times Magazine* article ("Chief Guru of the Western World") and
Lapham's two-part feature in the *Saturday Evening Post* ("There Once Was a
Guru from Rishikesh") ultimately adopt such a stance. In "Chief Guru of the
Western World," Barney Lefferts believes that Mahesh's followers are "decent
and articulate people; seemingly not a loon in the lot."[42] Juxtaposed to their
seemingly genuine commitment, the guru's means and motivations are far
more suspect:

> The only people who cavil at the Maharishi's way of life are other
> gurus in India who are not privileged to scamper around Europe and
> America propagating the faith and charging admission. They
> periodically go on record as saying that the Sage's methods are
> unscientific and that he is in meditation to make money. The
> Maharishi, confronted with those accusations, shrugs and smiles,
> and it would be most difficult to prepare a balance sheet for the last
> eight years of Transcendental Meditation.[43]

Indeed, Lefferts insinuates that Mahesh may be just another clever salesman
interested in his own personal status and gain. As the article's opening caption
reads: "Maharishi Mahesh Yogi . . . is an apostle of the contemplative life but
makes waves like any celebrity when he goes on tour."[44] Here, Lefferts suggests

underneath Mahesh's spiritual guise lurks less than noble intentions. The most disturbing aspect of the Maharishi's emergent fame (and his movement's rising fortune) is his followers' apparent blindness to an institutional, worldly success that is achieved at their expense. Lefferts ironically states:

> When a person is initiated into the movement, he pays a week's salary. Additional fees are charged for courses of instruction. The Maharishi never handles money. "He himself has nothing," says a disciple. "Of course, there are certain rich believers who fill the gaps." (One of the "gaps" was a private airplane, purchased recently for the Sage's use in India this winter.)[45]

Mahesh's followers apparently see no contradiction between the monetary and spiritual aspects of the movement, but to the reporter, the conflict is most glaring.

Young people—who "respond quicker [to the Maharishi's philosophy], without hesitation"[46]—are portrayed as particularly susceptible to the Mahesh's wiles. Lefferts represents TM's youthful constituency through the figure of a "rather striking blonde 19-year old" follower named Monika: "The thing about the Maharishi," says Monika, "is that when you travel with him you don't have time to meditate—which is the whole thing."[47] By including the young disciple's statement, Lefferts demonstrates how Mahesh's enterprise is given priority over the individual's spiritual development. Monika's gullibility is further highlighted when immediately after her observation, she asks the interviewer: "When are you going to start to meditate?"[48]

As its selection of images acutely expresses, Lefferts's piece portrays well-meaning, enthusiastic, and energetic followers as victims who have fallen under the yogi's suspicious spell.[49] Lefferts does not probe why these individuals are drawn to Mahesh but simply presents them as folks who have been swept away by the Maharishi phenomenon. Other critical pieces are similarly constructed but highlight how Mahesh's Anglo followers in the West participate in their own self-deception. Lapham's *Saturday Evening Post* article figures this ironic situation particularly well. Like Lefferts, he points out Mahesh's questionable personality (the way he dotes over the Beatles and Farrow, his preoccupation with image and publicity). However, Lapham also reveals how the Maharishi's guests at Rishikesh, despite these obvious signs, are able to maintain their positive image of the guru:

> Simcox and two or three of the other young Americans raised mild objections to the Maharishi's involvement with modern technology.

> Like O'Shea, they had expected romantic asceticism, of the kind
> they'd read about in books and they'd been prepared to live on roots
> and berries. Their dissent was never harsh, reflecting instead a
> wistful disillusionment.[50]
>
> The night the balloons appeared in the lecture hall, Geoffrey
> mistook them for decorations in honor of the god Shiva's marriage to
> the goddess Parvati. The musicians seated on the stage, among them
> a Sikh wearing slippers that curled at the toes, seemed to support his
> assumption
> "How nice," he said, "Shiva day."
> We talked of Shiva's many tricks and disguises, which so pleased
> Geoffrey that he didn't mind when it turned out he was wrong about
> the balloons. Like the musicians, they had to do with George
> Harrison's birthday.[51]

Here, Orientalist notions seem to predetermine both Simcox's and Geoffrey's spiritual commitment to Mahesh. Geoffrey's case, in particular, demonstrates that these notions override the actualities that may challenge his positive view. The article, hence, suggests how romantic visions unwittingly upheld by Mahesh's followers distort any clear perception they may have of "the truth."

The different ways in which critical assessments of the Maharishi are drawn demonstrate the complexity of the stance and the various ways they are constructed. Despite the variation, they share one thing in common besides their skeptical attitude. In these commentaries, author and audience *collude* in their outlook.[52] Both seem to "know better" than the characters involved, especially Mahesh's young followers in the West. Within these accounts, participants embody a fatal flaw—namely, a lack of maturity—and the wise judgment and discipline that come with such maturity. The American mass audience also views the events of the Mahesh's visits abroad and the pilgrimages made by various celebrities to his Himalayan compound as a tragic comedy filled with eccentric characters. Given the targeted readership of popular magazines, such a stance is wholly comprehensible. These periodicals were geared mainly to adults over thirty,[53] whose views were shaped by the disciplined ethic of the Second World War and the religious conservatism of the early 1950s. Many of these readers undoubtedly were the parents of adolescent and college-age children, whose preoccupations and emerging outlook seemed to differ greatly from their own.

Hence, the ironic stance held by the American press reflected the views of their constituency. As Hayden White writes: "Irony is the linguistic strategy underlying and sanctioning skepticism as an explanatory tactic, satire as a mode of emplotment and either agnosticism or cynicism as a moral posture."[54] Indeed, such a *strategy*, by allowing the covert expression of such attitudes, served to contain the growing popularity of the Maharishi's alternative spiritual movement. In a vast number of reports, the International Meditation Society's increasing membership worldwide, most particularly within its student organization, SIMS, on college campuses in the United States, was often cited. Transcendental Meditation's burgeoning presence, as well as celebrity interest, was enough to generate not only the attention but also the proactive, critical view of American media and audience alike.

But the pervasiveness of an ironic strategy and the ambivalence it characteristically entails suggest a deeper issue at play. Popular press accounts, both reverent and critical, participated in a debate that had, in essence, very little to do with the Maharishi Mahesh Yogi and his Spiritual Regeneration Movement. The intense focus on famous converts, especially the Beatles, betrayed a riveting shift in the structure of cultural authority. Indeed, Mahesh's popularity emerged from a new countercultural outlook that seemed to resonate with the younger generation. This outlook eschewed traditional forms of American religion and embraced more mystical alternatives focused on individual fulfillment.

However, even more radically, this emerging sensibility brought forth a new authorial framework that featured pop celebrity as legitimating force and was inherently media driven in nature—a hallmark of Virtual Orientalism's method. *Look*, in its report registering the "Campus Mood, Spring, '68," spoke with student editors from twenty-three universities and reported:

> The nearest thing to heroes for many students is the Beatles. "The
> Beatles grew up right along with us," says Notre Dame's [Pat] Collins.
> "If you take the time to go through their music, it is really neat to see
> how these people with all their money still manage to keep moving,
> to keep telling the story while we are thinking of it. They're like the
> great scribes of our era." Mostly, the Beatles are seen as the knights
> of rebellion. "We all get a kick out of the fact that they are like us; but
> they have managed to take on this whole monolithic system," says
> Art Johnston, "and they have it right by the short hair."[55]

A similar observation was made in the December 4, 1967, issue of *Newsweek*, whose education column explored the demise of the campus hero. The magazine hints at several reasons that "college students no longer idolize political leaders, or try to imitate authors like Salinger or Tolkien."[56] These young people are either "too jaded," or "too busy." However, the piece paradoxically realizes: "The most popular non-ideological idols are the Beatles, particularly John Lennon. . . . 'They are saying that youth can be more successful than adults,' says Jon Ratner, a senior at Berkeley, 'and that the values of youth are important. All the new ideas of everything that's going on begin with the Beatles.'"[57]

The ambivalence toward the Beatles as heroes emerges from the assumption that the pop group not only is "non-ideological" (i.e., not political) but also derives its cultural authority from illegitimate means. This insight can be intimated not only by the inclusion of mass media philosopher Marshall McLuhan in the report "as coming very close to what students would like to say"[58] but also by the quote with which the article ends: "Ron Scheer was astounded when his students could not identify Westmoreland, Albee and Rap Brown. But they all readily recognized Napoleon Solo, the hero of "The Man from U.N.C.L.E."[59] The fact that college students so readily recognize and identify with entertainment figures—real and fictional—reveals a new form of cultural authority.[60] Such authority appeared not only unwieldy but also formidable, as other powerful influences, such as Mahesh, were spun off these figures. Cultural sanction seemed based on nothing more than the fluffiness of pop stardom, as Lapham's characterization of one adherent suggests:

> Characteristic of another type I found prevalent among meditators, [Kip] Cohen was young, engaging, very articulate and very hip. He had long blond hair and a mustache, and he was just past 26, which depressed him. He'd first seen the Maharishi on the Johnny Carson show, and he's heard that Donovan and the Beatles were into meditation.
>
> "With their endorsement, he said, "I knew the thing couldn't be too far amiss."[61]

Indeed, sensationalized image was often put forth as the foundation of Mahesh's "success" in the West. If anything, it afforded the guru and his movement widespread publicity, whether one felt he deserved it or not. As Hedgepeth observed: "Even if there were some who hadn't seen [Mahesh] on [the Berkeley] campus last year, there wasn't one who didn't realize that he was the same jet-age guru who had guided the Beatles off the psychedelic drug scene by way of a new, nonchemical turn-on."[62] All in all, the majority of American reviewers seemed most troubled not necessarily by *what* Mahesh had to say (most of which perplexed commentators), but rather by *how* he achieved popular recognition, namely, through the authorial framework of celebrity. Critical accounts, ironically posed in a variety of ways, expressed their disdain or at least their ambivalence toward this new framework. In contrast, more reverent portrayals were readily at home within this framework or at least resigned to its presence.[63]

Amid the larger battle for cultural authority and significance, the Maharishi's image served as a convenient screen on which to project these more immediate concerns. Hayden White notes that such figurations "are crucially necessary when a culture or social group encounters phenomena that either elude or run afoul of normal expectations or quotidian experiences."[64] The ascendancy of television and other new media undoubtedly had transformed popular consciousness in ways that few predicted. The emphasis on more immediate experience (sight and sound) and the powerful circuits of pop celebrity[65] were just two of its many unintended effects with which Americans struggled. The fact that the Maharishi capitalized on both of these effects seemingly to his advantage made him the perfect figure on which to project the ambivalent feelings toward the new media enviroment Americans held. Such anxiety, especially over the emerging status of celebrity, was displaced onto Mahesh—a target made more acceptable through racial and colonial difference. The figure of the celebrity guru allowed an American audience to disavow pop culture's widening influence by drawing their suspicion onto the figure, while simultaneously indulging their desire for celebrity spectacle.

Maintaining the Orientalist Realm

In the rhetorical ways just discussed, the majority of press accounts dedicated to the Maharishi presented their subject with great ambivalence. They did not romantically embrace Mahesh as Oriental Monk, but this is not to say that the Oriental Monk as icon did not figure into the guru's representation. As symbolic resource and tool through which to measure the spiritual authenticity of the historical figure, it played an integral part in assessments of Mahesh. The degree to which real Asian teachers conformed to the icon, an Orientalist sign already well known in the minds of the American audience, determined the legitimacy of their mission.

Both critical and reverent accounts implicitly invoked the Oriental Monk icon within a Virtual Orientalist frame to substantiate their views. Reverent accounts harmonized Mahesh's motivations and behavior with those the icon

paradigmatically set forth. Conversely, critical assessments gained their persuasive power by creating an image of Mahesh that fell woefully short of this
measure. By implicitly referencing the icon, as well as other preconceived notions about East (and more specifically, India), representations of Mahesh, on
the whole, not only prescribed to but also reinforced an Virtual Orientalist
framework of assumptions and beliefs.

One can easily discern the connection between 1960s American press
reports of Mahesh and views upheld by Orientalists during the nineteenth century. As Edward Said astutely remarks about the latter:

> Language and race seemed inextricably tied, and the "good" Orient
> was invariably a classical period somewhere in a long-gone India,
> whereas the "bad" Orient lingered in present-day Asia, parts of
> North Africa, and Islam everywhere. "Aryans" were confined to
> Europe and the ancient Orient; . . . the Aryan myth dominated
> historical and cultural anthropology at the expense of the "lesser"
> peoples.[66]

Given Said's characterization, representations of Mahesh entail a significant
difficulty, because in these, he seems to embody both "a long-gone India" and
"present-day Asia." But any contradiction dissolves when one takes into consideration the conflicting opinions of the guru held by the popular media. Reverent accounts primarily chose to see Mahesh merely as representative of an
ancient Hindu tradition ("long-gone India"), whereas critical ones spoke only
of the yogi's corrupted concerns ("present-day Asia").

Mahesh's historical person and mission were informed by similar views
and expectations, and he could not escape this deeply ingrained Orientalist
frame of reference, no matter how he tried. For instance, American reviewers
could not adequately comprehend his attempts to creatively employ modern
means of communication and travel to disseminate his spiritual knowledge.
Mahesh's mobility became an index of his agency and controllability. A Monk
who stays put in his Asian country of origin or whose mobility is limited is
certainly preferred over one who seems on the go. The Maharishi was portrayed as always on the move, traveling from one locale to another.[67] Not only
had he made eight trips around the world (by 1968) but also these trips were
part of a conscious plan to establish TM centers and spread his teachings
throughout the globe. On the one hand, this conscious plan demonstrated initiative on Mahesh's part that discomforted critical commentators. On the other,
reverent reviewers, often followers of the movement, saw the guru's visits as a
response to their call. They also saw themselves as providing Mahesh with the
means to travel from one place to another. Hence, Mahesh, as historical figure,

maintains the romantic composure of the icon as long as he is seen as suitably passive, that is, stays within the geographical view of the white host society and/or travels according to their needs. In either case, his spiritual initiative was not something that could not be adequately conceived by the American press. Initiative constituted a characteristic reserved solely for his pupils in the West.

Mahesh's Orientalized image did not exist independently but was supported by an equally Orientalized India. In his "Open Letter to the Beatles," Arthur J. Dommen, the *Los Angeles Times* bureau chief in New Delhi, invoked these notions to critically comment on the pop group's impending trip to India. For example:

> But you will say, the mystical wisdom of India lies not in the illiterate, ill-nourished peasants, who are like the illiterate, ill-nourished peasants everywhere, but in the holy men, the gurus and the sadhus. Here indeed is an important difference. To observe these holy men in their faded pinkish orange robes trudging the roads of India, their bare feet stirring the dust and their matted hair their only protection from the beating sun or rain, does make one wonder whether they have not attained a higher plane of spirituality, where the afflictions of the body no longer exist.
>
> In so far as they do not collectively concern themselves with problems of bettering society, India's holy men have relinquished the temporal things of life, I agree.
>
> The influence of these holy men is said to be considerable, yet it seems insufficiently enlightening to prevent the suicide of an estimated 17,000 people every year, and it does not give salvation to the estimated 2 million beggars.
>
> I confess that the spirituality of the several thousand baked and near-naked sadhus who tried to storm the Parliament building last November in their frenzy to see a law enacted to ban the slaughter of cows, even if they had to lynch a few MPs in the process, still escapes me today.[68]

Here, Dommen references the stereotypical view of India as a third world country, typified by its teeming masses, superstitious tendencies, and chaotic mix of lifestyles. Like British writers such as Kipling, he uses this characterization to posit the spiritual, moral, and political inferiority of the Indian peoples. Ironically, this same view was also upheld in more reverent portrayals. These accounts assumed that Indians' superstitious nature and their penchant to cater to religious folk like Mahesh meant excellent service at the Rishikesh ashram. India's nontechnological, agrarian setting provided a romantic back-drop. And the disorderly nature of Indian life translated into local color to be enjoyed and experienced by spiritual tourists from the West. Lapham's description of Mia Farrow captures this well:

> [Farrow] appeared at lunch, wearing white cotton pajamas and gold-rimmed glasses. In conversation with John Lennon she said she'd been to Goa, and there, with her brother, she'd bought a stove for a few rupees and lived on the beach for a week.
>
> "You've got to do it right, to be with the people and never mind the rotten conditions," she said. "Otherwise you miss the magic of this magical land."[69]

Although Americans at the time saw themselves as distinct from British colonizers of the past, they still adopted many of the same dispositions toward the former colony. Indeed, after India had declared itself an independent state, the Asian country received financial and technical assistance from the United States.[70] In Americans' eyes, India could not survive on its own and would continue to be a "white man's burden."[71] And this view of India's dependency continued to underwrite lingering Orientalist attitudes of pessimism (Dommen) and privilege (Farrow).

One of the hallmarks of Orientalist knowledge is that it involves a "battery of desires, repressions, investments, and projections."[72] While Mahesh offered a convenient figure through which to process the ambivalent feelings toward an emerging authorial framework of media celebrity, popular portrayals of him also reveal a desire for an obedient Indian subject—acquiescent, passive, and dependent. The portrayals of the Maharishi's Indian followers as appropriately servile also betray this Orientalist hope. Two decades after Indian independence, representations of Mahesh and his Indian disciples reflected, respectively, what India had become (autonomous agent) in the eyes of Americans and what they had hoped it would be (compliant ally). In this sense, such images surreptitiously worked to manage various American investments in matters both at home and abroad.

Hyperreal Samadhi

Of all the images of Mahesh and his movement to make their way into American popular view during the late 1960s, perhaps the most representative of the entire phenomenon was the one of the Maharishi and Mia Farrow on their arrival in New Delhi (figure 3.25). The spectacular color photo highlights the startling difference in appearance; the guru's nut-brown complexion and dark features stand in stark contrast to Farrow's fair face. Indeed, the actress—her light features, smooth skin, boyish haircut, and intense gaze—seem to portray Western innocence and youth unavailable to the Oriental sage who appears much more "shady." Of the strange pair, it is difficult to tell whose image is more spiritually imbued.

The bright orange marigolds in which the two are entwined are significant. Offerings traditionally given to a spiritual leader in India, they also are draped around the actress's neck in deference to the promise of her youthful celebrity. The Maharishi may have emerged from a long line of Hindu sages, but Farrow also boasts her own lineage. As the daughter of actress Maureen O'Sullivan and director John Farrow, she represents the consummate actor, the progeny of the New York stage and Hollywood screen. The image, less a reflection of the characters portrayed, reflects the complicated view of the American popular audience, who brought the frames of both media celebrity and Orientalism to bear.

FIGURE 3.25. Mia Farrow with Mahesh (Photographer: Raghubir Singh/ Nancy Palmer Agency).

Mahesh was the first spiritual leader from the East to experience popular media attention. This event, in itself, reinforced a radically different epistemological framework in which image became just as authoritative as anything that could be called historical reality. To the American public, Mahesh's likeness gave witness to its own Orientalist truth, while serving as a convenient screen on which to project debates closer to home. *Hyperreal samadhi.*[73]

The Orientalism invoked in mass media reports differed greatly from the Orientalism deployed in traditional print culture (with its focus on literature, especially the novel). The proliferation of images—both photographic and televisual—provided a new arsenal for imaginative construction. They also gave an American audience an illusory sense that they were experiencing Mahesh firsthand. The seemingly objective eye of the camera and transparent nature of the visuals gave one the impression that one could perspicuously view the phenomenon at hand. Such images as we have just seen are never neutrally presented but rhetorically select and often reflect the audience's predetermined frames of reference. The images of the Maharishi invoked a set of assumptions that allowed for two primary interpretations of the phenomenon (critical or reverent). Although deployed in different ways, the Oriental Monk icon and narrative was an essential dimension of both interpretations, which used this frame of reference to enact a larger battle over cultural authority, as well as offer geopolitical commentary. Far from challenging preconceived notions of Eastern spirituality, mass media in the television age consolidated an Orientalist view, created an Orientalist realm of vision that became deceptively "real" in its immediacy.

The Guru Redux: *Deepak Chopra*

Critical reviewers perhaps felt justified in their suspicions as the Beatles and other celebrities lost interest in the Maharishi and his movement. In the summer of 1968, the Maharishi cut short his fifteen-city American tour for lack of attendance. TM had indeed been a fad that seemed to fade as quickly as it emerged. But history is an unfolding story, and what it reveals can be equally ironic. As the 1960s evolved into the 1970s, the nation's youth—who held a more reverent view of Mahesh—grew up. Although many would abandon their early preoccupations and alternative lifestyles, this generation's experience of the Maharishi through mass media images would not be without its effect. Transcendental Meditation would enjoy resurgence in the mid-1970s, both practically and discursively.[74] Practically, meditation would be a technique experimentally adopted in American schools and workplaces. Discursively, it would become a buzzword for an alternative way to handle anxiety and stress. The Maharishi's image also enjoyed its own discursive regeneration, and the guru became a frequent guest on popular talk shows during this period. All in all, it is questionable whether Mahesh achieved his goal of worldwide peace. However, he and his movement did manage to initiate a set of controversies in American life and Western science that are still being debated today. And TM practitioners, such as David Lynch, seem dedicated to the Maharishi's lofty aim more than ever.

The Maharishi Mahesh died on February 5, 2008. Despite the immeasurable influence he had on American culture, Mahesh would be most remembered for his association with the Beatles long after this relationship had soured. His image would be nostalgically invoked as part of the larger phenomenon of their enormous success, as well as the cultural revolution that took place during the 1960s. Although they viewed the legendary pop group as TM's most promising pupils at the time, both Mahesh and the American public could not foresee the way the movement's legacy would unfold. Indeed, the individual through whom Mahesh's ideas would reach their contemporary fruition would be none other than a South Asian American named Deepak Chopra.

Those Americans seeking an alternative spirituality in the new millennium have a plethora of charismatic leaders from which to choose. Among the most popular to arrive on the scene is "the Indian-born endocrinologist-turned-guru,"[75] Deepak Chopra, whose philosophy is based on a "simplified Hinduism that [is] fascinating to a nation of seekers."[76] If media coverage is any measure, Chopra has certainly gained popular recognition: a dozen *New York Times* best sellers, numerous PBS specials, an appearance on *Oprah*, and more than fifty articles in popular magazines, including *Time*, *Psychology Today*, and *Fortune*. Lauded by statesmen and celebrities alike and named one of the "top 100 heroes and icons of the century" by *Time* magazine, Chopra has come to represent the perfect blend of Eastern wisdom and Western know-how. Despite the glowing press, a cloud of suspicion looms over his mystical empire. *Newsweek* (October 20, 1997) disrupted Chopra's glistening aura in its cover story "Spirituality for Sale." The report critically questioned the underlying motivations of the New Age sensation ("Would you buy a used mantra from this man?") and likened Chopra to a "snake-oil salesman."

Recruited as a young physician during the "Vietnam-era doctor shortage," Chopra arrived in the United States in 1970. He would become increasingly disillusioned with many aspects of Western medicine and, in 1980, picked up a book on Transcendental Meditation. By 1989, he had become the chairman and sole stockholder of Mahesh's product line of Ayur-Veda herbal cures.[77] His efforts were so successful that the Maharishi bestowed on Chopra the title

"Lord of Immortality." Although he eventually split with his former teacher, Chopra maintained much of the philosophical outlook developed under Mahesh, as well as the guru's media savvy.

Chopra's own rise to spiritual celebrity is as colorful as Mahesh's, and mass media representations of him are no less conflicted. Perhaps the most significant difference between teacher and pupil is the latter's Westernized image. Chopra—clean-cut and immaculately dressed in Western clothing— seems diametrically opposed to Mahesh in appearance and style. Often portrayed as "an immigrant success story,"[78] Chopra's popular image bespeaks a view where the Oriental Monk icon and the American model minority myth merge. Despite this representational inflection, the New Age guru and his former teacher do share the same dark features, betraying their Indian origins and adding a powerful mystique to their spiritual missions. Many of the same representational dynamics that informed the American popular audience's view of Mahesh in the 1960s can be read in portrayals of Chopra today.[79]

Perhaps the most disconcerting feature of Chopra is not the self-help leader's financial success or his special attention to celebrity followers. As was the case with Mahesh, the most confounding aspect of Chopra's fame seems to be the dissimulation between reality and image that the popular press senses yet is not able to dispel or contain. As *Time* anxiously quotes: "It's my destiny to play an infinite number of roles, but I'm not the role I'm playing," says Chopra with characteristic inscrutability.[80]

No matter how much they are remade in its image, Mahesh and Chopra, as historical figures, demonstrate not only an initiative but also a Westernized flair for promotion that exceeds Virtual Orientalism's representational bounds. And Americans would turn to figures more of their making.

4

The Monk Goes Hollywood

Kung Fu

In one of the most popular films of the 1990s, Quentin Tarantino's *Pulp Fiction* (1994), mob hit man Jules Winnfield, played by Samuel L Jackson, has a near-death experience that leads him to reevaluate his life. In the film's final scene, Jules renounces his violent life as a killer for hire for one dedicated to a higher, more humane mission. He tells his partner, Vincent (John Travolta), that he will "walk the earth . . . like Caine in *Kung Fu*. Just walk from town to town, meet people, get in adventures . . . until God puts me where he wants me to be."

The audience gets a clear sense of Jules's newfound spiritual conviction, not only through his references to the Almighty Father and the biblical scripture he so rousingly cites, but also through his idiosyncratic nod to Caine, the wandering monk of the 1970s television series, *Kung Fu*. Both the humor and efficacy of this reference derive from the allusion to Caine as pop cultural icon, a wholly fictional figure whose spiritual authority has been made real through the medium of television.

While "real" Oriental Monks like the Maharishi Mahesh would disappoint, ones spun directly from imagination could not, as the television and film characters such as Kwai Chang Caine would prove. As Hollywood creations, these characters would take part in a new stage in the development of the Oriental Monk icon, firmly establishing Virtual Orientalism's hold. Kwai Chang Caine in the 1970s television series *Kung Fu* would be the first to assert a prominent visual image of the Monk, as well as consolidate the discrete Orientalist narrative that the image would meaningfully carry. As I will discuss, implicit attitudes, expectations, and hopes in circulation since the 1950s and further cultivated in the 1960s were made explicit through the popular media of film and television.

The fact that Oriental Monks in the 1970s and later decades emerged within fictional accounts is of great significance. Virtual Orientalism constitutes a new symbolic realm characterized by its obdurate self-sufficiency. Not only does Virtual Orientalism declare an independence from the real but also it co-opts or colonizes the real. As modern-day media intertwine the fictional characters and the actors who play them, the lines between fabrication and reality become blurred. Although labeled as pure entertainment, these "Hollywood Monks" are taken as a new kind of ethical guide, often supplementing, if not supplanting, more historical models.

"An Eastern Western"

The 1960s was a watershed period in American history—a time of unusual social, political, cultural, and religious transformation. The period saw the popular recognition of "alternative" lifestyles and spiritual experimentation, as well as a new tolerance toward "peoples of color" (in the form of the Civil Rights movement and the 1965 Immigration Act). At the same time, this transformation was underwritten by a sense of loss—a loss configured by the wounds of war, the impact of technology and global capitalism, domestic racial strife, and growing disillusionment with traditional forms of religious faith and worship. Out of this context emerged the archetype of the American religious subject as a "spiritual seeker" who journeys in search of new religious ground for reconciliation and healing.[1]

The cultures of Asia offered the unparalleled promise of finding such ground. Although the seeds of such promise were already sown, as we have seen in the cases of D. T. Suzuki and the Maharishi Mahesh Yogi, they would not bear fruit until the early 1970s, when the search for spiritual renewal in the East found popular expression in *Kung Fu* (1972–1975). *Kung Fu*, which had its humble beginnings as an ABC *Movie of the Week* in February 1972, follows the wanderings of a "half-Chinese, half-American" Shaolin priest named Kwai Chang Caine through the late-nineteenth-century Western frontier. Having justifiably killed the emperor's nephew, Caine is forced to flee China for the United States. But his deed follows him, as the young monk becomes a fugitive on both continents, and he attempts to atone for his "sin" by helping those in need. In America, Caine also discovers that he has a half-brother, Danny Caine, for whom he searches.

Kung Fu began as a discarded script written by comic writers Ed Spielman and Howard Friedlander. Their decision to pen an *"eastern* Western," initially inspired by Spielman's avid interest in Asian cultures (Japanese film, martial arts, Chinese language and philosophy), led to the movie script the pair would sell to Warner Brothers in 1970. Although the studio bought the script with their overseas market in mind, the project was subsequently shelved because of its high production cost and "violent and esoteric" nature.

During an earnings slump, Warner Brothers decided to take a gamble on the project and handed it over to producer-director Jerry Thorpe, who transformed the screenplay into a made-for-TV movie. The original ninety-minute movie pilot, *Kung Fu: The Way of the Tiger, the Sign of the Dragon*, first aired on February 22, 1972. It was so popular that ABC offered a second showing of the movie during its summer season and commissioned four new one-hour episodes for the following fall. By 1973, *Kung Fu* officially became part of ABC's regular lineup.

From its inception, *Kung Fu* was viewed as a revolutionary series in many ways. The success of the program is undoubtedly due to the novel ways it transformed the fading genre of the television Western to reflect the outlook of a new generation. As in traditional Westerns, the rugged frontier characterized by its vigilante justice provided much of the backdrop, but the story's protagonist, Kwai Chang Caine, was without precedent. As a fugitive who possessed none of the bravado of conventional Western heroes and espoused a pacifist philosophy that directly challenged such behavior, the character of Caine seemed quite radical indeed. Viewed within the context of the ongoing Vietnam War, *Kung Fu* offered indirect political commentary and an attractive alternative.

One of *Kung Fu*'s most characteristic features was its use of flashback, which was intimately linked to its pacifist philosophy.[2] In most episodes, Caine's contemporary situation in the United States interspersed with scenes from his Shaolin training in China offers the philosophical background for his unorthodox actions and views. The audience is also able to trace Caine's spiritual development through his relationships with the show's regular characters, his Oriental Monk teachers—Master Po and Master Kan (figure 4.1). Under their tutelage, the viewer, along with young Caine, learn the show's most important lessons. In one of the most memorable passages from the show, Master Kan's words resound:

Perceive the way of nature and no force of man can harm you. Do not meet a wave head on: avoid it. You do not have to stop force: It is

FIGURE 4.1. Caine with Master Po (Keye Luke).

easier to redirect it. Learn more ways to preserve rather than destroy.
Avoid rather than check. Check rather than hurt. Hurt rather than
maim. Maim rather than kill. For all life is precious nor can any be
replaced.

The show's success rested on linking its Eastern-influenced pacifist philosophy
with martial arts prowess—a specific brand of physical strength and agility
about which Americans had but a vague notion. And this blend of spirituality
and physicality would prove a potent combination.

To many, *Kung Fu* was a breakthrough series—not only because of the
novel way it inserted pacifist philosophy into the popular genre of Western but
also because of its unlikely hero, a "half-Chinese Buddhist monk." No television show before *Kung Fu* had featured a lead character of Asian descent, let
alone valorized his cultural and spiritual heritage. Reflective of a new consciousness about race and gender, the series also featured other unsung heroes
of the West in a more humane and dignified fashion—Chinese laborers, Native
Americans, black and Armenian sojourners, and women.

These elements—the show's philosophical pacifism, its martial arts spirituality, and its embrace of minorities and women—were televisually idiosyncratic at the time and would distinguish the show from anything that had come
before. No one could have predicted the series' amazing success. As one critic
acknowledged: "Its audience appeal is a network vice president's dream. Kids
love it. So do teens, young marrieds, and women of all ages."[3] *Kung Fu* would
enjoy a three-year run, garnering impressive Nielsen ratings and several Emmy
nominations. The show's popularity would spawn a book series and record, as

well as inspire a popular dance craze.[4] Overwhelming cultural acceptance of the series by the American public was best seen by the show's appearance in Philadelphia's inner-city public schools, where the program was used as an aid in teaching children to read.[5] By 1973, "The Kung Fu Craze" was sweeping the nation,[6] and Kwai Chang Caine was declared a "new American hero."[7]

A Double-Edged Chop: Reading Controversy

Without a doubt, *Kung Fu* represented an innovative program in the early 1970s, with its unprecedented inclusion of women and racial minorities, as well as its unorthodox view of violence, aimed at a mass audience in the United States. However, if one views *Kung Fu* within the historical representation of other Oriental Monks in the American mass media, the series loses its revolutionary cast. Through this frame, *Kung Fu* can be read as a hegemonic moment in which the American popular imaginary once again re-created its Asian spiritual "other." The fictional nature of the series allowed an unmitigated Orientalist portrayal of Eastern philosophy, as well as of the behavior of its Asian characters.

Understanding *Kung Fu* as an instance of cultural hegemony is a complex affair, and the best way to discern its operation is to start with the *contradictions* the series entailed. Contradictions emerge when there is a severe clash between the dominant narrative at hand and the social reality it is attempting to contain. Richard Dyer describes the relationship between hegemony and contradiction:

> [Hegemony is] the expression of the interests and world-views of a particular social group or class so expressed as to pass for the interest and world-view of the whole of society.
>
> Hegemony is something that a class, gender and/or race constantly has to work for—it is never permanently, statically established in a culture. It seems to me likely that the degree to which the suppression of contradictions in an art-work actually shows is a register of the hold of a particular hegemony at the moment of the film's production. Where there is a sense of strain at holding down contradiction, I would posit either the ruling groups' own lack of faith in their world-view (contradictions *within* dominant ideology) or the presence in other groups of a hard and disturbing challenge to the ruling groups' hegemony (contradictions *to* dominant ideology).[8]

Kung Fu expressed both types of contradictions that Dyer describes (*within* and *to* dominant ideology). These can best be read from the popular print commentary that accompanied the show (e.g., reviews, letters to the editor). By understanding these two primary contradictions, or what I call "controversies," we can begin to discern the narrative shape and visual mechanics of the show's hegemonic project.

Caine: Pacifist Hero or Violent Assailant?

In the early 1970s, as Americans emerged from a decade characterized by social unrest and generational conflict, it is not surprising that their view of themselves and society was undergoing a major change. Contradictions *within* the dominant ideology were plentiful and reflected the shifts and compromises being made. In relation to *Kung Fu*, these contradictions emerged in the critical reviews of the show that centered on the issue of violence. These reviews noted a glaring contradiction between the pacifist philosophy of the series and its equally dependable fight scenes. As a critic for the industry periodical *Variety* sarcastically wrote: "Bragged on by the network for its non-violent nature, each segment seems to wind up with a clutter of corpses probably unmatched by any other series on TV. But Carradine is never really responsible—it seems the dead ones were always bent on destroying him when they met death."[9]

Chicago Tribune columnist, Gary Deeb, in his commentary "You Can't Teach the Golden Rule with a Punch in the Nose," further condemned the show's morality as disingenuous: "And please don't twist my arm about Caine's live-and-let-live credo. Kung Fu is a violent TV show that exploits the mass audience's craving for blood and guts, and yet astonishingly wraps it all up in a pretty package topped by a stylish ribbon that proclaims the Golden Rule."[10]

These critics and others questioned the depth and sincerity of the philosophical aims of the series. Rather than challenge the conventional use of violence, they felt that *Kung Fu* simply made aggression more palatable by coating it with a thin spiritual veneer drawn from "night-school notions about Buddha, Confucius and Lao-tse."[11] Although the character of Caine espoused a rhetoric of nonviolence, he inevitably put his martial arts skills to good use in each episode, with self-defense providing the convenient escape clause. According to critics, the show's producers and writers had stumbled on a formula that allowed the audience to have their fortune cookie and eat it, too.

Critics also worried about the possible effects the show had on its young audience. Stephen Farber for *Esquire* magazine noted:

Although Caine preaches nonviolence, every episode includes at least one juicy fight, and many high-school kids have indicated more interest in Caine's exotic techniques of assault and battery than in his pacifist philosophy. A boy from Arlington, Virginia, put it very simply in his letter: "I would like to learn karate and judo because kids are always trying to beat me up at school."[12]

The fact that critics were concerned with *Kung Fu's* influence on the country's youngest viewers tells us much about the particular ideological contradiction involved. Since children represent the nation's future, any public discussion regarding their moral development necessarily encapsulates the values that the nation holds most dear. As the 1960s generation began to have children of their own, they had to decide which of their parents' values to keep and which ones to transform.

Kung Fu: Racially Progressive or Racially Regressive?

As mainstream critics argued over *Kung Fu's* pacifist vision, one of the strongest critiques of the show was lodged from a very different angle. A "minority" opinion would offer a bold challenge to the seemingly progressive portrayal of racial-ethnic peoples in the show, creating controversy from a different angle. In his editorial review for the *New York Times*, Asian American author Frank Chin focused on the representation of Asians, and especially of Asian men, in the series. In his controversial opening, he claims:

> The progress that Asians of all yellows have made in the movies and on television is pitiful compared to the great strides in determination made by apes, dinosaurs, zombies, the Creature from the Black Lagoon and other rubber creations of Hollywood's imagination.
>
> In 40 years, apes went from a naked, hairy King Kong, gigantic with nitwit sex fantasies about little human women, to a talking chimpanzee leading his fellow apes in a battle to take over the planet. We've progressed from Fu Manchu, the male Dragon Lady of silent movies, to Charlie Chan and then to "Kung Fu" on TV.[13]

Chin goes on to link the show's portrayal of Asian masculinity to the "'small, soft man' vision of the Chinese in America."[14] Ultimately for Chin, *Kung Fu* reinforces preexisting stereotypes and plays into a white fantasy of Chinese as "passive, docile, timid, mystical aliens." The series, far from being progressive, simply continues a legacy of racist misrepresentation.

Chin also insists that "a debate is raging" in Asian America—one between those who accept the series and those who vocally express their disdain. He writes:

> The yellows who are against "Kung Fu" are advised to sit down and be grateful that Charlie Chan reruns and the "Kung Fu" series are making us sympathetic in the white man's mind. And the majority never having had a serious thought about our people mining for gold and building the transcontinental railroad, are so grateful to "Kung Fu" for making us likable that they look on its insults and inaccuracies as merely the price of acceptance in America.

At the heart of this debate is a commentary about the insidiousness of the "good" stereotype and its power to disingenuously represent a racial politics that is not only sympathetic but also progressive. While "the majority" of Asian Americans are willing to settle for this representational compromise, Chin, a product of the ethnic consciousness movements of the 1960s, is not. *Kung Fu*, for him and other vocal dissidents, is racially regressive in its cunningly deceptive portrayal of the Chinese. As a minority opinion even within his own racial-ethnic community, Chin calls attention to and firmly establishes a contradiction *to* the show's dominant ideology.

Three weeks after the article appeared, *Kung Fu* producer-writer-director Ed Spielman responded to Chin's attack. In "I'm Proud to Have Created 'Kung Fu,'" Spielman pegs the Asian American author as simply a "malcontent in residence" and defends the series as one that portrays Chinese as "intelligent, brave, disciplined and humane."[15] He goes on to claim: "No one ever formed a negative opinion of a Chinese from having watched 'Kung Fu.' It is the mainstream of public opinion which indicates that 'Kung Fu' changed the negative Oriental stereotype to an image of sensitivity and dignity."[16]

For the most part, Spielman does not seem cognizant of one of Chin's primary criticisms, namely, how seemingly "good" stereotypes can be as harmful as "bad" ones. This lack of awareness is written into his related defense of Charlie Chan. Of the Chinese detective popularized in American film during the1930s and 1940s, Spielman writes: "I would willingly trade such a stereotype for any one of the passive Jews, servile blacks, or drunken Irish that I have seen depicted."[17] In an especially telling comment, the *Kung Fu* creator labels Chin's opinion as "radical" and "very much in the minority," citing "the countless letters of thanks which I have received from Oriental-Americans for my creation."[18] As Chin predicted, Spielman, as the voice of "the majority," once again commands him "to sit down and be grateful."[19]

In addition to Chin's scathing critique, letters from Asian Americans in newspapers and magazines registered notable discontent with the racial politics of the series. In her letter to *TV Guide*, Miss S. Y. Pon from Fort Collins, Colorado, comments: "I resent having a white actor play the role of a Chinese man, even if the character is supposed to be half-Chinese, half-white."[20] In a more extended submission, Katie San of New York City writes to the *New York Times*:

> It is incredible that the role of the main character, Caine who is half-Asian, is played by Carradine, who does not—not, not, not—look remotely Asian. And when he appears with Asians, it is completely absurd. Maybe on a theater stage, from the 15th row, with a lot of adhesive tape on his eyes, Carradine might look half Asian to a white audience. But not to Asians—or half Asians.
>
> Is anybody following this? Does anybody care? Can anyone see the extreme irony of the situation? Here is a TV series with a story line that can, at last, begin to show an Asian as a human being, and not as a stereotype of one. And that role is being played by a white actor.[21]

It seemed that, especially for a number of Asian Americans and other dissatisfied viewers, the politics of casting seriously undercut any racial progress that *Kung Fu* made. Objections such as these, like Chin's pointed criticisms, marked a contradiction to the dominant racial ideology that the show could not so readily suppress. And it is this "minor" controversy that would become one of the most prominent issues surrounding the show with the passage of time.

The Middle Way

The images included in the *Esquire* issue featuring *Kung Fu* captured these ongoing ideological tensions. On the cover, David Carradine, dressed as Kwai Chang Caine, is seen "kicking" the Lone Ranger out of the frame, as the caption proclaims: "Ah, so! A new American hero at last!" (figure 4.2). The scene suggests the triumph of a new set of values—including a conflicted sense of violence and the embrace of cultural diversity—and a generational shift. This shift is visually staged on the *Esquire* cover through a scene of physical aggression in which *Kung Fu*'s Oriental Monk literally "kicks butt." The interior image (by photographer Frank Cowan), which accompanies the cover article, "Kids! Now You Can Chop Up Your Old Comic-Book Heroes with Your Bare Hands!" features a young boy dressed up as Caine, replete with bald head, who rips up his old comic books as he stands in front of a television set—Caine's image onscreen. Stephen Farber's tongue-in-cheek piece on the show does suggest how *Kung Fu* has a potential positive influence on the younger members of its audience. Still, Cowan's image is disturbing—if not for the youth's disregard of tradition (ripping his old comics to shreds), then for the utter mimicry of Caine and his Asian ways. The questionable impact of television and consumer culture provides the subtext for these images.

FIGURE 4.2. The August 1973 cover of *Esquire* magazine (Photographer: Carl Fischer).

Kung Fu set the stage for a negotiation of different sociopolitical interests emergent during the period. The turmoil of the 1960s produced a younger generation with new ideals. This generation—whose ethos was defined by anti-war movements, free-love culture, countercultural skepticism, and Civil Rights struggles—created their own subaltern existences that radically challenged the dominant social, religious, and cultural hierarchies of their parents' world. As American youth entered adulthood in the 1970s, the evolution of American values was evident, marking the entrance of a new dominant group. Television, as mass medium, reflected this cultural ingression with new programming that was a great deal more ethnically diverse (e.g., *Sanford and Son*) and attempted to honestly capture the social reality of its time (e.g., *All in the Family*, *Room 222*).

This is not to say that the cultural values and perspectives of the 1960s generation simply replaced that of their parents, but rather the early 1970s saw the complex negotiation between these dominant groups, especially in the realm of mass media. *Kung Fu* paradigmatically captured this moment, as the series enacted a protracted generational compromise. The television Western was a format familiar to an older audience, who had made it the most popular fictional genre of the 1950s. *Kung Fu* maintained many of the elements of the traditional Western: the distinct dichotomy between good and evil (good guys versus bad guys), the lonely and misunderstood hero, and the unforgiving landscape that reflected the harsh social and physical conditions of the frontier.

The series also incorporated the sensibilities of the younger generation. Critics, who immediately saw the show as a "flower children's western,"[22] attributed its more innovative dimensions to this cultural influence. The bulk of the commentary centered on the character of Caine, who was tagged in one review as "the runaway Buddhist priest with all the Love-Peace-and-Happiness ideals."[23] Kwai Chang Caine, as an alternative Western hero, embodied the values of nonviolence, antiauthoritarianism, and ethnocultural diversity that spoke to a younger viewing audience and served as an expression of the changing times.

As an integrated discourse, *Kung Fu* did not only conjoin resonant themes of the old dominant group with the ones of the new but also emphasized values they had in common. Most notable of these were Caine's self-reliance and his spiritual individualism. As a biracial outcast in both China and the United States, Caine is left to fend for himself. In the flashbacks that recount his initiation into the Shaolin Temple, the young Caine perseveres both physically and morally over other boys who wish to enter. This dimension of self-reliance is even more apparent in the scenes that take place in America, in which Caine must depend on his own ingenuity and strength to survive as a fugitive. However, even as he seeks and finds human friendship along the frontier, his spiritual training sets him apart from those he meets—Chinese and American. In addition, he does not stray from his religious commitments, even in the intemperate social environment of the West. As one who is able to maintain his spiritual integrity in the hostile frontier, Caine stands out as a staunch individualist and reinscribes the myth of the American West in conventional form.

While the features of self-reliance and individualism struck a chord in both old and new dominant groups, perhaps the element that most contributed to *Kung Fu*'s mass appeal was the show's focus on human reconciliation and spiritual justice. Robert S. Ellwood has called the years leading up to the 1970s "the bitter years"[24]—when Americans witnessed the assassinations of Robert Kennedy and Martin Luther King Jr., the Chicago riots, the Kent State shootings, and the prolonged continuation of the Vietnam War. This environment of seemingly senseless violence and aggression, as Ellwood states, "seemed to exhaust the Sixties spirit and gave way to the more inward, disillusioned mood of the Watergate decade."[25]

In addition, the dominant culture also felt under siege by the growing political presence of a variety of subaltern groups. The late 1960s saw the emergence of the Black Power Movement, as well as similar movements by Chicanos, Asian Americans, and American Indians. These new movements brought their own challenges and distinguished themselves from the Civil Rights movement of the early 1960s in several ways. For one, they did not simply seek recognition in the political sphere (e.g., voting rights, school integration) but demanded full acknowledgment of racial minorities in all areas of life (most notably, education and culture and, for Native Americans, full-scale autonomy). Moving beyond the issue of assimilation and integration, ethnic consciousness movements also posed a direct affront to the state. "Liberation" entailed liberation from American imperialist efforts—on both international and domestic fronts—and gave rise to the emergence of various cultural nationalisms.[26] Finally, these movements did not necessarily adopt the pacifist means of protest espoused by Martin Luther King Jr. but entertained approaches that were more direct and confrontational. Indeed, both parties of the dominant group sought relief from the social unrest and confusion of the 1960s, especially the direct and proactive challenge from various subaltern movements regarding the state.

Emerging within this socially fraught environment, *Kung Fu* offered itself as an expression of these larger conflicts and provided a singular vision of how these conflicts could be overcome. As both acknowledgment and panacea, it constituted a type of regular and regulated *release* for its audience from these struggles, as its formulaic narrative was played out each week on the small screen. To understand the effectiveness of the series, it is helpful to look at the details of its narrative and the dynamic identifications it forged between the show's characters and its faithful audience.

Kung Fu: The Way of the Tiger, the Sign of the Dragon

Kung Fu effectively brought unexpected solace to the dominant culture suffering from the social upheavals just discussed. Caine's weekly encounters with Chinese laborers and other misfits enacted a pointed commentary concerning these groups that, at once, acknowledged their presence and the nobility of their struggle yet clearly denounced their methods. One of the most evident examples of this can be found in the series pilot, *Kung Fu: The Way of the Tiger, the Sign of the Dragon* (1972).[27] The made-for-TV movie centered on the plight of a group of Chinese railroad workers who are forced to dig through a rock formation filled with natural gas. As thirteen men are subsequently killed, Fong, a pragmatic and bitter worker, incites the rest of the camp to rebel. He is immediately shot to death by Raif, the surly white foreman. In the tense scene, Caine implores the laborers: "To fight for yourself is right. To die vainly without hope of winning is the action of stupid men. Let one death be enough." The workers, suitably pacified, return to their tents. The story takes a number of twists and turns, but eventually, Caine himself takes up militant means to disrupt the continued mining effort (e.g., by blowing up a new shipment of dynamite and eventually employing his Shaolin training to overcome his captors). As Dillon, the head boss, becomes the sole white person remaining and a prisoner in his own camp, the workers celebrate their victory. Throughout the events, Caine maintains a calm detachment. And in his final act before leaving the settlement, he sets ablaze the symbol of the workers' oppression—the wooden railway—with a spirit of both sadness and defiance.

The television movie that would launch the series is remarkable in both content and style. Per content, the story line was indeed revolutionary in that it not only brought to the small screen a most unconventional hero (a Shaolin Buddhist monk) but also focused attention on and sympathetically portrayed the plight of Chinese railroad workers, whose struggles were conspicuously absent in fictional accounts of the Western frontier.[28] The audience forges an identification with the workers through Caine, who is hired as "coolie" labor. In addition, the workers were not written as an undifferentiated mass; they reflected a range of character types that, at first glance, seemed to go beyond the conventional representations of Chinese.

On a stylistic level, the movie effectively incorporated several devices that not only gave *Kung Fu* its unique look and feel but also were visually innovative for television: "It was Jerry [Thorpe] who started the visuals with candles, . . . the slow motion, forced perspective, and long-lens rack focus techniques. The rest of us, certainly awe-inspired, tried our best to add to and increase the visual impact."[29] All these elements combined to visually capture the spiritual and philosophical dimensions of Caine's story. The use of slow motion made the martial arts scenes more ballet-like and highlighted the skillfulness and artistry behind the protagonist's Shaolin training. The slowed-down pace of the combat sequences was meant to reflect the deep thought behind the action and present a philosophical alternative to the viewing audience. One of the later producers of *Kung Fu*, John Furia Jr., would note:

> The whole show displayed a lack of the frantic, frenetic motion for its own sake that I think is part of the American culture and a lot of the American media. Our characters moved and spoke slowly and tersely. They used fewer words rather than more. They didn't repress their emotions, they controlled them, as well as their actions.[30]

This new philosophical view was enhanced further by other techniques as well. The use of flashback—a hallmark of both movie and series—allowed the viewer to reconstruct Caine's training at the Chinese temple, as well as trace the attachments and events that were formative in his emotional and spiritual development. The personal background that the flashbacks provide helped create a strong identification between Caine and the viewer. In *Kung Fu: The Way of the Tiger, the Sign of the Dragon*, form and content merged seamlessly, setting a precedent for a series that would introduce a new type of American hero.

However, both form and content would help carry out a greater ideological mission beyond these obvious achievements. Although it humanely portrayed the Chinese laborers' struggle against their white employers, the story line did enact a pointed commentary regarding how such struggles are most effectively resolved. Fong, who initially calls the men to arms, is immediately killed off. As angry upstart, his actions are portrayed as foolishly impulsive in relation to Kwai Chang Caine's calm and tactical approach. Even when Caine resorts to more destructive measures, his actions are always portrayed as somehow provoked and therefore always justified. For instance, one of the extended martial arts scenes is prompted by the stabbing death of an old man, Han Fei, who reminds Caine of his favorite teacher, Master Po (figure 4.3). Not only does the men's age make their murders abhorrent but also his (and the audience's) attachment to these spiritual men makes Caine's retribution seem necessary and fair. The movie, therefore, portrays the use of violence as a defensive measure and last resort.

FIGURE 4.3. Caine and Han Fei (Benson Fong) in the pilot movie for the television series *Kung Fu* (1972).

In this way, the movie's plot conveys its preference for one style of leadership over another: defensive over aggressive, thought over emotion, Caine over Fong. On a superficial level, this view seems benign and more reflective of a philosophical choice that has little to do with whether those being led are Chinese. However, because race plays a significant part in both story and visuals, the movie's contemporary message cannot be thus separated. One is able to discern this commentary through a close examination of the characters involved. Although a variety of Chinese railroad workers are portrayed, as a whole, they are represented as an oppressed group that is unable to organize effectively against their oppressors. Han Fei, the old man, possesses the spiritual insight but not the initiative. Fong, the young upstart, possesses the initiative but not the insight. And the rest of the Chinese characters who have speaking roles either resign themselves to their fate (Chuen) or exploit the situation to their own benefit (Hsiang). It is not until Caine arrives on the scene and takes control of the situation that the unjust system is properly handled, and much of this, he accomplishes mainly on his own.

Hence, old stereotypes of Chinese get written into the movie in a new, yet insidious way. For instance, the character of Han Fei, in his calm passivity and general goodwill, shares an affinity with the emasculated colored servant, who knows better than his oppressors but accepts his fate all the same. On the other end of the spectrum, the character of Hsiang alerts Dillon and Raif of the impending uprising and thus trades in his loyalty for a meal. As such, he is easily recognized as the immoral and essentially cunning Asian.[31]

Other stock characters, such as the racist bar patron and the brutish foreman (Raif), also take part in the story. However, the white men in the movie are, for the most part, written with greater depth. McKay, the mine surveyor, embodies a social conscience that eventually gets him killed. And out of all the characters (besides that of Caine), it is Dillon, the camp boss, who is portrayed in the most sophisticated manner. Although he sanctions continued blasting through the gas-laden hillside and is therefore directly responsible for the deaths of many Chinese laborers, he is not cast as an evil villain but rather as someone who is doing his best under the circumstances. His character is allowed to register doubt over his decisions, as well as a resigned remorse after the successful takeover of the camp by Caine and the other Chinese railroad workers.

Viewed as an ideological compromise between old and new dominant groups, one is able to understand Dillon's portrayal and the concurrent stereo-typing of the other characters—both Chinese and white. The concept for the film was obviously indebted to the genre of classic Westerns that fit squarely within the sensibility of the old dominant group. Within this genre, the protag-onist was usually a man who possessed unusual character that distinguished him from the more brutish types that he encountered in the Old West. He was also often portrayed as an individual who faced a difficult moral dilemma and who would eventually succumb to the fate he was unfairly dealt. Caine fits this mold, but, more interestingly, so does Dillon.

Caine and Dillon reflect the sensibilities and characteristics of new and old dominant parties, respectively, *in the new party's eyes*. Dillon is portrayed as the ultimate company man, a model citizen and by-product of capitalist expan-sion. With a firm belief in technological progress (railroad), he perseveres in his attempts to settle uncharted territory. On a more mundane level, he is a person caught up in a system that depends on such a belief. In *Kung Fu: The Way of the Tiger, the Sign of the Dragon*, Dillon embodies the old Western hero, now transformed into tragic victim. Indeed, Dillon's eventual insight is meant to parallel that of the audience members, who witnessed the promise of a new industrial age in the postwar period leading only to increased disillusionment and alienation in the 1960s.

While Dillon serves as the point of identification for older audience mem-bers, Caine serves as one for the movie's younger audience. For a generation eager to abandon, or at least call into question, their parents' way of life, Caine's anomalous character reflected their commentary on the conventional order. The system could not be challenged from within, given established ethical structures. It could only be transformed with the introduction of new models for behavior and action. The young generation that came of age during the

1960s found such models in the spiritual cultures of the East. Hence, the character of Kwai Chang Caine embodies this new sensibility that emerged in direct response to the old. As itinerant monk in a foreign setting, the character seemed to capture the alienation of a generation who saw themselves as seeking a new identity apart from their past.

The sympathetic portrayals of both Chinese (Han Fei) and whites (Dillon) at *Kung Fu*'s inauguration seemed to suggest a new representative egalitarianism. However, within the larger ideological frame, these sympathetic identifications functioned differently according to race and social position. On the one hand, the figure of Dillon, the movie's nod toward a dominant (white) ethos of the previous generation, acknowledged this generation's lingering authority yet demonstrated the tragic impotence of its claims. On the other, the film included a self-congratulatory recognition of a subaltern group (Chinese Americans) that was, as we have also seen, both limited and limiting it its vision. The character of Kwai Chang Caine stood at the center of the Virtual Orientalist stage. And as a unique expression of an emerging party of the dominant group (1960s moderate liberals), his figure would relativize and force silent commentary on the concerns and interests of both traditional dominant and subaltern groups through his narrative journey. As the pilot gave way to the television series, *Kung Fu* would come to stand as a generation's representational claim to a new social order.

Kung Fu: The Series

The way in which racial minorities are scripted into each episode reveals a potent commentary on contemporary race relations during the early 1970s. Unlike the movie pilot, which dealt with an exploited group (Chinese American laborers), the weekly episodes individualized the politics of race. In addition, they ideally configured a pacifist approach to social oppression. This ideological solution, although often complicated by plot and character development, became *Kung Fu*'s patterned and paternalizing answer to racial strife and misunderstanding.

Caine's struggle to live a peaceful existence in the not-so-peaceful environment of the Wild West is a focal point of each episode. It is apparent that the story writers were aware of the contradictions the show held regarding pacifism and violence, as well as attitudes toward the self-determination of minority groups. And the way these tensions were eased became formulaically scripted. Each episode that deals with the oppression of an ethnic individual by whites first recognizes and highlights the injustice of the situation. It also, at some point, gives expression to the anger inherently involved, especially how the minority characters experience this anger. When either side resorts to psychological or physical violence, Caine inevitably steps in and diffuses the scene as heroic and wise mediator. And as such, he becomes the only one who is justified in his use of physical force.

This formula can best be seen by examining several episodes that invoke its prowess and appeal. In "The Spirit Helper" (November 1, 1973), Caine befriends an Indian adolescent named Nashebo (played by a young Don Johnson), during the boy's spiritual rite of passage to becoming a man (figure 4.4). Alone in the wilderness and suffering extreme exhaustion from his quest, Nashebo opens his eyes to find Caine standing before him and immediately takes the wandering monk as an otherworldly presence, his "spirit helper." At the youth's encouragement, Caine follows him back to his family's camp, only to find Nashebo's father slain and his mother, Crucita, kidnapped by a band of outlaws. As Caine and Nashebo attempt to rescue Crucita, they, too, are captured. The story climaxes when the outlaw leader, an aggressive Irishman named Pike, challenges Caine to a fight. Mano a mano, Caine defeats the prideful Pike and wins the release of himself, the boy, and his mother. But when the ropes that bind Nashebo are cut, the young Indian immediately lunges for Pike with a machete to avenge his father's death. Both Crucita and Caine intervene, and as he holds Nashebo back, Caine utters: "Is it not better to embrace the living than avenge the dead?" Nashebo relents, and at the story's end, Caine declares: "Now, you have become a man."

FIGURE 4.4. Nashebo (Don Johnson) in "The Spirit Helper" (1973).

"The Spirit Helper" serves as a pointed commentary on the use of violence as a means to enact racial justice. The story line does much to develop viewers' identification with Nashebo, as he is portrayed with a youthful earnestness and passion. While the audience is also allowed to feel the young man's rage and helplessness when he discovers the violent demise of his family, they are steered away from embracing an equally violent response through Caine's intervention. Caine, as such, does not function as a conventional protagonist but rather as a moral measure for the actions of those he meets. Most notably, his character is meant to reveal how the edict of "an eye for an eye" is ethically bankrupt and only continues the cycle of vengeance and hate; the cycle can be overcome only through love and the embrace of all human life. On the surface, the solution to personal and racial strife that Caine provides seems not only dignified and morally sound but also simple.

Despite its elegance, the episode lacks both emotional and moral depth and does not adequately address the problems it raises. Nashebo's pain and suffering, as well as his mother's, remain at a superficial level—with the machete scene acting as the defining moment. In addition, any legacy of greater conflict between Native Americans and frontiersmen is completely absent from the narrative. The only mention of Nashebo's larger community is made in the episode's final moments, when he and his mother leave Caine to rejoin their people. The audience is left with the hope that Nashebo will take his pacifist lesson to heart and share its message with others of his kind—no doubt a commentary to racial and ethnic minorities in the present day.

A significant reason for this easy solution rests in the medium itself. Bound to a narrative format that requires the elements of intriguing conflict and satisfactory resolution within the space of less than an hour, the show's producers and writers are inevitably confined to this moral recipe. However, one must also acknowledge the ways in which the television format colludes with a larger ideological view that finds such a solution palatable. In the eyes of the dominant culture, the answer to racial oppression is indeed quite simple, or at least that is what it wishes it to be. And as it trades its panacean vision for Nielsen ratings, *Kung Fu* promotes an ideological contract that precludes other types of resolution. In these complex ways, the show reinforces a hegemonic view that not only ignores the deep wounds of racial injustice by offering easy solutions but also makes only one solution the morally correct one.[32]

This solution is given variegated expression in other episodes of *Kung Fu* that feature racial minorities. "The Well" (September 27, 1973), which kicked off the show's second season, centers on an ex-slave named Caleb and his family. In the small town of Crossroads, riddled by drought, Caleb hides a well on his property because of his inherent distrust of his white neighbors. He is also distrustful of Caine. But when Caine defends Caleb from a corrupt local deputy who discovers the well, he gains not only the black settler's trust but also the admiration of his young son. While the show's story line revolves around the struggle for a precious resource, it ultimately comments on racial distrust and the meaning of freedom. In one of the episode's crucial moments, the interaction between Caine and Caleb encapsulates the show's definitive take on the matter:

CAINE   "You look to others for your own freedom?"

CALEB   "Where else am I gonna find it?"

Caine's rhetorical question leads Caleb to look at the situation from a different angle. As John Furia, one of the producers of the show, later remarked about the episode's message, freedom comes by "freeing yourself of anger, and by freeing yourself of your own prejudices and by, in a sense, acting free."[33] This response to racial oppression, while superficially appealing, places the responsibility for reconciliation squarely on the shoulders of the minority individual in episodes such as "The Well." While the white settlers are greatly to blame for the situation, it is Caleb who must make the first move. Not only do larger social ills become individualized through Caine's intervention but also their remedy is one-sidedly cast. As a result, sustained oppression becomes the moral burden of minorities and outcasts.

Perhaps the most characteristic and insidious aspect of *Kung Fu*'s formulaic story lines involving minorities rests in its constant turn toward the psychospiritual realm for answers. In the two aforementioned episodes, Caine points both Nashebo and Caleb toward internal resolutions that erase the larger social context and material realities from which their hatred and anger spring. This process of internalization is especially highlighted in the episode "In Uncertain Bondage." The episode focuses on the kidnapping of a white southern belle, Dora, by her driver, Tait, and the complicity of her two black servants, Jenny and Seth. Although Jenny and Seth eventually rebel against the scheme, the episode centers most on Dora, whose heart is changed through her interaction with Caine; she thanks the fugitive monk for "teaching her that there is no less dignity in serving others than in being served." In this one variation of the usual formula, it is implied that Dora's attitude toward her servants has been radically altered and that she will treat them with greater respect. However, it again leaves intact her institutionalized relationship with Jenny and Seth (master-slave) and masks the inherent oppressions of the social economy, including her own gendered status within that economy; as privileged yet defenseless "southern belle," she exists as a commodity to be ransomed. The moral insight she adopts, the show's proffered solution, reconfigures the initial problem of social exploitation as one exclusively of the individual soul.

This turn toward an internalized solution is most pointedly expressed in the first-year episode "Blood Brother" (January 19, 1973), where Caine happens across the name of a man, Lin Wu, with whom he grew up in the Shaolin temple. He searches the town for his longtime friend but instead encounters Soong, an elderly Chinese man who is being viciously harassed by a group of drunken young men. Caine intervenes but is then thrown in jail "for his own protection," suggesting the town's racially fraught environment. As the story evolves, it is revealed that the same young men are also responsible for killing Lin Wu and abandoning his body in the marshlands. The episode's plot revolves around their eventual indictment, which Caine helps bring about. Through legal resolutions such as this, the show promotes the enactment of social justice via institutional channels of recourse (i.e., the law and the courts) and reaffirms the eventual effectiveness of these institutions. All alternative means of resistance to legal restitution are invariably written out of the scene, except one: pacifism.

It is the ideal of absolute pacifism as proper response to racial injustice that, in fact, becomes the show's significant message. Although Caine's efforts to have the racist gang tried in court move the story line along, it is the characteristic flashback scenes that are its true impetus. In these scenes, Caine recounts his early relationship with his friend, Lin Wu, at the temple. The Shaolin monk teachers arrange for a contest between the two young novitiates as a test of skill. When Caine wins the match, he feels that "his gentle friend let him win on purpose." Attempting to trace the events that led up to Lin Wu's senseless death in the arid terrain, namely, his failure to use his combative skills to defend himself in a socially hostile environment, Caine recalls Master Kan's lesson:

> Each living thing strives to survive. It is an instinct as deep as life. Yet,
> Lin Wu, given the ultimate choice of a death, a symbolic death in his
> contest with you, chose his own. At some time in the future,
> confronted with the honest choice, he will choose his own. It is,
> perhaps, the flaw of saintly men, condemning him to an early death.[34]

These words reflect the show's resolution to an acute moral dilemma that racism breeds—namely, that if given the choice to kill or be killed by one's oppressors, those who choose the latter are more spiritually noble. Through his severe treatment and seemingly nonsensical response, the physically absent Lin Wu becomes a pacifist model and spiritual ideal against which even Caine falls short.

The writer's choice to invoke such an ideal once again demonstrates how *Kung Fu* deftly deals with the contradictions that emerge in the series. Through Lin Wu and Caine's relationship to him, the show maintains its pacifist stance; it smooths over the protagonist's regular use of physical force by positing the ideal as something difficult to achieve (i.e., of the realm of "saintly men"). As such, it becomes all the more glorified, as Caine's admiration attests. But perhaps the most significant dimension of the show rests in the way it squarely situates this response within a racialized context. As Herbie J. Pilato, in *The Kung Fu Book of Caine*, comments:

> This episode directly addresses the racism of the West, particularly
> the racism against Chinese-Americans. Rather than ignore the
> complicated rage that results from racism, Caine addresses it head
> on. Referring to Lin Wu's apparent death, Caine says to Soong: "You
> are a man. What has happened must make you angry. To hide a
> feeling is to increase its force a thousand times."[35]

Often by subject matter alone, *Kung Fu* appears as a racially progressive show. And in views such as Pilato's that seek to acknowledge the psychological dimensions of racial discrimination, the series does an effective job. However, given the show's apparent response to how racism should be handled—through legal institutions or, in the extreme case, through unmitigated pacifism—one must question its ideological intent. The recognition of anger stemming from racist injustice is certainly important, but the ways in which the show suggests such anger should be channeled is most telling.

Indeed, the organic relationship of the characters in "Blood Brothers" further shapes the show's ideological agenda. The character of Soong's son, angrily asks Caine: "Why did he let it happen? He was a practitioner of *kung fu* like you! Why did he let it happen?" The Chinese American's outrage provides a human touch to the scene. But it also simultaneously highlights the equanimity with which Caine and Lin Wu deal with racial injustice and helps to establish their response as a model. The fact that the two are both Shaolin priests also emphasizes that response as essentially a spiritual one. Through this juxtaposition of character response, the show invalidates any other possible modes of social action and leads its audience to a foregone spiritualized solution.[36]

Individualization and Identification

The series' ideology toward racial conflict is shaped in two specific ways: first, through a process of *individualization* of social problems and, second, through the types of character *identification* it establishes. As we have seen, the weekly episodes *individualize* this oppression and often make it a problem for minority characters to solve. The social context and institutional racism that give rise to the characters' conflicts are practically erased, as Caine's spiritual direction leads these characters to an internalized resolution on an individual level.

Indeed, this focus on the protagonist's one-to-one encounters with marginalized peoples (Indians, blacks, Asians) is legibly apparent in the "Writer's Guide" for the show:

II. CONTENT

c. Ideally, stories and scenes should spring from character, rather than incident. Ambiguities should be apparent in character and in drama as they are in people and in life.

d. We prefer to avoid stories about Indians. It is virtually impossible to reproduce the culture of the American Indian with any sense of reality. Among other things, it was very rare to find an American Indian who spoke English, while still living in his own environment. Then, too, the limitations with Indian actors and extras, as well as authentic accoutrements tend to make everything seem like musical comedy. However, we have done and will continue to do stories about a single Indian character seen apart from his own civilization.[37]

Emphasis on character development (II.c) and the explicit avoidance of "the culture of the American Indian" (II.d) express a directed individualization that underwrites the series' take on social representation. Problems that minorities and women face in the show become the problem of the individual—ones that are produced and should be addressed on a deeply personal level. It is interesting to note the rationalization that underlies this process of individualization, especially in guideline II.d. Because the series is unable to duplicate without any *authenticity* the historical reality of the culture and conditions in which Native Americans lived during the period, the possibility of representing their social reality is dismissed in a cursory manner. While the guideline suggests a sensitivity and awareness regarding issues of racial representation, the show's writers ultimately choose not to deal these issues.

The Writer's Guide also bases its rationale to allow only a "single Indian character" per show on the "limitations with Indian actors and extras." What exactly those "limitations" are is not exactly clear and one is left to ponder: Are there not enough Indian actors to play these parts? Or are the Indian actors available not up to speed, that is, not considered good enough actors or not easy to direct? Or both? In any case, the obstacle of racial casting also provides a convenient excuse. Again, authenticity becomes an issue, as the series does not see itself able to re-create a marginalized social group on the most physical, in other words, visual level.

Kung Fu's concern for authenticity is obviously an effect of a new social consciousness regarding the racial representation emergent at the time. This consciousness reframed previous portrayals of ethnic individuals in film and television by white actors either as obscene, undignified, or ridiculous ("like musical comedy"). Whether these portrayals were actually seen as such, the fact of the matter is that they were clearly unacceptable, given the cultural milieu. Hence, *Kung Fu's* producers felt compelled to justify not only their casting decisions but also their reasons for avoiding the larger social reality of their characters.

Despite its attempt at toward broader representation, the show's move toward individualization was inevitably also the product of more suspect motives. In a *New York Times* article that reviewed the current state of the film industry in 1973, "How Do You Pick a Winner in Hollywood? You Don't," Aljean Harmetz reported that "the two biggest hits in America right now are 'The Mack,' about a black pimp, and some Chinese film Warner Brother picked up—'Five Fingers of Death.'"[38] Obviously, the success of films featuring minorities in subcultural contexts came as an unexpected surprise. However, Harmetz also reveals the executive philosophy at play in Hollywood's choices:

> Daniel Melnick, the articulate MGM vice president in charge of production, newly come West from—he mocks himself—"the Eastern lib-rad Establishment," expounds MGM's philosophy. "To make pictures that are movie movies, not polemics or minority entertainment, not for special groups, not downbeat or about losers."[39]

Although Melnick works within the medium of film, his comment is significant because it reflects a general dis-ease with racial representation shared by the general viewing audience. Pictures that are racially colored are acceptable as long as they are "not polemics or minority entertainment, not for special groups." Films that advocate such interests are not considered "movie movies," that is, ones that will appeal to a large number of the moviegoers. Melnick's view of the general public, as well as the rhetoric he employs, hints at a more large-scale backlash toward marginalized groups—their representation and political concerns.

Kung Fu's process of individualization similarly takes part in this backlash as the representation of the social ills experienced by racial minorities is routinely disciplined and rechanneled to make the show palatable for mass consumption. Under this rubric, it is assumed that *changing the hearts of individuals will automatically lead to changing society*. To a post-1960s liberal audience who obviously felt sympathy toward the plight of racial minorities but who nevertheless were wary of certain measures taken by these groups toward self-determination and weary from extended conflict, this simple adage proved seductive. Indeed, for a great many Americans, post–Civil Rights race relations had transformed the United States into an unruly site with different groups vying for cultural, economic, and political resources. In this way, *Kung Fu*'s Wild West setting—the uneven hand of justice, the social free-for-all, the generally inhospitable natural landscape— seemed to reflect the audience's view of their contemporary social environment. It also mirrored the overall impotence that Americans felt toward ameliorating the situation. Given such a scenario, individualizing racial oppression and other social inequities may have seemed like a final alternative.

While this process of individualization is key in deciphering the show's political stance, the types of *identifications* the series forged between character and audience more substantively reveal its ideological commitments. Although *Kung Fu*'s psychospiritualized vision was available to all of its audience members, one could argue that it was primarily framed as a commentary toward racial minorities and women who sought social change through means other than or in addition to inner transformation. It achieved this through a formulaic pattern of identifications. To discern this pattern, one must first understand the constraints placed on character development specific to a television series. Rita Parks, in her examination of Western heroes in film and television, remarks:

> Added to the exigencies of structure are the necessities developing
> about the recurring characters in any [television] series. These types
> must remain stable enough for audience identification and
> development of residual personality, yet they are also responsible for
> satisfying the constant demand for variety. Irwin Blacker indicates
> the problem of developing character as one of the difficulties of
> creating a classic Western in the television format. If the story is to
> have any significance, says Blacker, the people in it must change; yet
> in a Western series the hero cannot risk change. The writer,
> therefore, must constantly use "guest" characters who are able to
> develop, change, or die within the context of the weekly episode while
> the hero functions as a catalyst in that action. This constraint, though
> preventing the series from developing into a significant drama,
> achieves a twofold purpose necessary to the continuing story: the

> variety of secondary plots and characters retains audience interest;
> the stability of the continually developing (but basically unchanging)
> residual personality of the hero sustains audience loyalty.[40]

Kung Fu fit this mold for the television Western well, with Caine as the hero and figures such as Nashebo, Caleb, Dora, and Soong serving as rotating or "guest" characters. Hence, the latter provided color and variation, and the former offered a stable point of identification and entry into each week's plot.

As previously mentioned, the audience was indeed meant to identify with the guest characters—feel his or her anger and confusion. However, given the temporary status of these characters and the fact that they were often minorities, the connection the audience made with these figures was at best an *ancillary* identification—a link forged in sympathy and dependent on racial and gendered difference. As the series' protagonist and hero, Caine provided the *primary* identification for the viewer, who aspired to the show's vision of fair-mindedness and spiritual acumen.[41] Although Caine is obviously a minority as well, the fact that he is both Chinese *and* white allows a type of representational access for the dominant culture viewer that monoracial characters do not share. Indeed, his biracial status becomes the pivot point on which everything turns. Like Alan Watts and the Beats during the Zen phenomenon of the 1950s and the Beatles and other celebrities who flocked to the Maharishi Mahesh Yogi in the 1960s, the character of Kwai Chang Caine served as a *bridge figure* by which an American audience could enter a seemingly foreign worldview with ease.

As a biracial character, Caine represents the perfect blending of East and West. Although he was raised in China and his spiritual outlook informed by Chinese cultural traditions, Caine seems to retain behavioral traits that are marked for the audience as decidedly "Western." For instance, his instinctual defense of Master Po at the August Moon festival in which he kills the emperor's nephew—the event that serves as the impetus for Caine's exile—is a response that the audience can identify with, although morally denounce. Compared with the Chinese characters who appear in the series, Caine demonstrates an unusual degree of loyalty based on bonds of feeling, rather than bonds of honor. The difference between these motivations—feeling versus honor—are racially coded, Western versus Eastern, and within the narrative, highlight the character's link to the West even before he sets foot in America. The demonstration of active commitment also comes to distinguish Caine from his full-blooded Chinese compatriots. In "Blood Brother," Caine's ambivalent, yet heroic, fortitude is most evident. Whereas Lin Wu and his stance of extreme pacifism come to mark "Chineseness," Kwai Chang's decision to defend himself and other innocents—his unique sense of justice and his willingness to act on that sense—comes to be viewed as decidedly "American" in flavor.

Caine's biraciality also allows for a key transaction to take place both within the story and without: the transfer of Eastern spiritual knowledge to the West. Caine, unlike many of his fully Chinese counterparts, endures the rigorous training at the temple to be initiated into the order of Shaolin priests. The television series implicitly links his endurance and noble stoicism to the conditions that brought him to the temple in the first place: his marginal status in Chinese society as a "half-breed." As a marginal individual in a homogeneous society, the young Caine is intuitively aware that the temple is perhaps the only place he can call home and therefore seems determined to excel. He also seems to appreciate and respect the teachings of his elder monks and takes their lessons to heart in an unparalleled manner. In this way, Caine's biraciality allows him to embody Eastern spiritual teachings in a way no pupil fully Chinese could. And similarly, his hereditary connection to America that prompts him to travel to the United States both in exile and in search of his Anglo-American family also authorizes him to transmit those teachings from China to the West. Both these elements of the larger narrative offer extratextual license for the spectator to take part in a foreign spiritual heritage and potentially begin to adopt it as his own.

Perhaps the significance of Caine's biraciality is most apparent when one considers the visuals of casting. The producers' decision to cast David Carradine, a white actor, over other Asian American or Anglo-Asian actors is in itself telling. One of the actors considered was martial arts legend Bruce Lee, born in San Francisco and biracial in heritage (his mother, Grace Lee, was of Chinese and German descent). According to certain accounts, Lee not only helped in the development stages of *Kung Fu* but also competed with David Carradine for the role of Kwai Chang Caine. David Carradine would later comment:

> There are two stories about why Bruce Lee didn't get the part. One: that he was turned down because he was too short and too Chinese; which is a way of saying he was, ironically, a victim of the same prejudice we would be dealing with as our theme in the film. Two: that, for some reason I can't fathom, he was advised by his people not to take the part.
>
> I was told by someone in the production company that they weren't sure he could act well enough to handle the complexities of the character. I don't know. Whatever the reason, it caused him to quit Hollywood, go home to Hong Kong and embrace his destiny.[42]

Kareem Abdul-Jabbar, who claims the martial arts legend as a good friend, notes that Lee "would have been perfect [for the part], a master working his art before the national audience, but whoever it was that decided such things made it clear to [him] that they didn't think a Chinese man could be a hero in America. They passed over Bruce and gave the part, and the stardom, to David Carradine."[43]

The truth of the matter is difficult to discern. However, both Carradine's and Abdul-Jabbar's remarks point to a possible consideration when it came to casting the enigmatic figure of Caine. The producers perhaps felt that if the actor who played Kwai Chang looked "too Chinese," then the necessary identification between the series' main protagonist and the American audience could not be achieved, let alone sustained. To properly draw a sympathetic connection, the audience had to be able to visually see themselves in him, in other words, see at least a hint of recognizable whiteness somehow reflected back to them in the most visceral manner. At the same time, the actor who played Caine had to be able to "pass" as half-Chinese and convey somehow a character undoubtedly new and foreign in nature (figure 4.5).

During the early 1970s, David Carradine appeared to fit this bill. Seeing Carradine's "stunning and balletlike performance"[44] as Atahualpa Capac, the emperor of the Incas, in the Broadway play *The Royal Hunt of the Sun*, Jerry Thorpe recalls: "He had the same kind of dignity and lyricism that we wanted."[45] The way in which the young actor may have met the visual requirements of the role was never referred to by Thorpe. However, Carradine acknowledges the trend for producers to typecast him in ethnic roles:

> For a few years I had tried to escape my fascination with the Third
> World by turning down those parts. I'm not sure we even had that

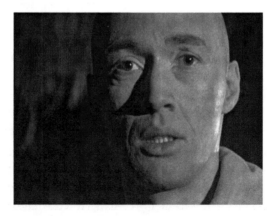

FIGURE 4.5. Close-up shot of Kwai Chang Caine (David Carradine).

term in those days: "Third World"—probably not. Then fatefully, one day, out in the woods in Arkansas, I decided that if there were some progressive function in society which I could perform by accepting these roles, and there seemed to be no one else to do it, and everybody else seemed to want me to say yes; well then, who was I to say no?

When the script, *Kung Fu, The Sign of the Dragon*, arrived at my door, I knew it was the one. Not because of the martial arts—none of us even knew anything about that. That was just the hook the movie hung on. It could have been basketball or downhill skiing. It was "the one" because it was a great story. It was about important things and it could make a significant movie, and it had that "Third-World thing" that I was looking for right then. The character of Caine was obviously perfect for me.[46]

Kung Fu constituted a propitious meeting of interests, as Carradine fulfilled the minimal visual requirements to play the part of Kwai Chang Caine, and the role itself met with the actor's own mission to promote the "Third-World thing." But the primary identification that was forged between Carradine's portrayal and the audience went beyond the superficial appearance and movement of the character. The young actor seemed to be able to capture the spiritual ethos of Caine as well.

Carradine's comment, that the appeal of *Kung Fu* was "not because of the martial arts—none of us even knew anything about that" is prescient in this context. In a more extended interview, Jerry Thorpe, the show's producer, relayed:

I'll never forget the day David first came in to see us. He arrived, seething with rebellion and accompanied by his dog, Buffalo, who is part Great Dane, part Labrador, plus a lot of other breeds, and who has one brown eye and one blue eye. David didn't say two words in that first interview. There were six of us on one side of the room and David and Buffalo on the other side of the room, and no communication between us whatsoever.

Finally David left and I got the idea that he was putting us on— sort of a slap at the Establishment. So I called his agent and asked if David and Buffalo would come back and see me alone. They did, and this time man and dog were totally co-operative. We made the deal for him to do the movie, little realizing then that it would become the pilot for a series. When I asked David why he had been so resistive the first time, he said, "Your brown office and your brown Mercedes outside the window turned me off."[47]

More than any connection that was distinctly Asian or spiritual that Carradine had with the role, his antiestablishment attitude seemed to define the producer's sense of the character, as well as their decision to cast the disaffected actor for the part. Indeed, the character of Caine was, in essence, more a reflection of the American counterculture—with its affront to Western institutions and attitudes, its pursuit of new ways of being and knowing, and its challenge to American aggression—than it was of Chinese life and spiritual traditions.

In unacknowledged yet significant ways, the character of Kwai Chang Caine, "the runaway Buddhist priest with all the Love-Peace-and Happiness ideals,"[48] was more akin to an American 1960s hippie than to an ancient Chinese monk. Both the casting of David Carradine for the role and his subsequent portrayal affirmed this in a variety of ways. To the audience who read about the actor in the *New York Times*, *TV Guide*, and other periodicals, Carradine seemed to embody the hippie almost to the point of caricature and would carry much of this ethos into his portrayal of Caine (figure 4.6). The actor's

FIGURE 4.6. Carradine as featured in the *TV Guide* article, "Does Not the Pebble, Entering the Water, Begin Fresh Journeys?" (Photographer: Jim Gill).

vision for the role included "a whole style of playing him that would be very quietly stylized, satirical, a sort of formal way of moving, the deadpan reading of those far-out lines of his."[49] In addition, he would add small but significant changes to the character: Caine's trademark flute (which the actor hand-carved) and his shoeless appearance (mirroring the actor's own preference for bare feet). But Carradine readily admitted that very little of this vision was based on any concrete knowledge of martial arts or Shaolin spirituality.[50] As one interviewer discovered, Carradine "is not interested in Zen [sic], and he has never studied Eastern religions. 'I couldn't get interested in Eastern mysticism or any of those things. I'm basically a pagan—but I'm very religious about it.'"[51]

Still, the actor saw his necessary mission as "keeping the character pure." For Carradine, this meant shielding Caine from a particular kind of representational compromise:

> You'd be amazed how many times they put in something just for convention's sake. When we were doing one of the first segments the director was trying to show me where to stand and he was standing there demonstrating it the way some macho actor would do it—with his hand cocked over one hip. I thought that was silly. I usually bend my knees and stoop a little. . . . The only reason I don't want [the show] to go down is that I keep seeing it actually approach an ideal. Left to its own devices, the studio would just turn the show into *The Rifleman.*[52]

The ideal of which Carradine speaks seemed to rely on conveying an authenticity based on his own beliefs and values. Kwai Chang Caine and his Shaolin background became a convenient vehicle through which this ideal could be achieved. And Warner Brothers, in tune with the changing demographics of its audience, exploited this convergence of actor and character to its advantage.

If the analogical relationship between the roaming Shaolin monk and the modern-day hippie was not apparent in the intertextual dynamics (casting, star interviews) surrounding the show, it was certainly was made manifest in the series' intratextual dynamics (narrative, character development). As Benjamin J. Stein for the *National Review* elaborates in his critique of the series:

> Caine has sprung up from that worship of the occult, the different, the alien that showed itself in the earlier teenybopper adoration of Spock (the half-other-world-half-human creature of *Star Trek*), and in the current fascination with things Chinese. The hippie's dream, he is, by birth and education, not part of this degenerate and violent society, yet he can defend himself in it. He lives by his own

standards, without allowing other people to impose their standards on him. Yet Caine always succeeds in imposing *his* standards (nonviolently, despite his lethal skills) on those around him. . . .

Caine never seeks out female attention. It always just seems to come to him (goading the Caucasian men in the show to fury), and he never reciprocates, always keeping himself in a position to make peace between the two men fighting for the woman. This too is part of the hippie's dream—a world in which sex is so readily available that it is a free good, one which can be turned down without any fear that there will not be more tomorrow, a world in which women are complaisant and eager, in which they have the (dubious and archaic) equality necessary to be sexual aggressors, but not sufficient equality to be able to harm Caine, or those who identify with him . . . [an] electronic incarnation of doped-up fantasies of an ideal way of life. . . .[53]

This stinging commentary peels back *Kung Fu*'s veneer to reveal the hippie ideal at the show's core. Although propelled by the reviewer's own particular motives, it does suggest the ways in which the series constitutes a patriarchal expression that relies on racial and gendered difference.[54]

To more readily understand how this ideal functions in relation to the identifications that the show depends on and, further, how these operations undergird the show's hegemonic impulse and efficacy, it is helpful to reframe these in psychoanalytic terms. In her seminal article, "Visual Pleasure and Narrative Cinema," Laura Mulvey explicates the "function of the woman in forming the unconscious" and the way this unconscious has structured film form.[55] She harnesses Jacques Lacan's theory of the mirror stage to speak of the primary identification that is reenacted in conventional Hollywood films. Similar to the child who recognizes himself in the mirror for the first time and posits this image as "more complete, more perfect than he experiences his own body," the spectator takes cinematic images as reflective of his "ego ideal." Mulvey further elaborates on "this long love affair/despair between image and self-image" as it is played out on the screen:[56]

An active/passive heterosexual division of labour has similarly controlled narrative structure. According to the principles of the ruling ideology and the psychical structures that back it up, the male figure cannot bear the burden of sexual objectification. Man is reluctant to gaze at his exhibitionist likeness. Hence the split between spectacle and narrative supports the man's role as the active one of forwarding the story, making things happen. The man controls the film phantasy and also emerges as the representative of power in a further sense: as the bearer of the look of spectator, transferring it behind the screen to neutralise the extra-diegetic tendencies represented by woman as spectacle. This is made possible through the processes set in motion by structuring the film around a main controlling figure with whom the spectator can identify.[57]

In the case of *Kung Fu*, Kwai Chang Caine serves as the "main controlling figure with whom the spectator can identify." And as the spectator's "screen surrogate," Caine becomes more than just a heroic character and functions as an ego ideal. With his Shaolin insight and martial arts skills, he certainly "can make things happen and control events better than the subject/spectator." Indeed, the seamless melding of spiritual wisdom and physical prowess that Caine embodies offers the viewer an irresistible integration of mind and body. And these acute powers make him especially equipped to negotiate his way through an uncharted frontier or landscape that is both physically and socially hostile.

As ego ideal, Caine also becomes the fair arbiter of the social conflicts he encounters. In the fashion of the philosopher-king, Caine is able to wisely intervene in situations that seem hopelessly deadlocked (e.g., racial misunderstanding) and, through seemingly noncoercive means, enlightens the parties involved. As is obvious from the series' inception, when dialogue fails, Caine is the only one justified in his use of physical force to ameliorate the situation. (For example, in the movie pilot, the Chinese workers' uprising is portrayed as futile, whereas Caine's tactics are seen as heroic.) This authority to judge both the oppressor and the oppressed and to morally engage in justifiable violence becomes the hallmark of the character as ego ideal. Through a Virtual Orientalist frame, Caine not only mirrors the audience's desire for such authority but also confers and reestablishes their claim to such.

Such an ideological vision is further confirmed when one considers the character description of Caine on which the show's producers and writers relied:

THE MARKS OF CAINE.
Caine is a duality. In a way, the familiar western hero, recognizable, satisfying. But in perhaps a larger way, he is unique. He is a man who seeks peaceful justice in a time of violent solution. He becomes almost the inadvertent symbol, the unsought-for (on his part) champion of the underdog, with whom he can empathize only too well—the Red man, the Brown Man, the Yellow Man, and the Black.

Though he doesn't seek out this kind of action, he yet attracts it, and, being what he is, a man who cannot endure injustice, he must act on it.

As a traditional western hero, we can see him in traditional stories, but with a new dimension. See him for instance, as Shane, drawn to the side of a small family fighting to keep their home against the incursions of the cattle barons, forming a relationship with both the man and the woman. The woman, like other women, will be drawn to him by his air of mystery, his aura of gentleness combined with strength. And because he is human, and because it is not forbidden to him, he may be attracted to her.[58]

Mulvey's theoretical insights regarding the male protagonist in conventional Hollywood film are especially apt here. An "active/passive heterosexual division of labour" is indeed written into *Kung Fu*'s overarching narrative, as Kwai Chang Caine becomes the unlikely protector of the "small family" against capitalist forces that seek to destroy it ("incursions of the cattle barons"). Perhaps more reflective of his role as screen surrogate, Caine attracts female attention as women are drawn to "his air of mystery, his aura of gentleness combined with strength." Reflective of women's changing roles in a post-1960s America, the female characters are granted a certain degree of agency within *Kung Fu*'s narrative field. However, this agency is undermined, as this description surreptitiously suggests. Sexual attraction becomes something that Caine naturally evinces and controls ("*his* air . . . *his* aura"), converting an apparently passive role into an active one and vice versa. Within this field of vision, the show paradoxically offers (in the words of Stein's unwittingly apt review), "a world in which women are complaisant and eager, in which they have the (dubious and archaic) equality necessary to be sexual aggressors, but not sufficient equality to be able to harm Caine." Women are once again transformed into objects that Caine, as well as the male audience member, is able to control and in whom they can take pleasure (figure 4.7).

The fact that Caine becomes involved in amorous conquests is doubly telling. Moral license is given to the character, according to the show's description, because "he is human, and because it is not forbidden to him." But his couplings with women appear to be a privilege and a need that his Oriental monk teachers do not seem to share. Here, we are able to fully examine the visual and narrative plane on which race and the heterosexual division of labor intersect. The full-blooded minorities that Caine encounters are either reinscribed back into a family (e.g., Nashebo, Caleb) or, in the case of certain women of color, resexualized for the pleasure of Caine and the male viewer. Any minority

FIGURE 4.7. Mayli Ho (Nancy Kwan) captures Caine's interest in "The Cenotaph" (1974).

character who falls outside this configuration is taken as a threat (e.g., the Emperor's avengers) and is quickly disciplined by our Shaolin hero.

Master Po and Master Kan, at first, appear to be an exception to this rule (figure 4.8). As monks, they seem to fall outside the domain of the family. In addition, they are never viewed as a threat but are, in fact, featured as caring figures to whom Caine is emotionally attached. But if one conceives the Shaolin order as offering a type of family structure in which Master Po and Master Kan serve as father figures for the young Caine, the domestic scene is reconstituted (and a homosocial order established). Also, the fact that the older monks do not leave the temple except on rare occasions precludes them from sexual liaisons with women. As such, they fit squarely within the stereotype of the desexualized (i.e., impotent) Asian male who poses no threat to Caine's masculine authority.[59] In these ways, race and gender form an inseparable matrix from which the ego ideal gains its potency and the male spectator, in turn, gains his sense of control.

If "good" Asian males are sexually neutralized within *Kung Fu's* televisual realm, then one may wonder why the main protagonist is himself half-Asian. As mentioned earlier, Caine's biraciality allows a type of spiritual crossing to occur that reflects the audience's own interests and desires. At the very least, viewers could entertain an alternative identity—"try on" a different way of being with all its attendant pleasures. But perhaps more than that, the ambivalence that the protagonist literally embodies (white/Oriental, American/ Chinese) reflects the inner turmoil experienced by a generation coming into its hegemonic own. The figure of Caine offered an identification through which a post-1960s audience could channel their disappointment and guilt over promises lost and promises gained.

FIGURE 4.8. Master Kan (Philip Ahn).

Of promises lost, the emergent dominant group, whose views and ideals *Kung Fu* readily expressed, undoubtedly suffered the disappointment of broken alliances with subaltern groups, such as those embodied by women's liberation and ethnic consciousness movements. Antiestablishment whites, especially white males, perhaps could not understand how they could be shunned by these subaltern groups. In their efforts toward self-determination, such groups exhibited an agency that directly threatened the existing social structure and those who enjoyed privilege under that structure. However, such agency was easily wrested away through the medium of television—a medium that was still controlled by white American men. Within this context, Kwai Chang Caine would represent a protagonist that mirrored the affinity or "love" that antiestablishment white males had once felt toward their subaltern compatriots, as well as their grief over the loss of that love. The character of Caine achieves this psychic negotiation of an unrequited love through incorporation of the idealized traits of the Other—a certain level of passivity, unusual calm, and spiritual wisdom. Yet the character also maintains the patriarchal privilege to speak, act, and fight on behalf of the Other. Put in other words, the series' continual emphasis on Caine's biraciality reveals a need to maintain the ego's claim to agency (American male initiative), while holding onto its vision of the submissive Other (Chinese feminized passivity) that had been so seriously challenged. Hence, a racial and gendered equilibrium—on which American white male privilege relies—is achieved via the unlikely hero of the exiled and itinerant, half-American, half-Chinese Shaolin priest. Viewing itself as both itself and the Other through the figure of Caine, the new dominant group staves off its disappointment. Returning to a psychoanalytic frame, this unusual representation that serves as both ego ideal and fetish is also reflective of a transitional moment in American cultural power, in which the new dominant group ambivalently eschews its subaltern affiliations. The character of Caine, at once, serves as a declarative statement of the group's emerging dominant status, as well as a symbolic substitute for alliances hoped for but never achieved.

Of promises gained, the generation of viewers that embraced *Kung Fu* and its unconventional hero saw themselves as helping to establish a new social and spiritual order. But this did not come without its psychic repercussions. As the new dominant group sought to challenge the old, it inevitably suffered a degree of ambivalence and guilt over its emerging authority. In many ways, this guilt is reflected in *Kung Fu*'s larger narrative and the diegetic event that set that narrative in motion: the death of Master Po and Caine's inadvertent yet subsequent slaying of the Emperor's nephew. This formative incident eerily reenacts the Oedipal drama itself, namely, Oedipus' unwitting murder of his father and his attendant guilt. Like the Greek character, Caine is intimately connected with the demise of a father figure. Also, the two characters appear blameless as far as intention. Acting out of instinct, Caine is portrayed as not directly responsible for the death of the Emperor's nephew and even less so for that of Master Po. At the same time, Kwai Chang accepts responsibility—if only based on the mere feeling that through his actions, he has devalued all that he has learned from his beloved teacher.

Through Caine's moral dilemma, the emerging dominant group reenacts the psychic trauma that emerges from the foreclosure of possible futures (subaltern groups) and an ambivalent break from the past (older dominant group).[60] Guilt's lingering presence throughout *Kung Fu*'s narrative again reveals a love for an Other (this time, for the new dominant group's predecessors). In her explication of guilt as a psychic process, Judith Butler elaborates:

> If the object goes, so goes a source of love. In one sense, guilt works to thwart the aggressive expression of love that might do in the loved object, an object understood to be a source of love; in a counter sense, however, guilt works to preserve the object as an object of love (its idealization) and hence (via idealization) to preserve the possibility of loving and being loved.[61]

In *Kung Fu*, guilt becomes a way for antiestablishment white males to forge and maintain what they see as their link to their fathers' ideals. While the love for the subaltern is expressed by incorporating (i.e., consuming) the Other's idealized traits, the love for the dominant expresses itself through an alternative path—one that ceaselessly recalls the initial trauma of separation and loss. Read within this frame, Master Po's death gains its full significance. The new dominant group, through Caine's representational guilt, both acknowledges its aggression toward the older dominant group and preserves it as an object of love. On this tenuous psychic foundation so readily expressed in *Kung Fu*, anti-establishment white males who emerged out of the 1960s began to negotiate and establish their own cultural authority.

As we have seen, the audience's primary identification with the ego ideal (Caine) is characterized by a desire for agency and an alleviation of guilt and disappointment. But no single identification is seamless or universal. No doubt there were those who saw the guest characters (e.g., outcasts, misfits, children, pioneer women) as more a reflection of themselves. In this ingenious way, *Kung Fu* also employed ancillary identifications most efficiently to cover an audience with diverse claims and interests. However, even these characters gained their significance in relation to the main protagonist, who serves as their teacher, defender, protector, and friend. When these ancillary identifications failed to interpellate the viewer both visually and psychically, one witnesses the breakdown of the hegemonic frame and the expression of contradiction, as the critical commentaries attest.

We began with two sets of contradictions to which *Kung Fu* gave rise—ones that focused on the show's violence (contradiction *within* the dominant ideology) and others that criticized the series' racial politics (contradiction *to* the dominant ideology). By exploring the narrative, character development, visuals, and casting decisions of the show in depth, one is able to discern the inextricability of these two contradictions. *Kung Fu*, as a hegemonic statement of a post-1960s liberal audience, can be viewed as the patriarchal assertion of a new group of the dominant ideology, in which older forms of authority are delicately cast aside, and minorities and women shrewdly disciplined. And Kwai Chang Caine, as enigmatic hero, stands as the remnant of this historical move.

Not So Long Ago in China

Kung Fu would reflect back not only on domestic relations in the United States but also on American involvement in the global arena. As *Kung Fu* entered the American popular imagination in 1972, a watershed event in foreign relations between the United States and China simultaneously occurred—President Richard Nixon's visit to Communist China. The historic meeting between the president and Chairman Mao Tse-tung coincides perfectly with the series' inception. As David Carradine would later recall:

It seemed that a lot of people hadn't watched the show the first time it was aired because they had no idea what it was. Now, they all wanted to see it. The network scheduled a second showing and, then, just when the whole country was tuned in to see this Chinese western they'd all heard about, the show was preempted by Richard Nixon shaking hands with Chairman Mao, to commemorate the acceptance of Red China into the United Nations. This seemed, to me, remarkably synchronistic.[62]

Indeed, the American audience's openness to *Kung Fu* seemed to mirror that of its government's. Whereas China had literally dropped from Americans' representational view during the time of the Communist takeover,[63] it was granted a positive reappearance on the small screen.

This is not to say that a certain level of ambivalence and distrust did not accompany both political and representational rapprochement. Impressions of China, which had developed since the Cold War, were not simply abandoned but continued to feed into Americans' contemporary views of the Communist superpower. During Mao's official takeover in the 1950s, these images included the resurrection of the Chinese as the "evil and untrustworthy Oriental."[64] In Harold R. Isaacs's survey of Americans' attitudes toward the Chinese in the late 1950s, he notes:

> In the images of the Chinese that they see in the Communist mirrors, these Americans see no more deferential politeness, no more gratitude, and distressingly little humor; no more philosophic calm, no more sage wisdom, no more respect for antiquity or tradition, or passive and smiling reliance on timeless verities— almost none, in short, of all the features that made the Chinese so attractive and often so dear.[65]

Although "twenty-two years of hostile nonrelations had clearly reached a sterile end"[66] and the United States had begun to positively entertain the idea of China once again, these images still lingered in the American imagination, even as its attractiveness was on the verge of being restored.

From *Kung Fu*'s inception, such mixed impressions were woven into the story's larger narrative. The Asian characters who were featured as regulars— Kwai Chang Caine, Master Kan, and Master Po—all exhibited the traits of a desirable China: deferentially polite, humble, philosophically calm and wise, suitably passive, and respectful of their spiritual tradition. In addition, the fig-ure of Master Po, with his easy smile and good humor, gained a special place in the viewing audience's hearts. In both the series pilot and subsequent episodes, the majority of the scenes in which these characters take part occur within the confines of the temple. Although squarely located in China, the temple takes on an other-worldly character that is carefully constructed: the chimes that transition Caine and the audience into the flashback mode, the darkened halls of the temple eerily lit by candles that produce an otherworldly sense of time, the neatly manicured gardens where Master Po imparts his wisdom to the novice Caine (figure 4.9). The culmination of these effects transforms the site into a space that is untouched by the outside world, in which the physical environment reflects the eternal truths that are sequestered within the temple walls. As such, Caine's education takes place not in China per se but in an idealized storehouse of its spiritual and cultural traditions. Invoking the cherished Orientalist myth of an undisturbed "heaven on earth," the Shaolin temple becomes for the Western audience a Shangri-La, evoking "an eternal classical age . . . outside time and history."[67]

As soon as the monks leave the temple, they encounter a very different environment—one that is characteristically brutal. This is symbolically captured in the show's opening credits that display Caine's full initiation into the Shaolin brotherhood. As he successfully maneuvers through a set of physical tests and brands himself with the marks of the dragon and the phoenix within the darkened corridors of the temple, he stumbles out into the harsh snow and glaring light. Barefoot and clad only in a monk's humble robe, he must now journey out into an unsympathetic world. This synecdochic scene figures the China that Caine enters as an unusually cruel place. The scene in which the

FIGURE 4.9. The use of flashbacks was a hallmark of *Kung Fu* and included many scenes in the Shaolin temple.

audience, along with Caine, witnesses the disrespectful treatment and eventual death of Master Po sets in marked contrast the humble values of the Shaolin order versus the arrogance of the Emperor's court. Sacred and profane systems of order are pitted against one another to highlight their antithetical nature. The fact that the Emperor's young nephew is the one who kills Master Po further suggests an archaic system of rulership that has become both egotistical and childish in its old age. Although there is an obvious distinction between China's rule under the Emperor and its rule under Mao, a parallel can be drawn between the two that probably was not lost on *Kung Fu*'s audience. In the American viewer's eye, both regimes seemed to hold little regard for the nation's rich spiritual resources and had lost a sense of individual human dignity linked with its cultural and religious traditions. The legacy of a great civilization was threatened by the ineptitude of its leadership. Only within the temple walls forged in the American imagination was this legacy fully protected.

Hence, positive images of Chinese in *Kung Fu* as Oriental Monks (i.e., spiritual men) served as a pointed commentary on Red China, which, under Mao, had labeled religious practices and beliefs as superstitious and misleading. For the first two seasons, the show's representational bearing on China would be confined to this implicit critique. However, by in the final year, "the production staff was beginning to realize that the American West was invariably the West—that is, predictable. Thus, at the end of . . . the second season, there was a turn to Asia. More of the episodes were to be set in China and, in the third season, the show became decidedly more mystical."[68]

As the story lines began to take China as their setting, the guest characters (and that of Caine as well) seemed to lack human depth and, instead, often served as the archetypal figures of good and evil. For instance, in "The Devil's Champion" (December 20, 1974), Caine confronts the devil himself. The narrative begins with Yi Lien, an individual unknown to the temple, challenging Master Kan to a ritualistic combat to the death. As Master Kan finally is made to concede (since Yi Lien has started killing innocent peasants for every day his request is not met), he first requires the bloodthirsty warrior to fight the novitiate Huo. Through a dream, Caine realizes that Yi Lien has been possessed by the devil Hsiang and subsequently travels to Hsiang's lair to confront and eventually defeat the evil spirit. By doing so, he releases Yi Lien from the devil's possession and saves Huo in the process.

Through episodes such as this, *Kung Fu* took a decidedly mystical, otherworldly turn, supported by trick visuals; for example, Hsiang's image doubles and quadruples as he and Caine battle (figure 4.10). "The Devil's Champion" is perhaps one of the show's most over-the-top episodes. However, other Chinese characters did not escape such crude portrayal. In many cases, they are spiritually dehumanized—shells for evil spirits that Caine must vanquish. In other cases, they are greedy individuals (e.g., feudal lords and princes) who threaten the temple. Interactions with these figures are often marked as trials in Caine's spiritual development, which he eventually confronts and triumphantly overcomes.

Women's roles in Chinese society are also commented on in the series. In "Besieged" (parts 1 and 2), Barbara Seagull/Hershey (Carradine's real-life wife at the time) plays Nan Chi, an independent woman determined to enter the Shaolin order. Although she attempts to disguise herself as a man, Nan Chi's gender is revealed, and she challenges Master Kan to accept her into the priesthood as an opportunity to change the temple's institutional practices:

MASTER KAN   "I do not regard it as an opportunity, and I certainly do not regard you as a remedy. I regard you, on the contrary, as a remarkably impudent child whose unacceptability is only exceeded by her capacity for showing disrespect."

NAN CHI   "Surely not because I am a woman . . ."

Master Kan is forced to acknowledge Nan Chi's point. For the scene, the scriptwriter's note elaborates on his mind-set: "Master Kan is most cruelly caught

FIGURE 4.10. Caine battling with the evil Hsiang (John Fujioka) in "The Devil's Champion" (1974).

out . . . not because of dishonesty or duplicity . . . but simply because of a centuries-laden way of thinking of females. Hell yes, it's because she's a woman . . .
and the truth of it hangs in the echoes . . . and Master Kan is too honest an old
man to deny the truth."[69] Here, it is not just Master Kan who is "caught out"
but China as well. According to the American view so readily expressed here,
the Asian nation, despite its move toward Communism, cannot escape its
patriarchal, nonegalitarian tendencies because of its "centuries-laden way of
thinking of females" (figure 4.11).

Although *Kung Fu* attempts to make a progressive statement on gender
in shows such as this, its portrayal of Chinese women especially reenacts
the timeworn narrative of female sacrifice. In "Besieged" and "The Cenotaph"—both two-part episodes that take place in China—the female protagonists, out of love, give up their lives in some way to save Caine. Nan Chi
("Besieged") throws herself in front of Kwai Chang and is killed in his
defense; Mayli Ho ("The Cenotaph"), in her belief that she will inevitably
"destroy" the young monk, unselfishly rejects him. These stories of ardent
sacrifice seem to take as their impetus the Western tale of *Madame Butterfly*.
Although originally invoking the fantasy of "the submissive Oriental
women and the cruel white man,"[70] *Kung Fu* twists the narrative and makes

FIGURE 4.11. Caine gets to know Nan Chi (Barbara Seagull/Hershey) in "Besieged"
(1974).

the women (Mayli Ho, Nan Chi) less submissive and the man (Caine) less cruel. Despite this seemingly progressive variation, both episodes leave intact the eventual sacrifice of the Chinese woman on which (white) male subjectivity depends. The ego ideal is shored up and made worthy through her abandonment.

The two instances in which Caine enjoys sexual relations are with Chinese women (Mayli Ho in "The Cenotaph," Su Yen in "The Tide"). Through this specificity, the biracial protagonist at once crosses boundaries and maintains them. *Kung Fu*'s story lines maintain ethnic-racial boundaries by keeping sexual relations within a certain culture (Chinese doing Chinese). But at the same time, the narrative transgresses them by allowing an "experience" with the fetishized Asian woman. The fact that both Mayli Ho and Su Yen are played by actresses of Chinese or half-Chinese descent (Tina Chen and Nancy Kwan, respectively) seems to visually authorize their role as objects of temptation and pleasure. (Nan Chi,—played by Barbara Seagull/Hershey who is white—loves Caine but does not have sexual relations with him.)

Through narratives of self-sacrifice and of sexual love, *Kung Fu* symbolically appropriates the figure of the Chinese woman to once again reconfirm and secure patriarchal and racial privilege. Again, these female characters are granted a degree of agency, but it is eventually turned against them toward the masculine reconfiguration of Caine. As in the case of subalterns who would be disciplined by the series' representations, China would suffer a similar fate. Both American desire for a pacified state (Mayli Ho, Su Yen, and Nan Chi) and disappointment over political and cultural affairs (Emperor's nephew) would be mirrored in the show. Far from treating China as its symbolic equal, *Kung Fu* would assert an Orientalist scene that representationally maintained a self-portrait of American dominance.

Carradine/Caine

On June 28, 1975, the final episode of *Kung Fu* aired on ABC. Apparently, the end of the series was not due to lack of ratings (it still enjoyed a high Nielsen share) but rather was based on David Carradine's decision to leave the show to pursue other projects. He recalls: "You know the mystique of the character sort of began to take me over. I think actually that's why I left the series. The series was never cancelled . . . I just left."[71] Although Carradine eschewed any similarity to Caine in public interviews at the time, he could not seem to escape this slippage between himself and the character. As Alex Beaton, one of the show's producers and directors, would remark:

David had always been interested in mystery and in the mystical elements of life. And *Kung Fu* was a great opportunity to explore that interest. . . . David was a peaceful guy. He really just wanted to bring joy to himself and the world. I believe he wanted his life to be as Caine's. In other words, his intentions and Caine's were one and the same. And he had Caine's principles.[72]

Zealous fans would carry out the confusion even further and, when happening upon the actor, often challenge Carradine to a fight.[73] As for those who looked to Carradine for spiritual wisdom and advice, he would comment: "I'm not about to present myself as a potential guru."[74]

Carradine would go on to enjoy modest acclaim and success as an actor in movies such as *Bound for Glory* (1976), in which he played folksinger Woody Guthrie, and *Death Race 2000* (1976), a science fiction film and a "deliberate move to kill the image of Caine." However, he could never escape his most famous role.[75] By 1976, only a year after the end of the series, he began to embrace martial arts and train with *Kung Fu* consultant and *sifu*, Kam Yuen. During that time, he pursued production of *The Circle of Iron (The Silent Flute)* (1979), an allegorical tale initially conceived by Bruce Lee that attempted to present the "true essence of kung fu."[76]

In the early 1980s, with *Kung Fu* in syndication around the world, Carradine, along with original costar Radames Pera (young Grasshopper), came up with the idea for *Kung Fu: The Movie* that would have Kwai Chang Caine pass his spiritual legacy to his son. Warner Brothers embraced the idea, and production soon began. Carradine reprised his role, and Brandon Lee (Bruce Lee's son) was cast as Caine's son. The movie obviously was successful enough for the studio to pursue a sixty-minute television movie pilot, *Kung Fu: The Next Generation* (1987). This time, Carradine nixed playing the role of Caine because the potential series featured "kung-fu car crashes" and compromised the original series' spiritual integrity.

However, by the 1990s, David Carradine appeared fully ensconced in his role as Caine. In 1991, he wrote *The Spirit of Shaolin*, a book that includes autobiographical stories, as well as the philosophical background and explication of kung fu. Per the impetus for writing the work, Carradine recounts:

A few years ago, I received a message on my answering machine from Sifu Kam Yuen, my nominal Master for the last eighteen years. I called him back and he said, "David, I want you to write a book about the true essence of kung fu. People associate it with violence and aggressiveness. They have lost track of the spiritual and philosophical aspects. I know, however, that you will never get around to it, so I'm going to write it and put your name on it. There is a great need for this book."

Every once in a while, the Master gives me a task, and I must perform it or suffer because of it. Yet, from time to time, I have taught the Master. We have grown up side by side.

So, I said to him, "Sifu, I have always agreed with everything you have ever said or written, but if I must do this task, I must DO it. Will you help me?"

After some thought, Sifu Kam Yuen agreed. "All right, David, but don't take too long. The world needs this book."[77]

Subsequently Warner Brothers resurrected Kwai Chang Caine (this time as the grandson of the original protagonist and in a contemporary urban setting) in *Kung Fu: The Legend Continues* (1993–1997). Gone were the philosophy and flashbacks to China and the alternative sense of Caine's responses, and in their place were other-worldly plots and martial arts scenes filled with implausible stunts. Most notable was the absence of a bridge figure: Caine's son, ironically named David, is a middle-class, thirty-something, white-identified law enforcement official who totes a pistol and shares little in common with his father. As he says in the opening credits: "I don't do that kung fu stuff . . . I'm a cop, a cop." Although canceled in the late 1990s, *Kung Fu: The Legend Continues* received heavy airplay in syndication ten years later,[78] and numerous Web sites catered to its loyal fan base. One wonders whether it stood as the entrenchment of what was once an emergent dominant group now firmly established or as the hegemonic claim of a new generation with ambivalent ties to their hippie parents.

In 2003, Caine/Carradine finally came home. Although Quentin Tarantino's fondness for the itinerant monk would find its way into *Pulp Fiction*, his homage to *Kung Fu* was even greater in *Kill Bill, Vol. 1* and *Kill Bill, Vol. 2* (2004). Indeed, Tarantino used his audience's affection for Caine to good effect, as Carradine is transformed from the peace-loving ascetic to a cold-blooded master assassin. Bill's portrayal depends on this shocking, if not strangely pleasurable contrast; however, he is safely circumscribed within the martial arts genre.

David Carradine often reprised the character of Kwai Chang Caine in skits and satires up until his death in 2009. On June 4 of that year, the actor was found dead—hung from a rope in a hotel room in Bangkok. The cause of death was officially ruled accidental asphyxiation, and tawdry details of his personal life and unorthodox sexual practices became fodder for news reports and gossip columns. Truth became more sensational than fiction. Despite the revelations,

Carradine's legacy remained intact. As one commentator noted: "David Carradine will best be remembered as 'Grasshopper' Kwai Chang Caine to Keye Luke's Master Po in the original 'Kung Fu' and has left an indelibly positive mark on the minds and spirits of many as a result of that singular role."[79] Or put more colloquially, "R.I.P., David Carradine. The interdependent ways of the world are odd, and I don't know if representing pseudo-Eastern spirituality is generous or not, but you probably got more than a few fannies on the cushions and into the zendos."[80] The mark of Caine remains.

As mass media helped make Carradine and Caine inseparable in the minds of both actor and viewing public, *Kung Fu* represents the ideological legacy of a generation and its full-fledged induction of that generation into the realm of the hyperreal. Visual media, and most notably television, transformed the fictional characters of Caine and his Oriental Monk teachers into messengers of spiritual substance and transformed the actors who played them into their fictional characters. Indeed, the protagonist's "search for truth" parallels that of the American viewer who, through the show, searches for his or her own Orientalist truth and finds it virtually real.

5

Conclusion

Spiritual Romance Today

As the millennium approaches, "God is in" and everyone is searching for meaning beyond the material—even in materialistic Hollywood. It's now chic in Tinseltown to have a spiritual path that goes beyond mainstream religion. *Hollywood Spirituality* is a one-hour long look at celebrities' search for meaning in the esoteric spiritual disciplines of yoga, kabbalah, witchcraft, Buddhism and alternative forms of healing.
—E! cable network promo

Can you not flick the shit out of your fingernail these days and not have it hit one of those damn White Buddhists right in the lotus?

Just a few years ago, it seemed like they were all Hindu, buying up all the sitar music at Street Light, and taking cooking lessons at the Bombay Culinary Institute in Sunnyvale. The lucky ones who dared venture to Chinatown to the cheap cheap travel agents managed to find a good ticket, dashing off to India for a good deal of Indiany stuff, swimming in the holy Ganges and coming home with parasites swimming in their blood, which I'm sure many mistook for some kind of divine blessing of enlightenment. Until the harsh reality of blood in the stools took over.

But now, nothing beats the calm, centered, self-actualization of the Buddhist Thing.

. . . Welcome to Lamapalooza
—Justin Chin, "Attack of the White Buddhists"[1]

Americans' fascination with Asian religions remains surprisingly intact over the past half-century. However, as the tagline for the E! cable network special *Hollywood Spirituality* (1998) seems to suggest, this fascination is marked by an unusual type of amnesia—an amnesia that allows its subjects to experience their fascination each time anew. For a younger generation, D. T. Suzuki, the Maharishi Mahesh Yogi, and Kwai Chang Caine are names that mean very little. All held the attraction of a particular generation; all were "chic" in their given time.

Since "Caine walked the earth" in the early 1970s, reincarnations of the Oriental Monk made their steady appearance in Hollywood fictional accounts. There have been more anonymous sightings of the iconic figure in a multitude of films—from *Ace Ventura: When Nature Calls* (1995) to *Holy Smoke* (1999), *Bulletproof Monk* (2003), and *The Forbidden Kingdom* (2008)—and across different platforms: in television shows, such as *Walker Texas Ranger*, Airwalk print ads, Mortal Kombat video games, and Second Life "islands." The monk's ingress in kid-oriented fare is especially noteworthy.

Entertainment supersystems aimed toward children deploy a range of media and consumer products (toys, figurines, and games) that symbolically rely on the Oriental Monk narrative and draw on Virtual Orientalism's potential to engage young viewers. The popularity of the narrative among teens and youths is undeniable and can be seen in such "classics" as the *Star Wars* enterprise and the *Karate Kid* and its sequels (with Yoda and Mr. Miyagi, respectively, as enduring Oriental Monk figures). In *The Teenage Mutant Ninja Turtles*, the figure is given animated expression, and the narrative has become a staple of children's cartoons in the new millennium (e.g., *Xiaolin Showdown* and *Avatar: The Last Airbender*).[2]

The Oriental Monk would indeed come full circle with *Kung Fu Panda*, perhaps one of the closest relatives to *Kung Fu* in the 1970s. Set in China, the movie utilized one of the most potent symbols of U.S.–China relations, the panda, as its sympathetic hero and protagonist. Similar to *Kung Fu*, Po is a character that represents a dual existence: on the one hand, as a Chinese peasant subject and, on the other, as a fun-loving, martial arts–obsessed youth (voiced by comic actor Jack Black). Faith in oneself and faith in others, attachment and nonattachment become religiously inflected challenges that the film explores. Grand themes, wrapped in stunning animation and a lush score, transform an otherwise summer blockbuster into a epic for the entire family.

Whereas *Kung Fu* marks a generational compromise between "the Greatest Generation" (World War II contemporaries) and their postwar, baby boomer offspring through the marriage of countercultural values with the form of the classic Western, *Kung Fu Panda* demonstrates the realization of the latter's vision and hope for their own children. Indeed, these values, accentuated by the discourse of liberal multiculturalism, are written into the story line of *Kung Fu Panda*. The relationships between monks and pupils are multigenerational in the film, as the ancient (and most overtly Orientalized) Oogway counsels his long-time student, Master Shifu, and Shifu in turn reluctantly trains the physically hapless Po. The spiritual struggle of the embittered red panda, one could reasonably argue, is as much a focus as that of his lovable student. Here, the fears and challenges that Master Shifu faces—his prideful, yet abiding love of Tai Lung, his lack of confidence in training his new pupil, and his disillusionment or inability to no longer "believe"— mirror those of *Kung Fu Panda*'s adult audience.

The shift from adult dramatic story lines that feature Oriental Monks to the Monks' increased appearance in kid-oriented fare becomes an important turn of the representational wheel. Indeed, the mediums of film and television— once suspiciously assessed for their negative influence—become the "skillful means" by which values newly embraced by the boomer generation are passed on to their children. For an American audience whose members increasingly identify themselves as "spiritual but not religious," these opportunities of encounter offer a moral touchstone and hip alternative. New media and a host of consumer products further stimulate interest in Oriental Monk–inspired features. Indeed, the work of Virtual Orientalism is especially strong in story lines and products aimed at a younger generation, socializing youth not only as consumer agents but also into a spiritualized, competitive individualism demanded by late capitalism.

In each of these examples, the characters may change, but they play the same role, serve the same function, and tell the same story—time and time again. Virtual Orientalism relies on this repetitive promise, on the reliability of iconic performance, and on a Western audience's spiritual needs and desires, as it masks the ideological interests and geopolitical concerns that invisibly drive its cultural imperialist enterprise. It relies heavily on new technologies and visual media that allow a constant stream of images. The seemingly uninterrupted flow of representations and their easy access make stereotypes of Asians and Asian religions all the more obdurate. In a consumer-oriented society, we have seen how Virtual Orientalism accommodates the demand for novelty by introducing new versions of the icon. As Justin Chin's diatribe hyperbolically (yet truthfully) states: It may be a guru one year and a lama the next. Beyond the fact that the specific heritage of a given representation is dictated by the U.S. political terrain, manifestations of the icon are marked by their relative substitutability in the pop cultural realm. This substitutability is possible because a mass audience is less concerned with the distinctiveness of the figure or the religious tradition he represents than with the desires the iconic figure meets and the operations he performs. The preceding chapters have been an attempt to trace the emergence of the development in Orientalism's broader history, as well as unveil Virtual Orientalism's hegemonic work.

Today, the situation seems more complex than ever. In the past decades, we have seen a burst in communications technology in the form of wireless telephones, MP3 recordings, digital game consoles, and most notably, the Internet, and we have experienced the effects of these technologies in our everyday lives and consciousness. This explosive "multiplication of the media" (to borrow Umberto Eco's prescient phrase), far from challenging stereotypical views of Asians and Asian cultures, in many ways has further strengthened Orientalism's virtual hold. An ongoing case study of this fact can be seen in the unprecedented popularity of the Dalai Lama in the United States.

With much acclaim, the Fourteenth Dalai Lama received the Nobel Peace Prize in 1989. In the tradition of Martin Luther King Jr., his selection for the honor continued a new line of world peacemakers whose vision was simultaneously shaped and influenced by a mixture of a profound spirituality and political awareness. The Nobel Peace Prize hurled the Dalai Lama and the small Asian country of Tibet into the public eye and therefore marks the most contemporary stage in the development of the icon of the Oriental Monk.

What happened next solidified the Dalai Lama's inception as an American pop cultural figure.[3] Hollywood actor and celebrity Richard Gere personally adopted the Dalai Lama's spiritual and political mission as his own—promoting the cause at the 1993 Academy Awards and becoming the founding chair of the Tibet House in New York. Many of Gere's contemporaries followed: "the Power Buddhist/Free Tibet contingent" included Harrison Ford, Willem Dafoe, Sharon Stone, Steven Seagal, and Adam Yauch of the Beastie Boys.[4] These celebrity endorsements offered a Buddhist way of life unprecedented Western exposure and shepherded in a new variation of the icon. The power of these celebrity networks proved vital in keeping the Dalai Lama's name in the headlines and his image in the news.[5]

This attention has had enormous payoffs, as "Lama fever" spread to famous Hollywood directors. The 1990s saw the production of several big studio films that centered around the life of the Dalai Lama and Tibetan Buddhism: Bernardo Bertolucci's *Little Buddha* (1993); Martin Scorsese's *Kundun* (1997), and Jean-Jacques Annaud's *Seven Years in Tibet* (1997). To add to this media mix, the Dalai Lama himself published several best-selling books, made public appearances across the United States, and even chatted online in an e-public forum. This acclaim has afforded the spiritual leader private meetings with leading political figures and heads of state, including Bill Clinton, George

W. Bush, and Barack Obama. One can find further evidence of Americans' love affair with Dalai Lama on the World Wide Web and the innumerable sites dedicated to him, as well as to Tibetan Buddhism and culture. His influence similarly shows up in the commercial realm: One can buy audio CDs of Tibetan mantras and chants, spirit bead bracelets, meditation pillows, Buddha wall and garden statues, and mandala posters. One can purchase, in stores and online, the live box set of CD recordings from the Tibetan Freedom Concerts. Stylized religion has come home and caters not only to aging yuppies but also to their children—a new generation of spiritual seekers.

Despite opportunities to experience the Dalai Lama through books, iPod apps, Twitter, and sound recordings, it is again the image of the Tibetan patriarch that proves most compelling. The Oriental Monk has become increasingly modeled after His Holiness (note the saffron-robed, shaved-head version has been featured in ads for IBM and Mercedes Benz in the past decade). Psychically, this monk descendant continues the work of its predecessors in the critique of American society—its religious and secular preoccupations:

> We don't need these Buddhist temples, we don't need these Christian Churches, What we need, [the Dalai Lama] says, are the values of the human heart. . . . There's a lot of talk about [the baby boomer] generation being materially satisfied, but the next level of need is not satisfied and that's the spiritual level. (Martin Wassell, documentary filmmaker)

> Buddhism is seen as one way that we might re-create a sense of spiritual meaning and purpose within a directionless society. Amid widespread despair, those who have found Buddhism have a sense of joy and inspiration. (Steven Batchelor, English Buddhist monk and scholar)[6]

The Dalai Lama obviously fulfills certain cultural and spiritual needs. But this version of the icon also constitutes a shift in political focus and mission. At different moments, Americans demonstrate a preference for the Japanese or Chinese model; this selectivity is not coincidental. Japan and China are still seen as cultures possessing great spiritual richness. But this recognition emerges only when relations between these countries and the United States are good, and their challenge in the arena of international politics and the world market is perceived as fairly contained. Ideally, they are seen as less modernized than the West or, in the case of Japan, possess some inexplicable nature that accounts for their (economic) success. Only when these conditions are met are Japanese and Chinese Oriental Monks suitable representatives of the East in the American popular imagination.

The late 1980s into the 1990s brought transformed relations with Japan and China. Whereas Japan became transfigured as America's economic competitor in the global market, China emerged as its primary political adversary. In 1989—a year that included the fall of the Berlin wall, as well as the Tiananmen Square massacre— a "giant, powerful, merciless China" was inaugurated. Richard Bernstein, in his analysis into "The Hollywood Love Affair with Tibet," remarks: "The answer [to why Tibet has become the cause du jour for celebrities and noncelebrities alike] has several factors. There is the ferocity of China's actions in Tibet, and China's status in the post-cold-war world as the most important large country still holding another land in subjugation."[7] Previous variations of the Oriental Monk as a result were traded in for a less compromised Tibetan model. The Tibetan version of the icon through his dress and religious practices paradigmatically signifies a mythic spiritual past. The nation to which he is attached is actually no nation at all—except in its past and its promise. Under Chinese rule, Tibetans have been scattered throughout the globe, and the Dalai Lama, as their leader, remains in exile. Out of this political situation, Americans have developed a unique affinity to spiritual patriarch and his people.

The Dalai Lama as Oriental Monk also provides his American charges with a concrete political mission: Free Tibet. The Tibetan monk's politico-spiritual mission and the forces that he opposes are well defined. They are succinctly summarized in the inaugural issue of *Tricycle*:

- 1.2 million Tibetans have died (one-sixth of the population)
- 70 percent of Tibet's virgin forest has been clear cut
- More than 6,000 monasteries, temples, and historic sites have been looted and razed
- All religious practices have been outlawed.[8]

This scenario portrays a marginalized people who are fighting against a global power (China) for their very physical, cultural, and spiritual survival—a noble cause with which to align oneself. But unrecognized desires underlie American interest in this mission. Tibet's predicament mirrors and emerges from America's own guilt within its own borders and without—the millions of human lives it has taken, the deforestation it is responsible for, and its judgment on ways of life foreign to a democratic, secular, late capitalist model. Indeed, Tibet represents a manageable cosmos where sins—past and present—can be atoned. Hence, the Tibetan model of the Oriental Monk enacts an exchange: a model of ethical behavior and spiritual direction for political and economic support. But this exchange serves the West well: America gains not only psychic resolution and healing but also unchallenged political and cultural influence over the exiled nation.

I surmise that we have yet to see the full potential of the Dalai Lama in his role as an Oriental Monk figure. His representation or image constitutes an unfolding phenomenon. However, we perhaps are now able to better understand what fuels Americans' attraction. We can isolate and recognize the conventionalized narrative that draws his audience in close relation with him. We are better able to discern how his image and personality meet certain Orientalist protocols and why an American pop culture audience is more consumed with what he represents than with what he necessarily has to say (Suzuki). We have a better clue about what makes his representation especially attractive to young people (Maharishi) and especially apt for a youth-oriented market. And we now perhaps realize how the radical pacifism he seems to embody can actually works against other liberatory efforts (*Kung Fu*).

For Americans, the Oriental Monk has certainly arrived—he can be found on a television set in Des Moines, a movie screen in Tampa, a computer monitor in Minneapolis, or a billboard ad in Oakland. You can carry him around in your book bag or hang him on your bedroom wall. His image adorns the meditation rooms in Second Life. At our immediate disposal and making no demands of his own, he has indeed become virtually ours. *Welcome to Lamapalooza. . . .*

Notes

1 INTRODUCTION

1. David Morgan, "The Image of Religion in American *Life*, 1936–1951," in *Looking at* Life Magazine, ed. Erika Doss, 139–157 (Washington, DC: Smithsonian Institution Press, 2001).

2. South Asian Hindus and Sikhs are often mistaken for Muslim extremists. An examination of the "religious oppression" that South Asian Americans face can be found in Khyati Joshi, *New Roots in America's Sacred Ground* (Brunswick, NJ: Rutgers University Press, 2006). The controversy over the invocation of a Hindu prayer at the opening of the U.S. Congress in 2000 attests to the lingering suspicion of particular Asian religions that certain Americans hold and their continuing view that the United States is a (white) Christian nation.

3. Americans' contemporary fascination with Asian religions and its link to consumer culture is readily documented and explored by scholars. Two notable examples are Kimberly Lau, *New Age Capitalism: Making Money East of Eden* (Philadelphia: University of Pennsylvania Press, 2000); and J. Carrette and Richard King, *Selling Spirituality: The Silent Takeover of Religion* (New York: Routledge, 2004).

4. For a discussion of how icons operate, see S. Paige Baty, *American Monroe: The Making of a Body Politic* (Berkeley: University of California Press, 1995); and Margaret R. Miles, *Image as Icon: Visual Understanding in Western Christianity and Secular Culture* (Boston: Beacon, 1987).

5. See Edward Said, *Orientalism* (New York: Vintage, 1979).

6. A compelling interpretation of Orientalism's outcome, especially as it relates to new digital media can be found in the work of Lisa Nakamura.

See *Cybertypes: Race, Ethnicity, and Identity on the Internet* (New York: Routledge, 2002) and *Digitizing Race: Visual Cultures of the Internet* (Minneapolis: University of Minnesota Press, 2008).

7. Although the hyperreal operates as its own type of reality, this does not mean that its provenance is divorced from the material conditions in which we live. The fact that the images that the media project can be readily identified as "representations," rather than the truth of the matter, works to further mask the political, social, and cultural interests involved. At the same time, these images have the force of reality and serve as a conduit of meaning. No doubt, viewers can recognize the Arab terrorists in the Arnold Schwarzenegger film *True Lies* (1994) as fictional characters ("It's just a movie!"), but these images undoubtedly reinforce, if not substantively inform, American viewers' notions of Islam and the U.S.-Middle East conflict.

8. Vijay Prashad, *The Karma of Brown Folk* (Minneapolis: University of Minnesota Press, 2000), 20.

9. M. K. Naik, S. K. Desai, and S. T. Kallapur, eds., *The Image of India in Western Creative Writing* (London: Macmillan, 1971), preface.

10. Rudyard Kipling, *Kim* (1900; repr., New York: Doubleday, 1956). The description is taken from the book cover. E. M. Forster's *A Passage to India* and Somerset Maugham's *The Razor's Edge* are literary staples that are still being read today. (Both novels have been translated for the big screen.) However, Kipling's *Kim* arguably remains the quintessential British novel about India, whose influence is unsurpassed except by his *The Jungle Book*, written for children.

11. Rudyard Kipling, *Life's Handicap.*

12. Avtar Singh Bhullar, *India, Myth and Reality: Images of India in the Fiction by English Writers* (Delhi, India: Ajanta, 1985), 92. Patrick Williams, in his essay on *Kim*, also discusses the "widespread negativity in the text towards Indian religion." See Patrick Williams, "Kim and *Orientalism*," in *Colonial Discourse and Post-Colonial Theory: A Reader*, ed. Patrick Williams and Laura Chrisman, 484–485 (New York: Columbia University Press, 1994).

13. Patrick Williams carefully notes that "neither Kipling the author nor the range of positions offered by his texts is reducible to the merely imperialist." I agree that such a qualification needs to be made. However, like Williams, I also believe that although *Kim* represents an exceptional work in Kipling's oeuvre for its sympathetic portrayal of Indians, its dominant ideological effect remains imperialist in nature. See Williams, "Kim and *Orientalism*," 480–497.

14. Laurie Maffly Kipp, "Engaging Habits and Besotted Idolatry: Viewing Chinese Religions in the American West," *Material Religion: The Journal of Objects, Art and Belief* 1, no. 1 (2005): 72–97.

15. The engraving of Dharmapala, in fact, would appear twice during the *Tribune's* two-week coverage of the Parliament, a visual sign of religious and cultural difference, undoubtedly meant to highlight the unprecedented meeting of Occident and Orient.

16. See Kipp.

17. Barbara Greorich, *Harvard Magazine*, March–April 2000.

18. The ideological caregiver operates within what Sau-ling Wong calls the *psychospiritual plantation system*. Although Wong develops these concepts in relation to Asian

American literature and film, her observations are equally relevant here. See her "'Sugar Sisterhood': Situating the Amy Tan Phenomenon," in *The Ethnic Canon: Histories, Institutions, and Interventions*, ed. David Palumbo-Liu, 174–210 (Minneapolis: University of Minnesota Press, 1995); and "Diverted Mothering: Representations of Caregivers of Color in the Age of 'Multiculturalism,'" in *Mothering: Ideology, Experience, and Agency*, ed. Evelyn Nakano Glenn, Grace Chang, and Linda Rennie Forcie, 67–91 (New York: Routledge, 1994).

19. John Kuo Wei Tchen, "Modernizing White Patriarchy: Re-Viewing D. W. Griffith's *Broken Blossoms*," in *Moving the Image: Independent Asian Pacific American Media Arts*, ed. Russell Leong, 135 (Los Angeles: UCLA Asian American Studies Center, 1991).

20. Brian Massumi, *Parable for the Virtual: Movement, Affect, Sensation* (Durham, NC: Duke University Press, 2002), 133–134.

2 ZEN'S PERSONALITY

1. Winthrop Sargeant, "Profiles: Great Simplicity; Dr. Daisetz Teitaro Suzuki," *New Yorker*, August 31, 1957, 34.

2. William R. LaFleur, "Between America and Japan: The Case of Daisetsu Teitaro Suzuki," *Zen in American Life and Letters*, ed. Robert S. Ellwood (Malibu, CA: Undena, 1987), 67.

3. See Rick Fields's *How the Swans Came to the Lake: A Narrative History of Buddhism in America*, 3rd ed. (Boston: Shambhala, 1992); and Masao Abe, ed., *A Zen Life: D. T. Suzuki Remembered* (New York: Weatherhill, 1986).

4. See Benedict Anderson, *Imagined Communities* (New York: Verso, 1991). Although Anderson employs this term to speak of the "nation," his conceptualization is salient for my discussion here. Zen adherents "will never know most of their fellow-members, meet them, or even hear of them, yet in the minds of each lives the image of their communion" (6). They also view themselves ideally as "a deep, horizontal comradeship" (7). Suzuki's role in shaping Zen's "imagined community" in the West cannot be underestimated. His English-language works helped Western enthusiasts legitimate their beliefs by allowing them to reference Zen sources and authorities that were both geographically and historically remote. Also, his universalized portrait of Zen flattened the tradition's hierarchical elements and cleared the way for a Western "fraternity" of Zen proponents.

5. Jack Kerouac, *Berkeley Bussei*, 1960. Quoted in Fields, *How the Swans Came to the Lake*, 205.

6. For a general overview of Suzuki's work and its contributions, see Heinrich Dumoulin, *Zen Buddhism in the 20th Century*, trans. Joseph S. O'Leary (New York: Weatherhill, 1992); Abe, *A Zen Life*; "D.T. Suzuki, 'Suzuki Zen,' and the American Reception of Zen Buddhism," in *American Buddhism as a Way of Life*, ed. Gary Storhoff and John Whalen-Bridge (Albany: State University of New York Press, 2010); and the documentary, *A Zen Life: D. T. Suzuki* (Michael Goldman, 2006).

Suzuki's presentation of Buddhism has come under harsh criticism in academic circles. Buddhologists such as Bernard Faure and Robert H. Scharf have ideologically questioned the scholar's work and provided compelling analyses of its link with Japanese nationalism. See Bernard Faure, *Chan Insights and Oversights: An Epistemological Critique of the Chan Tradition* (Princeton, NJ: Princeton University Press, 1993), and "The Kyoto School and Reverse Orientalism," in *Japan in Traditional and Postmodern Perspectives*, ed. Charles Wei-hsun Fu and Steven Heine, 245–281 (Albany: State University of New York Press, 1995); Robert H. Scharf, "The Zen of Japanese Nationalism," in *Curators of the Buddha: The Study of Buddhism under Colonialism*, ed. Donald S. Lopez Jr., 107–160 (Chicago: University of Chicago Press, 1995); James W. Heisig and John C. Maraldo, eds., *Rude Awakenings: Zen, the Kyoto School, & the Question of Nationalism* (Honolulu: University of Hawai'i Press, 1994); and Brian Victoria, *Zen at War* (New York: Weatherhill, 1997). These interpretations, in turn, have been challenged by those who insist that Suzuki's position was much more philosophically and emotionally complex. See Kemmyo Taira Sato, "D.T. Suzuki and the Question of War," trans. by Thomas Kirchner, *The Eastern Buddhist* 39, no. 1 (2008): 61–120; and Michael Goldberg, Director, *A Zen Life – D.T. Suzuki*, 2006.

Suzuki may have participated in a reverse Orientalism of sorts and employed Zen "as an ideological instrument to promote a cultural image of Japan in the West," as Faure contends (*Chan Insights*, 86). But studies such as these appear to look at only one side of the rhetorical equation, focusing on the author's (i.e., Suzuki's) intention and not on the general Orientalist environment in the West in which his work was received. Despite their particular focus, Faure seems aware of the need for further analysis. He writes that it "may be relatively easy to denounce the *nihonjinron* ideology, while it is harder to see the *amerikajinron* (or *furansujinron*) ideology at work in this very process. We need to become aware of our own 'political ontology,' even as we perform the necessary task of deconstructing that of 'philosophical' movements like the Kyoto school" ("Kyoto School," 272).

7. In 1956, 20,000 television sets were being purchased per day.

8. "People Are Talking about . . . Dr. Daisetz Suzuki," *Vogue*, January 15, 1957, 98.

9. "Zen," *Time*, February 4, 1957, 65.

10. Daniel J. Bronstein, "Search for Inner Truth," *Saturday Review*, November 16, 1957, 22.

11. *Time*, February 4, 1957, 66.

12. *Harper's Bazaar* and the *New Yorker* were the only magazines to feature Suzuki in his usual white shirt and bow tie. Otherwise, photographs of him in Western dress came into print only from the 1960s on.

13. Sargeant, "Profiles," 34.

14. Ibid.

15. In her exploration of early-twentieth-century representations of non-Western indigenous peoples in film, Fatimah Tobing Rony notes: "When the average museum goer views a life group of Hopi dancers handling snakes, or a display of Wolof pottery, or an ethnographic film about trance and dance in Bali, he or she does not see the images for the first time. *The exotic is already known*" (6) (my emphasis). See *The Third Eye: Race, Cinema, and Ethnographic Spectacle* (Durham, NC: Duke University Press, 1996).

16. *Life* August 16, 1943: 94.

17. Christina Klein, *Cold War Orientalism: Asia in the Middlebrow Imagination, 1945–1961* (Berkeley: University of California Press, 2003).

18. Sargeant, "Profiles," 36.

19. This practice was often featured in articles about Zen during the period.

20. Sargeant makes special note: "During the Second World War, Dr. Suzuki was in Japan, where he held the unwavering interest of the Japanese secret police because of his relentless fight for greater tolerance and understanding and because of his denunciation of militarism in the national cult of Shinto" ("Profiles," 53). The critical distance he is able to achieve as a scholar in relation to the harsh practices of Zen Buddhist monks also seems to inform the perception of Suzuki's relation to politics. American commentators such as Sargeant distinguished Suzuki from other Japanese, who were portrayed as supporting their government's aggressive acts during World War II without question.

Suzuki's conscientiousness has fallen under scrutiny in recent times, but it remained effectively intact in the late 1950s (and for at least two subsequent decades).

21. Sargeant, "Profiles," 53.

22. The definition of Suzuki as a scholar is a peculiar one. Although he demonstrated a predisposition toward logical exposition, he also stressed Zen's nonlogical dimensions. Many American commentators also picked up on Zen's intuitive, anti-intellectual stance when they attempt to explain the sudden interest in Zen during the period. This paradox—the explication of an essentially inexplicable phenomenon—did not seem to undermine Suzuki's scholarly status. He would admit: "The Zen master, generally speaking, despises those who indulge in word- or idea-mongering, and in this respect Hu Shih and myself are great sinners, murderers of Buddhas and patriarchs; we are both destined for Hell" (quoted in Sargeant, "Profiles," 36). Such statements of self-deprecation only added to Suzuki's appeal. Here his "confession" seems sufficient for spiritual pardon and allows him to maintain in his scholarly role.

23. Sargeant, "Profiles," 49.

24. Ibid., 53.

25. Here, one must also take into account the thousands of Japanese war brides who immigrated to the United States with their GI husbands (under the 1952 McCarran-Walter Act). Unlike women from China, who primarily married coethnics, Japanese women more often married non-Asian men. See Sucheng Chan, *Asian Americans: An Interpretive History* (Boston: Twayne, 1991), 140.

Such interracial marriages between Japanese women and Euro-American men became somewhat of a phenomenon. For instance, *Life* magazine featured such a union in 1955 in an article written by James Michener, "Pursuit of Happiness by a GI and a Japanese: Marriage Surmounts Barriers of Language and Intolerance," February 21, 1955, 124. Popular films, such as *The Teahouse of the August Moon* (1956) and *Sayonara* (1957), also offered entertaining, if not "realist" narratives of this encounter. The politics of this gendered representation are explored in Gina Marchetti, *Romance and the "Yellow Peril": Race, Sex, and Discursive Strategies in Hollywood Fiction* (Berkeley: University of California Press, 1993).

26. LaFleur, "Between America and Japan," 81.

27. See William L. O'Neill, *American High: The Years of Confidence, 1945–1960* (New York: Free Press, 1986).

28. Personal reflections by those who met Suzuki note the ways in which he did *not* fit the image they had expected. These are important to note. For instance, Philip Kapleau remarks:

> Having read the romantic novels *The Lost Horizon* and *The Razor's Edge*, I expected to be greeted by a sage with long white hair and beard, flowing robes, and crooked walking stick. Instead I came upon a short, clean-shaven, almost bald Japanese who looked for all the world like an editor. His book-lined study, the visor shading his eyes, and his one-finger typing at an old Underwood all strengthened this impression. (Abe, *A Zen Life*, 204)

Richard DeMartino, in his reminiscence of Suzuki, offers a very similar account (in Abe, *A Zen Life*, 195–196). Alan Watts also mentions the way in which Suzuki did not conform to a different stereotype—one of the austere and seemingly unapproachable Japanese Zen monk.

One of the most shocking features for each of these individuals is how Westernized Suzuki is: his typewriter, the green eyeshade he wears as he types, and the "Western-style section of his house" in Japan where he engaged in his studies. In these ways, he did not fit their image of the timeless and ahistorical sage who stood apart from historical innovations of the West.

On a popular level, though, Suzuki's representation remained fairly conventionalized, since the press preferred to portray him without his Western accoutrements. Perhaps the only remnant of Western influence is the spectacles that lend Suzuki his scholarly air. In any case, these inflections do not compromise Suzuki's overall role as an Oriental Monk. The Underwood typewriter, visor, and modest eyewear all seem antiquated and somewhat obsolete, even as they help recall the achievements of Western society. This strange amalgam of East and West would later functionally serve the larger narrative of the Oriental Monk: the Monk's openness to the West symbolized by his use of Western technology, his obsolescence by the outdatedness of these objects, and the timelessness of his vision through their "classic" nature.

29. Nancy Wilson Ross, "What Is Zen?" *Mademoiselle*, January 1958, 64.

30. Ibid.

31. Ibid.

32. Ibid., 65.

33. Ibid., 117.

34. Stuart Ewen, *All Consuming Image: The Politics of Style in Contemporary Culture* (New York: Basic Books, 1988), 23.

35. John Kenneth Galbraith, *The Affluent Society* (Boston: Houghton-Mifflin, 1958), 345.

36. Japhy Ryder's phrase in Jack Kerouac's *The Dharma Bums* (New York: Penguin, 1976), 39.

37. Eugene Burdick, "The Innocent Nihilists Adrift in Squaresville," *Reporter*, April 3, 1958, 30–31.

38. Tim A. Ross, "Rise and Fall of the Beats," *Nation*, May 27, 1961, 456.

39. Ibid.

40. Ibid., 457.

41. Again, see the December 31, 1950, issue of *Life* magazine, in which Asia's open markets are featured.

42. Both Beat and elite constituencies expressed strong objections to the rampant consumerism of their age. For the Beat, the thoughtless accumulation of wealth had a numbing effect and only disengaged Americans from any genuine form of experience and feeling. The elite related consumerism to mass culture; objects and goods were too readily available to a less discriminating audience and slowly eroded any distinction of taste. Despite these objections, Beat and elite styles were easily co-opted by the American capitalist culture.

43. Ewen, *All Consuming Image*, 113.

44. Indeed, Beat and elite subcultures seem ineluctably opposed in their values. The fact that Zen held interest for both factions helped highlight the philosophy's different valences and its representational potential to captivate different constituencies of a popular audience.

45. "Beat Mystics," *Time*, February 3, 1958, 56.

46. Kerouac, *Dharma Bums*, 9.

47. Ibid., 18.

48. Ibid., 13.

49. Ibid., 20.

50. Indeed, Kerouac dedicates *The Dharma Bums* to Han Shan.

51. Before this meeting, Kerouac's knowledge of Suzuki was secondhand at best. Although Allen Ginsberg and Gary Snyder both had their first encounters with Buddhism via Suzuki's oeuvre, there is little evidence that Kerouac had ever read the scholar's work. Ann Charters, in her autobiography of Kerouac, does note that Ginsberg had mentioned his study of Buddhism (including Suzuki's essays) to his fellow Beat, but that Kerouac "wasn't greatly impressed at the time" (191). His brief reference in *Dharma Bums* does relay the fact that he knew who Suzuki was. See Ann Charters, *Kerouac: A Biography* (New York: St. Martin's Press, 1973).

52. Fields, *How the Swans Came to the Lake*, 223–224. See note 55.

53. Daisetz T. Suzuki, "Zen in the Modern World," *Japan Quarterly* 5, no. 4 (1958): 452.

54. Ibid., 454.

55. Per my knowledge, there exist two different versions of Kerouac's encounter with Suzuki: the one recorded by Alfred G. Aronowitz and another published in the *Berkeley Bussei*. Aronowitz's was the first to appear, in his article "The Beat Generation," *New York Post*, March 19, 1959. The journalist provided a more extended version in his October 1960 article for *Escapade*, "The Year of Zen." This account was later published in *Big Sky Mind: Buddhism and the Beat Generation*, ed. Carole Tonkinson, 80–83 (New York: Riverhead, 1995).

Kerouac's reminiscence was also printed in *Berkeley Bussei* (1960), a periodical published by the Young Men's Buddhist Association of Berkeley. Rick Fields cites this version in his book, *How the Swans Came to the Lake*, 223–224. Fields's account was subsequently excerpted by *Tricycle: The Buddhist Review* 5, no. 1 (1995): 82, and retitled "Buddhism Beat & Square."

Although the two versions vary somewhat in length, detail, and the succession of the narrative, they are fairly similar in nature. I have relied mainly on the *Bussei* account, since it is the most succinct and dynamic. It is also the one that is probably the most widely read because of its inclusion in Fields's popular history of Buddhism in the United States (now in its third edition).

56. Gary Snyder, "On the Road with D. T. Suzuki," in *A Zen Life*, ed. Abe, 280.

57. Alan Watts, *In My Own Way: An Autobiography 1915–1965* (New York: Pantheon, 1972), 24.

58. "Eager Exponent of Zen," *Life*, April 21, 1961, 88A.

59. Watts, *In My Own Way*, 27.

60. Ibid., 78.

61. Ibid.

62. Ibid., 119.

63. Ibid., 122.

64. Watts notes in his autobiography: "It is therefore also said—perhaps with truth—that my easy and free-floating attitude to Zen *was largely responsible* for the notorious 'Zen boom' which flourished among artists and 'pseudointellectuals' in the late 1950s, and led on to the frivolous 'Beat Zen' of Kerouac's *Dharma Bums*, of Franz Kline's black and white abstractions, and of John Cage's silent concerts" (262) (my emphasis). Although he was certainly one of Zen's most prominent exponents in the 1950s, it is difficult to trace the claim that Watts intimates. For instance, Watts and his wife, Dorothy, did entertain Cage at one of their many dinner parties in the early 1950s, but it is Suzuki's lectures that seemed to have the most profound effect on the musician. (See Fields, *How the Swans Came to the Lake*, 196.)

As for the Beats, their view of Buddhism could only be called their own. It is true that Watts met Gary Snyder in the early 1950s and was responsible for introducing him to a number of Buddhist luminaries. But collectively, the Beats' interest in Zen was cultivated before they had ever met Watts and included an eclectic mix of influences.

65. The intellectual and spiritual connection that Watts felt he shared with Suzuki is unmistakable. Watts defends Suzuki's views as vehemently as if he were defending his own: "The time has come for someone to defend him like the swordsman Miyamoto Musashi, and smash his critics to pieces with a wooden oar against their finely tempered steels. I am not, at present, going to undertake this task, but no one who actually knew the man could possibly question the profundity of his spiritual insight—and I use this phrase advisedly although it is a little trite" (*In My Own Way*, 119).

66. Alan Watts, "The 'Mind-less' Scholar," in *A Zen Life*, ed. Abe, 189.

67. Watts, *In My Own Way*, 78.

68. Alan Watts, "Beat Zen, Square Zen, and Zen," *Chicago Review*, Summer 1958, 5.

69. Ibid., 6–7.

70. Ibid., 7.

71. Ibid., 10.

72. Ibid., 8.

73. Ibid., 11.

74. Ibid., 9.

75. Suzuki seems exempt from the Watts's criticism. Watts distinguished Suzuki from the institutional Zen of Japan in the following way: "The mood or atmosphere of Suzuki was more Taoist than Zen Buddhist. He didn't have the skin-headed military zip that is characteristic of so many Zen monks, nor their obedient seriousness" (Watts, *In My Own Way*, 120).

76. "The Zen Priest," *Time*, May 26, 1958, 65.

77. Sasaki was assisted in her duties by another English-speaking priest and "serious" student of Zen, Walter Nowick. Nowick had been tagged as "the real future of Zen in the U.S." in one of the earliest American popular accounts on the subject. See "Zen," *Time*, February 4, 1957, 65–66.

78. Watts comments: "Much of what I learned from Sokei-an and Ruth has so become part of me that I cannot now sort it out" (Watts, *In My Own Way*, 146).

79. Watts, *In My Own Way*, 126.

80. Ibid., 7.

81. Institutional Zen, in the United States, is a direct descendant of Watts; these individuals and organizations often view themselves as serious practitioners working toward the viability of Zen in a new environment. Although indebted to their Japanese ancestors, they often eschew many of the Japanese conventions, rituals, and practices, as they confidently define Zen on their own terms. They see themselves as the new direction of Zen—beyond both the faddish belief of their Beat counterparts and the sedimentary practices of Japanese tradition.

82. Watts, *In My Own Way*, 179–180.

83. Ibid., 211.

84. Watts, "Beat Zen, Square Zen, and Zen," 9.

85. "Zen: Beat & Square," *Time*, July 21, 1958, 49.

86. J. Donald Adams, "Speaking of Books," *New York Times Book Review*, October 26, 1958, 2.

87. Stephen Mahoney, "Prevalence of Zen," *Nation*, November 1, 1958, 311.

88. Ibid.

89. Ibid., 313.

90. Ibid.

91. Watts, "Beat Zen, Square Zen, and Zen," 8–9. See also "Zen: Beat & Square," 49.

92. "People Are Talking about . . . Alan Watts," *Vogue*, September 15, 1959, 140.

93. Nancy Wilson Ross, "The What and Why of Wabi and Sabi," *New York Times Book Review*, July 12, 1959, 4.

94. Peter Fingesten, "Beat and Buddhist," *Christian Century*, February 25, 1959, 226–227.

95. Alfred G. Aronowitz, "The Beat Generation," *New York Post*, March 19, 1959.

96. Barnaby Conrad, "Barefoot Boy with Dreams of Zen," *Saturday Review* May 2, 1959, 23–24.

97. "Beat Mystics," 56.

98. "Lions & Cubs," *Time*, September 14, 1962, 106.

99. Kerouac especially seemed to exhibit this "lack of seriousness." As Ann Charters writes in her biography of the writer: Kerouac's "interest in Buddhism, alive and expanding in 1955 with Gary Snyder, had diminished in 1960 to the point where he implied he was sick of the subject" (*Kerouac*, 339).

Many commentators also share Charters's view that "Kerouac was . . . born a Catholic, raised a Catholic and died a Catholic. His interest in Buddhism was a discovery of different religious images for his fundamentally constant religious feelings. He always remained a believing Catholic" (*Kerouac*, 190). Kerouac's Catholicism was most evident in his 1961 book, *Big Sur*.

See also Tonkinson, *Big Sky Mind*, 27; and Fields, *How the Swans Came to the Lake*, 248.

100. Mahoney, "Prevalence of Zen," 313.

101. "Eager Exponent of Zen," 88A.

102. Ibid.

103. Ibid., 88C.

104. Ibid.

105. This is not to say that Watts remained content with the sexual mores of his day. In 1958, he published *Nature, Man, and Woman: A New Approach to Sexual Experience*, in which he promoted a more open attitude toward sex. But his views conformed to fairly conventional heterosexist notions on the subject ("nature, *man, and woman*," my emphasis), albeit with a Zen twist, and he himself lived within the acceptable bounds of marriage and family.

106. This characteristic of Beat Zen was positively received in some cases. Both Stephen Mahoney and Seymour Krim laud the lively way in which Kerouac's writing captures a Zen sensibility. But what is admired is the author's ability to *express*, rather than his capacity to *articulate*.

107. Except for love of the nation. Jack Kerouac especially embraced America and its impulse toward freedom.

108. Watts, *In My Own Way*, 309.

109. See "The Beat Way of Life," in *Zen and the Beat Way*, 15–25 (Boston: Tuttle, 1997).

110. Watts, *In My Own Way*, 267.

111. Monica Furlong, *Zen Effects: The Life of Alan Watts* (Boston: Houghton Mifflin, 1986), 160.

112. One can interpret this geographical shift in the writings of both Watts and Kerouac. Watts put it this way: "I acquired an interior compass which led me to the East through the West. . . . This interior compass eventually drew me across the Atlantic, first to New York, then to Chicago, and at last to California—at which destination I saw a fog-clouded horizon and knew that this was the end of the West" (*In My Own Way*, 25, 27).

Kerouac saw himself as traveling a similar path. In the *Dharma Bums*, Ray Smith travels from his home on the East Coast to the spiritual center of the West (California). Also, Japhy Ryder, "the number one Dharma Bum of them all," hails from the back-woods of Oregon. In many ways, California represents the perfect geographical compromise as it is situated between Europe (and the European-defined American East Coast) and Asia.

Hence, the Orient-Occident binary is complexified as American Zenists situate themselves in between. Although the power relations between Orient and Occident remain intact, the designations *East* and *West* become confused as the center of Orientalism's power shifts from Europe to the United States.

113. This passion was inherently fueled by a clear disillusionment with Western culture, evident in the writings of both Kerouac and Watts. In *The Dharma Bums*, Kerouac would make pointed reference to the leveling effects of America's mass consumerism (Japhy Ryder's well-known monologue at 97) and the "millions and millions of the One Eye [America's love of television]" (104). In the February 1960 issue of *Escapade*, he also examines the West's "bloody mad history"—the Crusades, Thirty Years' War, Napoleon, Bismarck, and on and on—and wonders if humans will learn their lesson.

Watts, too, shared these sentiments, and in many ways his criticism is more wide-spread. He saw in Buddhism a possible solution to Western society's psychological and ecological woes. Both Watts's and Kerouac's disillusionment is also coupled with a kind of nostalgia for the past. In Watts's articulation:

> In retrospect, I believe that I entered the ministry under the influence of a tendency which has become rather widespread—a tendency to seek refuge from the confusion of our times by giving in to a kind of nostalgia. In a world where all the traditions in which men have found security are crumbling, the mind seeks peace and sanity in an attempt to return to a former state of faith. It envies the inner calm and certitude of an earlier age, where men could put absolute and childlike trust in the authority of the Church, and in the ordered beauty of an ancient doctrine. (*In My Own Way*, 207)

Although Watts is discussing his relationship to Christianity in this passage, one wonders if his embrace of Zen Buddhism and Eastern spirituality is not informed by the same nostalgia. For both Watts and Kerouac, this nostalgia speaks of a loss of a spiritual framework that they attempt to fill through alternative means. Ultimately, their longing is displaced onto the newfound object of their affection (Zen) as they attempt to recuperate its originary title. This psychological profile has become an integral part of the Oriental Monk narrative and helps to explain its appeal.

To Watts's and Kerouac's credit, they both exhibit a degree of reflection on the matter. As discussed earlier, Watts would insist on the necessity of coming to terms with one's Christian background in "Beat Zen, Square Zen, and Zen." And in *The Dharma Bums*, Kerouac would have Japhy Ryder exclaim to pal Ray (in a passage that was edited out of the book), "You old son of a bitch, you're going to end up asking for the Catholic rites on your death bed." However, in both cases, the gesture toward self-reflexivity is made but never fully realized.

114. Watts, *In My Own Way*, 119.

115. Tsuchiya had already planned for her photographs to be exhibited in the United States, "where enthusiasm for Zen's ego-smashing techniques ha[d] become a semi-religious phenomenon."

116. "Zensation," *Time*, February 23, 1959, 52.

117. "The Real Spirit of Zen?" *Newsweek*, September 21, 1959, 122.

118. Ibid.

119. These two explanations were not necessarily exclusive of one another; both were sometimes taken as contributing factors.

120. In *The Lotus and the Robot* (New York: Macmillan, 1961), Koestler also lodges a damning critique against Suzuki (sarcastically referring to him as "the Master"). Indeed, Suzuki serves as the authoritative figure of Zen from whose writings one could most notably detect "the stink of Zen." In response to the criticisms his book received ("Neither Lotus nor Robot," *Encounter*, February 1960), Koestler would launch his most inflammatory rebuke: "It is time for the Professor to shut up and for Western intelligentsia to recognize contemporary Zen as one of the 'sick' jokes, slightly gangrened, which are always fashionable in ages of anxiety" (58). Suzuki offered his rejoinder in a later edition ("A Reply," *Encounter*, October 1961, 55–58). He felt that most of Koestler's objections were due to "misinterpretations" of his views. Although most of Suzuki's essay was devoted to a generous rearticulation of his philosophical position, it did include its own retort: Koestler "unfortunately seems not to be cognisant of the 'the stink' radiating from his own 'Zen'" (58).

Koestler's views, as well as those of his critics, are much more complex than I am able to articulate here. For a cogent summary of *The Lotus and the Robot*, see the first half of Larry A. Fader's "Arthur Koestler's Critique of D. T. Suzuki's Interpretation of Zen," *Eastern Buddhist* 8, no. 2 (1980): 47–72. Bernard Faure also explores the "Suzuki/Koestler Controversy" in *Chan Insights and Oversights*, 67–72. Both Fader and Faure take different sides in the debate—a testimony that the controversy still continues.

121. Arthur Koestler, "The Decline of the East," *Esquire*, December 1960, 157.

122. Ibid.

123. Ibid.

124. Ibid., 156.

125. Ibid., 157.

126. Ibid., 158.

127. I should point out that Arthur Koestler writes as a European. He describes his own background as "born in Hungary, educated in Austria, the formative years spent in France, British by naturalization" (158). In this regard, he remained somewhat critical of the United States, which he viewed as an example of a culture involved in "change without a deep awareness of continuity with the past" (Koestler, "The Decline of the East," 158).

128. G. W. F. Hegel is the most notable figure of this tradition. According to the philosopher's teleological framework, Asian religions—Hinduism, Confucianism, Taoism, Buddhism, and Lamaism—represented the middle diremptive stage of mankind's philosophical and religious development. According to Hegel, these religious

movements emphasized a separation between consciousness and reality. In Hegel's scheme, Christianity embodied the reconciliation of consciousness with the material realm—the consummation of Spirit. See his *Lectures on the Philosophy of Religion*, ed. Peter C. Hodgson (Berkeley: University of California Press, 1988).

129. Koestler's book also drew criticisms from Christmas Humphreys and John Strachey.

130. Alan W. Watts, "Aftermath: The Decline of the East," *Esquire*, April 1961, 156.

131. Ibid.

132. Ibid.

133. Ibid.

134. Ibid.

135. Daisetz Teitaro Suzuki, *Zen and Japanese Culture*, 2nd ed. (New York: Pantheon, 1959), 346.

136. China also entered into American Zen discourse in the most oblique way. Zen (or Ch'an) originated in China, and commentators such as Watts emphasized Zen's interconnectedness with Chinese philosophy. The same was true for Suzuki. Although he felt Zen reached its most paradigmatic expression in Japanese culture, he also recognized the significance of its Chinese roots. As William Sargeant relates:

> The important point that Dr. Suzuki makes is that Zen is a peculiarly Chinese contribution to mysticism, and would probably never have existed if the non-speculative and practical Chinese mind had not evolved it. And though the cult has since died out in China, it still retains its Chinese flavor. ("Profiles," 46)

Hence, Americans' interest in Zen could also be viewed as a "preservative" not only of the rich spiritual heritage of Japan but also of China. This seemed especially pertinent since China had gone the way of Communism.

During the 1950s Cold War, the United States distinguished itself from Communist nations such as China by emphasizing its democratic impulse toward religious expression. If Zen had not "died out," it would have eventually been eradicated (as in the case of Tibetan Buddhism, which was also popularly featured). In a paternalistic gesture, America would remember what China wished to forget.

137. Fields, *How the Swans Came to the Lake*, 196.

138. Ibid., 215.

139. Watts was also asked to speak at one of the "large-scale seminars" sponsored by the Buddhist Churches of America (BCA) in 1952. The seminars were noteworthy in that they represented an ecumenical approach to Buddhism. They included not only speakers from the BCA's Jodo Shin sect but also Dr. Haridas Chaudhuri, who spoke on Indian philosophy, and Watts, who spoke on Buddhism and psychology. See *Buddhist Churches of America: 75 year History, 1899–1972*, vol. 1 (Chicago: Nobart, 1974), 96–97, 239–240.

140. This is a photo taken by Francis Haar at Diamond Sangha Kokoan, Honolulu, in 1964. I find it particularly revealing not only because of the positioning of Miss Okamura but also because of the other individuals as well. Suzuki is centrally located underneath the icon of the Buddha. On Suzuki's right are Tai Shimano and Robert Aitken.

Shimano was a Japanese monk who trained under Shaku Soyen and later helped establish a Zen Buddhist community in New York (along with Hakuun Yasutani). Aitken became the roshi of the Diamond Sangha in Maui, as well as a well-known popular writer on matters Zen. Together, they signify the extent of Suzuki's influence during his lifetime (in Japan and the United States). They also represent Zen's eventual institutionalization in America—from Hawaii to New York.

141. Sargeant, "Profiles," 38.

142. The internment of Japanese Americans during the Second World War is most likely another factor that contributed to Sargeant's apologetic tone. More than 100,000 persons of Japanese ancestry were forced to evacuate their homes on the West Coast of the United States. The mass evacuation order was revoked in December 1944, and no evidence of espionage or sabotage by Japanese Americans was ever found.

It is unknown whether Okamura's family had been interned during the war. In any case, she and her family were probably not excluded from the extreme racial prejudice toward Japanese Americans during this period. See Chan, *Asian Americans*, 121–142; and Ronald Takaki, *Strangers from a Different Shore: A History of Asian Americans* (New York: Penguin, 1989), 379–405.

143. Women played a significant role in cultivating a better understanding of Zen in the United States during the late 1950s. I have already mentioned two: Ruth Fuller Sasaki and Nancy Wilson Ross. Sasaki tirelessly worked to translate Buddhist scriptures and maintained the subtemple she established in Daitokuji. Nancy Wilson Ross served as an important commentator on Buddhism and wrote for a variety of publications, including *Vogue*. She also published the earliest English anthology on Zen, *The World of Zen: An East-West Anthology* (New York: Random House, 1960).

Elizabeth Gray Vining, who had tutored Prince Akihito in the postwar years, chronicled her life with the Japanese royal family in the best seller *Windows for a Crown Prince* (1952). In her follow-up, *Return to Japan* (1960), she details her encounter with tea ceremony and Zen meditation in "The Search for the Ox." Suzuki served as her guide during this time.

Although each of these women helped build a cultural bridge between East and West, their contributions are seldom recognized (except perhaps for Sasaki, who worked more within institutional bounds). Like Japanese Americans, they were viewed as assisting the larger movement and were secondary figures at best.

144. Sargeant, "Profiles," 68.

145. The division of a religion into sects is based on a denominational model of religious affiliation developed in Europe and the United States. This is not to say that Japanese Buddhists make no distinctions between different schools of Buddhism, but the separation does not allow one to consider the permeability and interchange that takes place between these different schools.

146. Sargeant, "Profiles," 86.

147. "Buddhism in America," *Time*, October 26, 1962, 60.

148. Sargeant, "Profiles," 86.

149. See Homi K. Bhabha, "Of Mimicry and Man: The Ambivalence of Colonial Discourse," in *The Location of Culture*, 85–92 (New York: Routledge, 1994). Bhabha's

articulation of the "mimic man" is most appropriate in discussing Japanese American attempts at assimilation. According to Bhabha, the mimic man "is the effect of a flawed colonial mimesis, in which to be Anglicized is *emphatically* not to be English" (87). In the case of Japanese American Buddhists, to be Americanized is *emphatically* not to be American; this is what is implied in the *Time* report's description. The Japanese American Buddhist becomes "*almost the same but not quite*" (89). She or he, in essence, is a failed copy. As Bhabha goes on to point out what this really means in racial and cultural terms is that she or he is "*almost the same but not white*" (and Christian, I might add).

Bhabha's model of mimicry serves as an excellent way to unearth and evaluate the strategies of Japanese American Buddhists, whose religious presentation appears to be simply a flawed mimesis. As the theorist insightfully uncovers, a more ambivalent reading is certainly called for.

150. An interesting example of the throwback strategy can be found in Kerouac's *Dharma Bums*. In a scene with Japhy, narrator Ray Smith describes: "Strangely Japhy wasn't interested in the Buddhism of San Francisco Chinatown because it was traditional Buddhism, not the Zen intellectual artistic Buddhism he loved—but I was trying to make him see that everything was the same" (113). Although Ray's description emphasizes the youths' assimilated nature and appearance, their faith is seen as "traditional" in Japhy's eyes. However, this paradox is easily overcome. For Japhy, these Chinese Americans have not escaped their racial past. Although Asian Americans have reclothed and redefined their religious faith in American terms, their interest and enthusiasm remain essentially Chinese. For an insightful analysis of the complex negotiation between Asian ethnic and white convert Buddhism that took place during this period, see Michael K. Masatsugu, "'Beyond This World of Transiency and Impermanence': Japanese Americans, Dharma Bums, and the Making of American Buddhism in the Early Cold War Years," *Pacific Historical Review* 77, no. 3 (2008): 423–451.

151. Okamura did commit to paper an account of her close relationship with Suzuki ("Wondrous Activity," in *A Zen Life*, ed. Abe, 160–172). More than reminiscence, it reveals dimensions of Suzuki's personality often unknown to more authoritative commentators and frames these slices in Okamura's own Buddhist perspective. She is also given new acknowledgment and voice in Ellen Pearlman's piece, "My Lunch with Mihoko," in *American Buddhism as a Way of Life*, ed. Gary Storhoff and John Whalen-Bridge, 57–67 (Albany: State University of New York Press, 2010) and Michael Goldman's 2006 documentary, *A Zen Life – D.T. Suzuki*.

152. Watts, "The 'Mind-less' Scholar," in *A Zen Life*, ed. Abe, 192.

153. Roland Barthes, *Mythologies*, trans. Annette Lavers (New York: Hill and Wang, 1972), 109.

154. Ibid., 108.

3 HYPERREAL SAMADHI

1. Although Mahesh's practice and philosophy were greatly informed by Hinduism, he continually stressed that TM did not require its adherents to shift their spiritual

beliefs; it was not a religion. Many of his followers found the technique attractive for just this reason. Despite this self-definition, pieces on the guru continued to be published in the Religion section of periodicals and newspapers. The American legal system would later consolidate this view; in 1976, both religious fundamentalists and civil libertarians brought about a federal suit challenging the constitutionality of Transcendental Meditation classes being taught in New Jersey schools. A federal district court judge in Newark subsequently barred the teaching of such classes, designating TM as a religious practice whose instruction violated the doctrine of the separation of church and state.

2. Barry Lefferts, "Chief Guru of the Western World," *New York Times Magazine*, December 17, 1967, 44–45, 48, 50, 52, 54, 57–58, statistic from 45.

3. Henry Idema III, *Before Our Time: A Theory of the Sixties* (Lanham, MD: University Press of America, 1996), 118.

4. "Yogi Speaks Here on Peace Teachings," *New York Times*, January 20, 1968, 14.

5. A fifth full-length article appeared in *Ebony*, a periodical targeted to a Black American audience. I chose not to include this article because it speaks to a particular demographic with specific assumptions and issues; I feel that the relationship between Asian religions and African Americans in the United States is deserving of its own study. See Era Bell Thompson, "Meditation Can Solve Race Problem," *Ebony*, May 1, 1968, 78–80, 82–84, 86–88. For a compelling introduction to the interaction between African Americans and Asian culture, see Vijay Prashad, *Everybody was Kung Fu Fighting: Afro-Asian Connections and the Myth of Cultural Purity* (Boston: Beacon Press, 2001).

6. Harold R. Isaacs, *Scratches on Our Minds: American Views of China and India* (1958. Reprint, White Plains, NY: M. E. Sharpe, 1990), xxxviii.

7. Unfortunately, video footage of Mahesh's guest appearance no longer exists. Only a couple of stills from the broadcast remain.

8. Here, I set up a dichotomy between the media of television and print. However, the two are much more mutually defined. As Meyrowitz elaborates, different media often operate in concert. As television emerged as the dominant form of mass communication, print media "emulate[d] the type and form of information that television provide[d]." Meyrowitz asserts that the immediacy of television established a "presumption of intimacy" on which print journalism capitalized. He notes: "Ironically, in *following* electronic media's pursuit of intimacy, print media often appear to *lead*. For the more private (and less regulated) nature of print forums allows books and magazines to reveal deeper back region behaviors."

"Back region behaviors" are spontaneous and informal and often betray the underlying feelings and emotions of the social actors involved. They represent more "private" moments of an individual's life. Television interviews with Mahesh, in which his everyday life and personal background were not discussed, fueled interest in such details that, at the time, magazines provided. Inversely, magazine and newspaper reports prompted an interest in the more immediate experience of the guru's "onstage" television appearance. See Joshua Meyrowitz, *No Sense of Place: The Impact of Electronic Media on Social Behavior* (Oxford: Oxford University Press, 1985), quotation from 177.

9. Here, I should stress that I am talking about the view of the popular media. Mahesh did write *The Science of Being and Art of Living* (1963), as well as *On the*

Bhagavad-Gita. A New Translation and Commentary, Chapters 1–6 (1967), before this time. Popular commentators rarely mention these works.

10. See "Yogi Speaks Here on Peace Teachings"; Paul Hoffman, "36,000 Hear Guru Urge Meditation," *New York Times*, January 22, 1968, 24; and "Preacher of Peace," *New York Times*, January 22, 1968, 24.

11. See "Yogi Confers with Thant—to Aid 'Permanent Peace,'" *New York Times*, January 21, 1968, 60.

12. This view was not commonly held by Western reporters, who painted Mahesh as more concerned with pleasing his Western audience than with the plight of the native population.

13. Paul Horn, "A Visit with India's High-Powered New Prophet," *Look*, February 6, 1968, 66.

14. Ibid., 65.

15. Ibid.

16. Ibid., 64.

17. One of the requirements to become an initiate of SIMS was that the individual must not have taken "hallucinatory drugs for 15 days prior to personal instruction in the technique" (Hedgepeth, "The Non-Drug Turn-on Hits Campus," 71). Other reports also mention this fact. The antidrug dimension of TM was probably the one feature that an older, more conservative adult audience could applaud. Drug usage among the nation's young was a top concern of parents during this time. See the *Time* issue "Drugs and the Young," September 26, 1968, 68–70, 72–74, 78.

18. The most obvious example here is Mahatma Gandhi, whose political and spiritual mission was primarily aimed at fellow South Asians. For Westerners, he also dressed the part, as he abandoned Western clothing for a more ascetic look.

19. Lewis H. Lapham, "There Once Was a Guru from Rishikesh, Part 1," *Saturday Evening Post*, May 4, 1968, 26.

20. Ibid., 29.

21. Lapham does eventually call into question O'Shea's spiritual journey in part 2 of the series ("There Once Was a Guru from Rishikesh, Part 2," *Saturday Evening Post*, May 18, 1968, 30), but the visual image of the wandering seeker in part 1 does not betray any such folly.

22. The caption does reveal: "John Lennon referred to the Beatles' photographs and records as diaries of their developing consciousness" (Lapham, "Part 2," 30).

23. Ibid., 31.

24. Ibid.

25. Ibid., 32.

26. Ibid., 33.

27. Ibid., 28.

28. Instances of verbal irony, according to Seymour Chatman, usually involve an *ironist* and a *target* (or an object of irony). "The ironist intends that somebody (though not necessarily the target) grasp the disparity between the words she utters and the underlying reality that she wishes to convey." In accounts of Mahesh, the reporter (ironist) cleverly and critically comments on the Maharishi and/or his followers (target)

in this indirect manner. Ironists need not be entirely opposed to the phenomenon at hand; they can be sympathetic to the selected target. However, the distance that the implied author maintains from the target lends ironic accounts their critical edge. See Seymour Chatman, *Reading Narrative Fiction* (New York: Macmillan, 1993), 187–188; and Chatman, *Story and Discourse* (Ithaca, NY: Cornell University Press, 1978), 156, 229.

29. Loudon Wainwright, "Invitation to Instant Bliss," *Life*, November 10, 1967, 26.

30. Ibid.

31. Ibid.

32. "Soothsayer for Everyman," *Time*, October 20, 1967, 86.

33. "The Guru," *Newsweek*, December 18, 1967, 67.

34. William Brandt notes: "When one is ironic about a subject, one refuses to assent to the usual view of it, and at the same time one does not flatly condemn the usual view." Such an ironic posture is useful especially in the genre of news magazines, where reporters are usually compelled to sensationalize information yet still maintain a semblance of reportorial objectivity. See William J. Brandt, *The Rhetoric of Argumentation* (Indianapolis, IN: Bobbs-Merrill, 1970), 157.

35. As Brandt and other rhetorical theorists maintain: "We are aware of the disparity [between what is said and what the author really thinks] either by reason of what we know of the speaker or by the context." See Brandt, *Rhetoric of Argumentation*, 157.

36. "Soothsayer for Everyman," *Time*, October 20, 1967, 86.

37. Harriet Van Horne, *New York Post*, March 1968.

38. Brandt, *Rhetoric of Argumentation*, 156–158, 283.

39. "Year of the Guru," *Life*, February 9, 1968, 54.

40. Arnold M. Auerbach, "When West Goes East," *New York Times*, December 17, 1967.

41. This is not to say that Auerbach sympathized with Mahesh and viewed him as a genuine spiritual figure. It is the fictional guru, fashioned somewhat according to the Oriental Monk icon, that the commentator envisions and deploys to make his larger criticism aimed at Mahesh's privileged followers.

42. Lefferts, "Chief Guru of the Western World," 50.

43. Ibid., 48.

44. Ibid., 44.

45. Ibid., 48.

46. Ibid., 50.

47. Ibid., 57.

48. Ibid.

49. The article does not proclaim such deceit outright. But the ambiguous and contradictory way it presents Mahesh and his movement certainly raises such doubts in the reader's mind. Such ambiguity is the hallmark of ironic accounts.

50. Lapham, "Part 2," 32.

51. Ibid., 33. In his piece, there is also a dimension of self-irony along the same lines, which can be discerned in the article's conclusion:

I still remembered them smiling at me as I turned away toward the ferry and the passage across the Ganges. From the opposite shore, I saw them all again, at a distance and for the last time. By a trick of the weather on that sudden, shifting day, it was raining on my side of the river, but they remained in the clear sunlight. I saw them as small bright figures, sitting in a circle on the stony beach against a background of immense trees. I thought I could see the light reflecting from the Maharishi's white robe and I knew they had gathered to listen to Donovan sing. (88)

52. Chatman notes that irony relies on a "secret communication" between ironist and audience. See *Story and Discourse*, 156.

53. Magazine publications were driven not by circulation numbers but rather by their advertising constituency. In response, magazines sought to appeal to potential consumers of their advertisers' goods and viewed adults, age thirty or older, as their most promising market.

In the late 1960s, commercial sponsors shifted their advertising dollars to specialty magazines that catered to discrete markets (e.g., *Field and Stream*, *Car and Driver*). Even though these general-interest periodicals still maintained their popularity and a fairly wide readership, *Look*, *Life*, and the *Saturday Evening Post* suffered eventual demise. See Don R. Pember, *Mass Media in America*, 3rd ed. (Chicago: Science Research Associates, 1981), 90–91; and David Abrahamson, *Magazine-Made America: The Cultural Transformation of the Postwar Periodical* (Cresskill, NJ: Hampton, 1996).

54. Hayden White, *Tropics of Discourse: Essays in Cultural Criticism* (Baltimore: Johns Hopkins University Press, 1978), 73–74.

55. Ernest Dunbar, "Campus Mood, Spring, '68," *Look*, April 2, 1968, 26.

56. "The Urug and the Grungey," *Newsweek*, December 4, 1967, 54.

57. Ibid.

58. Ibid. Arthur Marwick, in his sweeping cultural overview of the sixties, heralds McLuhan as one of the decade's intellectual "gurus," who was "undoubtedly a central figure in some of the key beliefs of the sixties" and its "post-literature culture." Indeed, McLuhan's 1964 publication, *Understanding Media*, which focused on the impact of new media and its pervasive influence, as well as its liberatory potential, had a tremendous impact. Slogans that emerged from his work, such as "the medium is the message," and the concept of the "global village" seemed to resonate with an American popular audience, especially its younger members. See Arthur Marwick, *The Sixties: Cultural Revolution in Britain, France, Italy, and the United States, c. 1958–c.1974* (Oxford: Oxford University Press, 1998), quotation from 309; and Kurt Von Meier, "Love Mysticism, and the Hippies," *Vogue*, November 15, 1967, 86.

59. "The Urug and the Grungey," 54.

60. An American audience certainly feared the truth of John Lennon's controversial statement; the Beatles may *actually* be more popular than Jesus.

61. Lapham, "Part 1," 25.

62. Hedgepeth, "The Non-Drug Turn-on Hits Campus," 68–69.

63. As one reverent account, which relates the media frenzy surrounding Mahesh's 1968 visit to New York, comments:

If all this sounds like "show biz" and rather commercial, it really shouldn't. That is how things are done in New York. The town is quick on its feet, particularly if you use "established channels." One of Maharishi's means of success has been his use of modern means of communications: airplanes, television interviews, wireless photographs, a readiness to answer the repetitive questions of press agency interviewers.

The piece interestingly maintains that the unique attitude toward the media hype that Mahesh's Felt Forum audience held allowed them to hear the guru in a way others could not. "Immunized by television commercials and the oratory of politicians, the audience was quite prepared not to hold the hyperbole of advance publicity against the diminutive, quietly smiling, white-robed speaker." True or not, the reporter's assertion does suggest a high comfort level with the new styles of communication that the Maharishi's movement utilized and embraced. See John C. Newhouse, "New York Is Ready," in *Maharishi, the Guru; An International Symposium*, ed. Martin Ebon, 12–20 (New York: New American Library, 1968), quotations from 13, 15.

64. White, *Tropics of Discourse*, 184. White speaks of metaphor in this manner as part of his analysis of the "noble savage." He demonstrates how this particular figure was used to express the ambivalent views that the bourgeoisie held toward aristocratic nobility in the eighteenth century.

65. For an interesting examination of these circuits, as well as the function of celebrity in contemporary society, see P. David Marshall, *Celebrity and Power, Fame in Contemporary Culture* (Minneapolis: University of Minnesota Press, 1997).

66. Said, *Orientalism* (New York: Vintage, 1979), 99. Here, Said generalizes upon the view of nineteenth century, "Darwinian anthropologists and phrenologists."

67. The mobility of the pupil is also implicated in the scheme. For instance, Watts and Kerouac never leave the West, whereas the Beatles and Mia Farrow travel to the Maharishi's retreat in Rishikesh, India. This pilgrimage east does not, in itself, degrade the spirituality of the adherents. (In fact, it is an essential element of the Monk narrative.) However, the celebrities' ease of travel, as well as the haphazard nature in which they approach the journey (as holiday), calls into question the legitimacy of their spiritual commitment.

68. Arthur J. Dommen, "India Offers Plenty for Meditation," *Los Angeles Times*, September 10, 1967, J1.

69. Lapham, "Part 2," 88.

70. Ernest Dunbar, "India," *Look*, March 19, 1968, 31–37, quotation from 31.

71. Kipling's famous phrase.

72. Said, *Orientalism*, 8.

73. *Samadhi* is a Hindu term that denotes a "meditative trance in which the highest truth is experienced." This definition is taken from Raymond B. William, ed., *A Sacred Thread: Modern Transmission of Hindu Traditions in India and Abroad* (Chambersburg, PA: Anima, 1992), 303.

74. See Gerald Clarke and Anne Hopkins, "The TM Craze: Forty Minutes to Bliss," *Time*, October 13, 1975, 70–74.

75. John Leland and Carla Power, "Deepak's Instant Karma," *Newsweek*, October 20, 1997, 53.

76. David Van Biema, "Emperor of the Soul," *Time*, June 24, 1996, 64–68.

77. Chopra, along with two coauthors, published an article that touted a "glowing assessment" of Ayur-Veda in the *Journal of the American Medical Association* in 1991. However, the editors of *JAMA* soon discovered the authors' link to the commercial venture and, in a piece commissioned for the publication, charged Chopra's findings as "misrepresentative." Chopra countered with a $194 million libel suit against the journal that was later dropped. Because of the bad publicity generated from incident, Mahesh encouraged Chopra to "stop writing books and doing workshops," and the two parted ways. See Van Biema, "Emperor of the Soul," 67; Chip Brown, "Deepak Chopra Has a Cold," *Esquire*, October 1995, 123; Robert Barnett and Cathy Sears, "JAMA Gets into an Indian Herbal Jam," *Science* 254, no. 29 (1991): 188–189; and Andrew A. Skolnick, "Maharishi Ayur-Veda: Guru's Marketing Scheme Promises the World Eternal 'Perfect Health,'" *JAMA* 266, no. 13 (1991): 1741–1746.

78. Leland and Power, "Deepak's Instant Karma," 54.

79. Vijay Prashad offers a trenchant critique of Chopra in *The Karma of Brown Folk* (Minneapolis: University of Minnesota, 2000). Prashad historically situates the New Age figure within a tradition of "sly babas" that includes Mahesh. Indeed, he denigrates Chopra and Mahesh as "gurus of green," who capitalize on Orientalized notions of the Indian as "a passive character absorbed in the pursuit of pleasure and success without a developed social consciousness, one who embodies the script of U.S. Orientalism from its dawn to its yawn" (68).

80. "Help Yourself," *Time*, June 14, 1999, 206. This edition of *Time* was the fifth in a series of special issues, "Heroes and Icons." Although Bill Wilson, the founder of Alcoholics Anonymous, was selected for the honor as one of the hundred "most influential people of the century," Chopra was featured in the subgroup of four gurus of the self-help movement, "who taught us to rely on ourselves—to heal both body and mind." (The other three were Betty Ford, Norman Vincent Peale, and Andrew Weil.)

4 THE MONK GOES HOLLYWOOD

1. See Wade Clark Roof, *A Generation of Seekers: The Spiritual Journeys of the Baby Boom Generation* (San Francisco: HarperCollins, 1993).

2. This pacifist philosophy, as well as the spiritual nature of the martial arts practice of kung fu, was also communicated by the way in which the program's more violent moments are portrayed. These slow-motion scenes were presumably meant to emphasize the wages of brute force and highlight Caine's artful and disciplined method.

3. Gary Deeb, "You Can't Teach the Golden Rule with a Punch in the Nose," *Chicago Tribune* October 1, 1973, 13.

4. "Kicking with Kung Fu," *Time*, January 27, 1975, 70.

5. "'Kung Fu' and 'Sanford' Praised as Aids in Teaching of Reading," *New York Times* June 24, 1973, 46.

6. "The Kung Fu Craze," *Newsweek* May 7, 1973, 76.

7. "Ah, So! A New American Hero at Last! (Kung Fu and All That)," *Esquire*, August 1973 cover.

8. Richard Dyer, *The Matter of Images: Essays on Representations* (New York: Routledge, 1993), 93–94.

9. Review of *Kung Fu*, *Variety*, September 18, 1974.

10. Deeb, "You Can't Teach the Golden Rule," 13.

11. Cyclops, "Kung Foolishness," *Newsweek*, February 12, 1973, 51.

12. Stephen Farber, "Kids! Now You Can Chop Up Your Old Comic-Book Heroes with Your Bare Hands!" *Esquire*, August 1973, 74.

13. Frank Chin, "*Kung Fu* Is Unfair to Chinese," *New York Times*, March 24, 1974, 137. The "talking chimpanzee" to which Chin is referring is Cornelius, one of the central characters in a series of movies popular at the time, *Planet of the Apes* (1968).

14. Ibid.

15. Ed Spielman, "I'm Proud to Have Created 'Kung Fu,'" *New York Times*, April 14, 1974, 109.

16. Ibid.

17. Ibid.

18. Ibid.

19. Chin, "*Kung Fu* Is Unfair to Chinese, 137."

20. S. Y. Pon, Letter, *TV Guide*, June 30, 1973, A-2.

21. Katie San, Letter, *New York Times*, June 17, 1973, 19.

22. Benjamin J. Stein, "Kung Fu," *National Review*, March 1, 1974, 265.

23. Deeb, "You Can't Teach the Golden Rule," 13.

24. Robert S. Ellwood, *The Sixties Spiritual Awakening* (New Brunswick, NJ: Rutgers University Press, 1974), 247–325.

25. Ibid., 249.

26. Ibid., 290. The "internal colonialism" paradigm acted as the philosophical model for action among many of these groups. The paradigm linked imperialist efforts abroad (in Asia, Africa, and Latin America) to the continued subjugation of Asian Americans, Blacks, and Chicanos in the United States and united these groups under the banner of the Third World—the continuing source of exploited labor in a capitalist-dominated world economy. Liberation therefore necessarily involved "self-determination" or autonomy from the state and its sanctioned institutions. See William Wei, *The Asian American Movement* (Philadelphia: Temple University Press, 1993), 41–42.

27. Warner Home Video has released the episodes from all three seasons of *Kung Fu*, including the made-for-television movie, on DVD.

28. Perhaps the best known Chinese character to appear in a television Western is Hop Sing, the loyal domestic of the Cartwright family on *Bonanza* (1959–1973). Darrell Hamamoto offers a survey of these characters in his chapter "Asians in the American West," in *Monitored Peril: Asian Americans and the Politics of TV Representation*, 32–63 (Minneapolis: University of Minnesota Press, 1994).

29. Herbie J. Pilato, *The Kung Fu Book of Caine* (Boston: Charles E. Tuttle, 1993), 9.

30. Ibid., 8.

31. For a discussion of stereotypes that haunt American portrayals of Asians and Asian Americans, see Elaine H. Kim, "Images of Asians in Anglo-American Literature," in *Asian American Literature: An Introduction to the Writings and Their Social Context*, 3–22 (Philadelphia: Temple University Press, 1982); and Robert G. Lee, *Orientals: Asian Americans in Popular Culture* (Philadelphia: Temple University Press, 1999).

32. In "The Spirit Helper," this solution is legitimated through a masculinist discourse. Only after Nashebo decides to follow Caine's advice and allow Pike to live is he declared "a man."

33. Pilato, *The Kung Fu Book of Caine*, 94.

34. Ibid., 70.

35. Ibid., 70–71.

36. I am aware that spiritual healing need not be divorced from social justice. But in the case of *Kung Fu*, the relationship between spiritual healing and social justice takes place *only* on the individual level, that is, posits individual healing as the source of social justice, instead of vice versa.

37. Pilato, *The Kung Fu Book of Caine*, 63.

38. Aljean Harmetz, "How Do You Pick a Winner in Hollywood? You Don't," *New York Times*, April 29, 1973.

39. Ibid.

40. Rita Parks, *The Western Hero in Film and Television: Mass Media Mythology* (Ann Arbor, MI: UMI Research Press, 1982), 152.

41. Identification is a complex term that has its own history of definition in cinema studies. Psychoanalytic film theorist Christian Metz is perhaps best known for articulating this psychic phenomenon, linking it to the mirror stage and the Oedipal narrative. According to Metz's framework, "primary cinematic identification" is squarely located between the spectator and the apparatus (i.e., camera and/or projector), and "secondary cinematic identification" is constituted by identifications with characters. See *The Imaginary Signifier: Psychoanalysis and the Cinema* trans. Celia Britton et al. (Bloomington: Indiana University Press, 1982.)

My use of primary and ancillary identifications here obviously differs from Metz. What he takes for secondary cinematic identification is the representational field in which the set of identifications of which I speak occur. Although his delineation is significant in understanding the epistemology of spectatorship, my use of these terms is meant to reveal the way in which a particular narrative with a particular set of characters operates and how that operation is informed both intratextually (within the story itself) and intertextually (through the dynamics of casting).

42. David Carradine, *The Spirit of Shaolin* (Boston: Charles E. Tuttle, 1991), 18–19.

43. Kareem Abdul-Jabbar and Peter Knobler, *Giant Steps* (New York: Bantam, 1983), 188–189. See also Hamamoto, "Asians in the American West," 59–63.

44. Here described by Gerald Leider, television chief of Warner Brothers, who recommended Carradine to Jerry Thorpe. See Bill Davidson, "'Does Not the Pebble, Entering the Water, Begin Fresh Journeys?'" *TV Guide*, January 26, 1974, 22.

45. Farber, "Kids!" 74.

46. Carradine, *The Spirit of Shaolin*, 13.

47. Davidson, "Does Not the Pebble," 22, 24.

48. Deeb, "You Can't Teach the Golden Rule," 13.

49. Tom Burke, "David Carradine, King of 'Kung Fu,'" *New York Times*, April 29, 1973, 141.

50. The exception to this is the flute, which Carradine explained grew out of the appreciation of *kung fu* as traditionally defined in Chinese culture as "the art of." As he explains: "A true martial artist must be well-rounded. Traditionally, the warrior should also be an artist. He should draw or paint, or make things with his hands, or play a musical instrument. This was my thinking when I introduced the bamboo flute into the series." But even this added accoutrement bore the actor's inflection; a silver concert flute was used as the model. See Carradine, *The Spirit of Shaolin*, 32–34.

51. Farber, "Kids!" 75.

52. Ibid, 76, 137.

53. Stein, "Kung Fu," 265, 273.

54. Lodged from within the conservative milieu of the *National Review*, Stein's review has an investment in unmasking the ideological interests at hand. However, whether it be through critiques such as Stein's (a representation of a competing dominant group) or ones similar to Chin's (mentioned earlier as a subaltern example), the show's hegemonic vision is further exposed and challenged.

55. Laura Mulvey, "Visual Pleasure and Narrative Cinema," *Screen* 16, no. 3 (1975).

56. Mulvey deals with the medium of film and not that of television. John Ellis argues that, when it comes to television, sound is a more significant aspect of reception than image due to the difference in format expectation and viewing environment. Although these differences certainly exist, Mulvey's work is still significant here, because through an extended interaction with a series, the viewer does garner visual impressions of character and scenery and links these to the show's overall narrative intent. Furthermore, Caine's long pauses and halting speech, as well the number of action scenes devoid of dialogue, draw the viewer to the visual text. See John Ellis, *Visible Fictions: Cinema, Television, Video* (New York: Routledge, 1982).

57. Mulvey, "Visual Pleasure," 838.

58. Pilato, *The Kung Fu Book of Caine*, 28.

59. The desexualization of Master Po and Master Kan should also be viewed as a resexualization. In his article examining the contemporary play and movie, *M Butterfly*, David L. Eng speaks of "racial castration" and "reverse fetishism" as a means by which Asian males are feminized (i.e., castrated) in order to maintain racist and heterosexist structures on which a colonial order depends. In Freudian terms, fetishism is reversed and involves a "blatant refusal to see on the body of an Asian male the penis that *is* clearly there for him to see" (346). See "Heterosexuality in the Face of Whiteness: Divided Belief in *M Butterfly*," in *Q&A: Queer in Asian America*, ed. David L. Eng and Alice Y. Hom, 333–365 (Philadelphia: Temple University Press, 1998); and David L. Eng, *Racial Castration: Managing Masculinity in Asian America* (Durham: Duke University Press, 2001).

60. This pivotal event can also be read along the lines of original sin. Caine (like Adam and also like Cain), through his moral transgression, is exiled from an idyllic

setting and is condemned to live out his existence in an arid and inhospitable land. His primary goal becomes reconciliation with the Father, which is represented through Caine's search for his patriarchal lineage in America, as well as his mission to maintain his spiritual beliefs passed down through his adopted Shaolin heritage.

61. Judith Butler, *The Psychic Life of Power* (Stanford, CA: Stanford University Press, 1997), 26. Here, Butler's explanation reiterates the theoretical framework of Melanie Klein.

62. Carradine, *The Spirit of Shaolin*, 25. The timing was perhaps less "synchronistic" than suggested. Although Nixon's landmark visit took place in 1972, the two nations had begun to edge toward renewed relations almost a year before.

63. Harold R. Isaacs comments on this lack of interest in China as a "nearly total severance" (212). See his *Scratches on Our Minds: American Views of China and India* (White Plains, NY: M. E. Sharpe, 1980).

64. Ibid., 218.

65. Ibid., 219.

66. Ibid., xx.

67. Donald S. Lopez Jr., *Prisoners of Shangri-La: Tibetan Buddhism and the West* (Chicago: Chicago University Press, 1998), 7. Shangri-La is often associated with Tibetan Buddhism and the contested kingdom of Lhasa, but as a notion that speaks of an imagined and imaginary repository of an ancient spiritual tradition in the East, it can be similarly applied to *Kung Fu*'s depiction of the Shaolin temple.

68. Pilato, *The Kung Fu Book of Caine*, 123.

69. Ibid., 140.

70. Ironically stated in David Henry Hwang's play, *M Butterfly* (New York: Plume, 1988), 17.

71. "Interview with David Carradine," *TNT.tv* (Series: *Kung Fu: The Legend Continues*). http://www.tnt-tv.com/action/kungfu/media/index.html (accessed June 19, 1999).

72. Pilato, *The Kung Fu Book of Caine*, 33–34.

73. In response, Carradine would confess: "Every once in a while, I would have to demonstrate a technique, but that's it." If the interaction began to border on actually physical combat, he would "see it coming and just walk away" (ibid., 35).

74. Ibid.

75. Carradine, *The Spirit of Shaolin*, 49.

76. Ibid., 51.

77. Ibid., 3.

78. In 2000, *Kung Fu: The Legend Continues* aired every weekday on the Turner Network (TNT).

79. Steve Curless, "David Carradine's Spiritual Legacy," *Sacramento Spirituality Examiner*, available at http://www.examiner.com/x-8637-Sacramento-Spirituality-Examiner~y2009m6d5-David-Carradines-spiritual-legacy.

80. Ellen Scordato, "David Carradine and the Lure of the East" at "One City: A Buddhist Blog for Everyone" on *Beliefnet*, available at http://blog.beliefnet.com/onecity/2009/06/david-carradine-and-the-lure-of-the-east.html.

5 CONCLUSION

1. Justin Chin, *Mongrel: Essays, Diatribes, and Pranks* (New York: St. Martin's, 1999), 113, 115.

2. See Marsha Kinder, *Playing with Power: In Movies, Television, and Video Games: From Muppet Babies to Teenage Mutant Ninja Turtles* (Berkeley: University of California Press, 1993).

3. This is not Americans' first engagement with the Dalai Lama and Tibetan culture. The encounter with Tibet was visually prefigured in James Hilton's novel *Lost Horizon* (1933) and Frank Capra's subsequent movie adaptation (1937). And the Dalai Lama's escape from the Chinese is prominently featured in 1950s news reports, including the April 23, 1951, *Life* cover story, "Flight of the Dalai Lama." While His Holiness was already positioned by the popular press as figurative resistance to Communism, the Dalai Lama did not achieve the iconic status he enjoys today.

4. See Edward Silver, "Finding a New Path," *Los Angeles Times*, April 11, 1995. This contingent has formally expanded into the Committee of 100 for Tibet. See its home page at http://www.c100tibet.org/Home.html.

5. An informal analysis of news coverage is revealing. A title word search on the *New York Times* database uncovers an interesting pattern. In the 1980s, the Dalai Lama receives the most coverage in 1989—the year he was granted the Nobel Peace Prize. Headlines drop in the early 1990s, until Richard Gere makes his much publicized statement of support at the 1993 Oscars. Since this time, the Dalai Lama has enjoyed regular coverage; his appeal remains constant throughout the decade and into the new millennium.

6. Silver, "Finding a New Path."

7. *New York Times*, March 19, 1997, C13-C14. See also Richard Bernstein, "Tibet is all set to enter Western consciousness via Hollywood," *New York Times*, March 27 1997, 13.

8. "The International Year of Tibet," *Tricycle: The Buddhist Review*, Fall 1991, 32.

Bibliography

Abdul-Jabbar, Kareem, and Peter Knobler. *Giant Steps.* New York: Bantam, 1983.

Abe, Masao, ed. *A Zen Life: D. T. Suzuki Remembered.* New York: Weatherhill, 1986.

Abrahamson, David. *Magazine-Made America, the Cultural Transformation of the Postwar Periodical.* Cresskill, NJ: Hampton, 1996.

Anderson, Benedict. *Imagined Communities.* New York: Verso, 1991.

Ang, Ien. *Living Room Wars: Rethinking Media Audiences for a Postmodern World.* London: Routledge, 1996.

Aron, Elaine, and Arthur Aron. *The Maharishi Effect: A Revolution through Meditation.* Walpole, NH: Stillpoint, 1986.

Banet-Weiser, Sarah. *Kids Rule! Nickelodeon and Consumer Citizenship, Console-ing Passions.* Durham, NC: Duke University Press, 2007.

Barthes, Roland. *Camera Lucida: Reflections on Photography.* Translated by Richard Howard. New York: Hill and Wang, 1981.

———. *Empire of Signs.* Translated by Richard Howard. New York: Noonday, 1983.

———. *The Fashion System.* Translated by Matthew Ward and Richard Howard. Berkeley: University of California Press, 1990.

———. *Mythologies.* Translated by Annette Lavers. New York: Hill and Wang, 1972.

———. *S/Z.* Translated by Richard Miller. New York: Noonday, 1991.

Bartholomeusz, Tessa. "Spiritual Wealth and Neo-Orientalism." *Journal of Ecumenical Studies* 35, no. 1 (1998): 19–32.

Baty, S. Paige. *American Monroe: The Making of a Body Politic.* Berkeley: University of California Press, 1995.

Baudrillard, Jean. *America*. Translated by Chris Turner. London: Verso, 1988.

———. *The Evil Demon of Images*. Sydney, Australia: Power Institute of Fine Arts, University of Sydney, 1987.

———. *For a Critique of the Political Economy of the Sign*. Translated by Charles Levin. St. Louis, MO: Telos, 1981.

———. *Paroxysm: Interviews with Philippe Petit*. Translated by Chris Turner. London: Verso, 1998.

———. *Simulacra and Simulation*. Translated by Sheila Faria Glaser. Ann Arbor: University of Michigan Press, 1999.

———. *The System of Objects*. Translated by James Benedict. New York: Verso, 1996.

———. *The Vital Illusion*. Translated by Julia Witwer. New York: Columbia University Press, 2000.

Belliappa, K. C. *The Image of India in English Fiction: Studies in Kipling, Myers, and Raja Rao*. Delhi, India: B.R. Publishing, 1991.

Berger, John. *Ways of Seeing*. New York: Penguin, 1977.

Bhabha, Homi K. *The Location of Culture*. New York: Routledge, 1994.

Bhullar, Avtar Singh. *India, Myth and Reality: Images of India in the Fiction by English Writers*. Delhi, India: Ajanta, 1985.

Bishop, Peter. *The Myth of Shangri-La: Tibet, Travel Writing, and the Western Creation of Sacred Landscape*. Berkeley: University of California Press, 1989.

Bodroghkozy, Aniko. *Groove Tube: Sixies Television and the Youth Rebellion, Console-Ing Passions*. Durham, NC: Duke University Press, 2001.

Brandt, William J. *The Rhetoric of Argumentation*. Indianapolis, IN: Bobbs-Merrill, 1970.

Brauer, Ralph. *The Horse, the Gun, and the Piece of Property: Changing Images of the TV Western*. Bowling Green, OH: Bowling Green University Popular Press, 1975.

Brennen, Bonnie, and Hanno Hardt. *Picturing the Past: Media, History and Photography*. Urbana: University of Illinois Press, 1999.

Buckley, Roger. *U.S.-Japan Alliance Diplomacy, 1945–1990*. Cambridge: Cambridge University Press, 1992.

Buscombe, Edward, and Roberta E. Pearson, eds. *Back in the Saddle Again: New Essays on the Western*. London: British Film Institute, 1998.

Butler, Judith. "Endangered/Endangering: Schematic Racism and White Paranoia." In *Reading Rodney King, Reading Urban Uprising*, edited by Robert Gooding-Williams, 15–22. New York: Routledge, 1993.

———. *The Psychic Life of Power*. Stanford, CA: Stanford University Press, 1997.

Carlebach, Michael L. *American Photojournalism Comes of Age*. Washington, DC: Smithsonian Institution Press, 1997.

———. *The Origins of Photojournalism in America*. Washington, DC: Smithsonian Institution Press, 1992.

Carradine, David. *The Spirit of Shaolin*. Boston: Charles E. Tuttle, 1991.

Carrette, Jeremy R., and Richard King. *Selling Spirituality: The Silent Takeover of Religion*. London: Routledge, 2005.

Chan, Jachinson. *Chinese American Masculinities: From Fu Manchu to Bruce Lee, Asian Americans*. New York: Garland, 2000.

Chan, Sucheng. *Asian Americans: An Interpretive History.* Boston: Twayne, 1991.

Charters, Ann. *Kerouac: A Biography.* New York: St. Martin's, 1973.

Chatman, Seymour. *Reading Narrative Fiction.* New York: Macmillan, 1993.

———. *Story and Discourse.* Ithaca, NY: Cornell University Press, 1978.

Chavez, Leo R. *Covering Immigration: Popular Images and the Politics of the Nation.* Berkeley: University of California Press, 2001.

———. *The Latino Threat: Constructing Immigrants, Citizens, and the Nation.* Stanford, CA: Stanford University Press, 2008.

Cheng, Anne Anlin. *The Melancholy of Race, Race and American Culture.* Oxford: Oxford University Press, 2001.

Chhaya, Mayank. *The Dalai Lama: Man, Monk, and Mystic.* New York: Doubleday, 2007.

Chidester, David. *Authentic Fakes: Religion and American Popular Culture.* Berkeley: University of California Press, 2005.

Chin, Frank. "Come All Ye Asian American Writers of the Real and the Fake." In *The Big Aiiieeeee! An Anthology of Chinese American and Japanese American Literature,* edited by Jeffery Paul Chan, 1–92. New York: Meridian, 1991.

Chin, Frank, and Jeffery Paul Chan. "Racist Love." In *Seeing through Shuck,* edited by Richard Kostelanetz, 65–79. New York: Ballantine, 1972.

Chin, Justin. *Mongrel: Essays, Diatribes, and Pranks.* New York: St. Martin's, 1999.

Chow, David, and Richard Spangler. *Kung Fu: History, Philosophy, and Technique.* Garden City, NY: Doubleday, 1977.

Clark, Lynn Schofield. *Religion, Media, and the Marketplace.* New Brunswick, NJ: Rutgers University Press, 2007.

Cox, Harvey Gallagher. *Turning East: The Promise and Peril of the New Orientalism.* New York: Simon and Schuster, 1977.

Debord, Guy. *The Society of Spectacle.* Translated by Donald Nicholson-Smith. New York: Zone, 1995.

Dodin, Thierry, and Heinz Rèather. *Imagining Tibet: Perceptions, Projections, & Fantasies.* Boston: Wisdom, 2001.

Donohue, John J. *Warrior Dreams: The Martial Arts and the American Imagination.* Westport, CT: Bergin & Garvey, 1994.

Doss, Erika Lee. *Looking at Life Magazine.* Washington, DC: Smithsonian Institution Press, 2001.

Douglas, George H. *The Smart Magazines: 50 Years of Literary Revelry and High Jinks at Vanity Fair, the New Yorker, Life, Esquire, and the Smart Set.* Hamden, CT: Archon, 1991.

Dower, John W. *War without Mercy: Race and Power in the Pacific War.* New York: Pantheon, 1986.

Dudziak, Mary L. *Cold War Civil Rights: Race and the Image of American Democracy, Politics and Society in Twentieth-Century America.* Princeton, NJ: Princeton University Press, 2000.

Dumoulin, Heinrich. *Zen Buddhism in the 20th Century.* Translated by Joseph S. O'Leary. New York: Weatherhill, 1992.

Dyer, Richard. *A Matter of Images: Essays on Representations.* New York: Routledge, 1993.

Ebon, Martin, ed. *Maharishi, the Guru; an International Symposium*. New York: New American Library, 1968.

Eco, Umberto. *Travels in Hyperreality: Essays*. Translated by William Weaver. San Diego, CA: Harcourt Brace Jovanovich, 1990.

Ellis, John. *Visible Fictions: Cinema, Television, Video*. New York: Routledge, 1982.

Ellwood, Robert S. *Alternative Altars: Unconventional and Eastern Spirituality in America*. Chicago: University of Chicago Press, 1979.

———. *Eastern Spirituality in America: Selected Writings, Sources of American Spirituality*. New York: Paulist, 1987.

———. *The Fifties Spiritual Marketplace: American Religion in a Decade of Conflict*. New Brunswick, NJ: Rutgers University Press, 1997.

———. *An Invitation to Japanese Civilization*. Belmont, CA: Wadsworth, 1980.

———. *Japanese Religion: A Cultural Perspective*. Englewood Cliffs, NJ: Prentice-Hall, 1985.

———. *Religious and Spiritual Groups in Modern America*. Englewood Cliffs, NJ: Prentice-Hall, 1988.

———. *The Sixties Spiritual Awakening: American Religion Moving from Modern to Postmodern*. New Brunswick, NJ: Rutgers University Press, 1994.

———, ed. *Zen in American Life and Letters*. Malibu, CA: Undena, 1987.

Elson, Robert T., Curtis Prendergast, and Geoffrey Colvin. *Time Inc.: The Intimate History of a Publishing Enterprise*. New York: Atheneum, 1968.

Eng, David L. "Heterosexuality in the Face of Whiteness: Divided Belief in *M. Butterfly*." In *Q&A: Queer in Asian America*, edited by David L. Eng and Alice Y. Hom, 333–365. Philadelphia: Temple University Press, 1998.

———. *Racial Castration: Managing Masculinity in Asian America*. Durham: Duke University Press, 2001.

Ewen, Stuart. *All Consuming Image: The Politics of Style in Contemporary Culture*. New York: Basic Books, 1988.

Fader, Larry A. "Arthur Koestler's Critique of D. T. Suzuki's Interpretation of Zen." *Eastern Buddhist* 8, no. 2 (1980): 47–72.

Faure, Bernard. *Chan Insights and Oversights: An Epistemological Critique of the Chan Tradition*. Princeton, NJ: Princeton University Press, 1993.

———. "The Kyoto School and Reverse Orientalism." In *Japan in Traditional and Postmodern Perspectives*, edited by Charles Wei-hsun Fu and Steven Heine, 245–281. Albany: State University of New York Press, 1995.

Fiebig-von Hase, Ragnhild, and Ursula Lehmkuhl. *Enemy Images in American History*. Providence, RI: Berghahn, 1997.

Fields, Rick. *How the Swans Came to the Lake: A Narrative History of Buddhism in America*. 3rd ed. Boston: Shambhala, 1992.

Fung, Richard. "Looking for My Penis: The Eroticized Asian in Gay Porn Video." In *How Do I Look? Queer and Film and Video*, edited by Bad Object Choices, 145–168. Seattle: Bay Press, 1991.

Furlong, Monica. *Zen Effects: The Life of Alan Watts*. Boston: Houghton Mifflin, 1986.

Galbraith, John Kenneth. *The Affluent Society*. Boston: Houghton-Mifflin, 1958.

Gane, Mike, ed. *Baudrillard Live: Selected Interviews*. London: Routledge, 1993.

Ginsburg, Faye D., Lila Abu-Lughod, and Brian Larkin, eds. *Media Worlds: Anthropology on New Terrain.* Berkeley, CA: University of California Press, 2002.

Gitlin, Todd. *The Sixties: Years of Hope, Days of Rage.* Toronto: Bantam, 1987.

Goldstein, Jonathan, Jerry Israel, and Hilary Conroy, eds. *America Views China: American Images of China Then and Now.* Bethlehem, PA: Lehigh University Press; London: Associated University Presses, 1991.

Goldstein, Melvyn C. "The United States, Tibet, and the Cold War." *Journal of Cold War Studies* 8, no. 3 (2006): 145.

Gramsci, Antonio. *Selections from Cultural Writings.* Translated by William Boelhower. Cambridge, MA: Harvard University Press, 1985.

———. *Selections from the Prison Notebooks.* Translated by Quintin Hoare and Geoffrey Nowell Smith. New York: International Publishers, 1971.

Greenberger, Allen J. *The British Image of India: A Study in the Literature of Imperialism 1880–1960.* Oxford: Oxford University Press, 1969.

Halberstam, David. *The Fifties.* New York: Villard, 1993.

Hamamoto, Darrell Y. *Monitored Peril: Asian Americans and the Politics of TV Representation.* Minneapolis: University of Minnesota Press, 1994.

Hammond, Phil, ed. *Cultural Difference, Media Memories: Anglo-American Images of Japan.* London: Cassell, 1997.

Hanke, Ken. *Charlie Chan at the Movies: History, Filmography, and Criticism.* Jefferson, NC: McFarland, 1989.

Harris, Michael D. *Colored Pictures: Race and Visual Representation.* Chapel Hill: University of North Carolina Press, 2003.

Heim, Michael. *The Metaphysics of Virtual Reality.* New York: Oxford University Press, 1993.

———. *Virtual Realism.* New York: Oxford University Press, 1998.

Heisig, James W., and John C. Maraldo, eds. *Rude Awakenings: Zen, the Kyoto School, & the Question of Nationalism.* Honolulu: University of Hawaii Press, 1994.

Hicks, Heather J. "Hoodoo Economics: White Men's Work and Black Men's Magic in Contemporary American Film." *Camera Obscura* 18, no. 2 (2003): 27.

Hodge, Bob, and David Tripp. *Children and Television: A Semiotic Approach.* Cambridge: Polity; Oxford: Basil Blackwell, 1986.

Hwang, David Henry. *M Butterfly.* New York: Plume, 1988.

Idema, Henry, III. *Before Our Time: A Theory of the Sixties.* Lanham, MD: University Press of America, 1996.

Inden, Ronald B. *Imagining India.* 1990. Reprint, Bloomington: Indiana University Press, 2000.

Iriye, Akira, and Warren I. Cohen. *The United States and Japan in the Postwar World.* Lexington: University of Kentucky Press, 1989.

Isaacs, Harold R. *Scratches on Our Minds: American Views of China and India.* 1958. Reprint, White Plains, NY: M. E. Sharpe, 1990.

Iwamura, Jane Naomi. "The Oriental Monk in American Popular Culture." In *Religion and Popular Culture in America,* edited by Bruce David Forbes and Jeffrey H. Mahan, 23-43 Berkeley: University of California Press, 2005.

Jackson, Carl T. *The Oriental Religions and American Thought: Nineteenth Century Explorations*. Westport, CT: Greenwood, 1981.

———. *Vedanta for the West: The Ramakrishna Movement in the United States*. Bloomington: Indiana University Press, 1994.

Jameson, Fredric. *Postmodernism, or, the Cultural Logic of Late Capitalism, Post-Contemporary Interventions*. Durham, NC: Duke University Press, 1991.

Jefferson, William. *The Story of the Maharishi*. New York: Pocket, 1976.

Jervis, John. *Transgressing the Modern: Explorations in the Western Experience of Otherness*. Oxford: Blackwell, 1999.

Jespersen, T. Christopher. *American Images of China, 1931–1949*. Stanford, CA: Stanford University Press, 1996.

Johnson, Sheila K. *The Japanese through American Eyes*. Stanford, CA: Stanford University Press, 1991.

Joshi, Khyati, *New Roots in America's Sacred Ground*. Brunswick, NJ: Rutgers University Press, 2006.

Kaiwar, Vasant, and Sucheta Mazumdar. *Antinomies of Modernity: Essays on Race, Orient, Nation*. Durham, NC: Duke University Press, 2003.

Kellner, Douglas. *Media Culture: Cultural Studies, Identity, and Politics between the Modern and the Postmodern*. London: Routledge, 1995.

———, ed. *Baudrillard: A Critical Reader*. Oxford: Blackwell, 1994.

Kerouac, Jack. *Big Sur*. New York: Farrar, Straus and Cudahy, 1962.

———. *The Dharma Bums*. New York: Penguin, 1976.

———. *Some of the Dharma*. New York: Viking, 1997.

Kim, Elaine H. *Asian American Literature: An Introduction to the Writings and Their Social Context*. Philadelphia: Temple University Press, 1982.

Kim, Jung Ha. "Spiritual Buffet: The Changing Diet of America." In *Off the Menu: Asian and Asian North American Women's Religion and Theology*, edited by Rita Nakashima Brock, Jung Ha Kim, Kwok Pui-Lan, and Seug Ai Yang, 69–86. Louisville, KY: Westminster John Knox Press, 2007.

Kim, Thomas W. "Being Modern: The Circulation of Oriental Objects." *American Quarterly* 58, no. 2 (2006): 379-406.

Kinder, Marsha. *Playing with Power in Movies, Television, and Video Games: From Muppet Babies to Teenage Mutant Ninja Turtles*. Berkeley: University of California Press, 1991.

King, Richard. *Orientalism and Religion: Postcolonial Theory, India and "the Mystic East."* London: Routledge, 1999.

Klein, Christina. *Cold War Orientalism: Asia in the Middlebrow Imagination, 1945–1961*. Berkeley: University of California Press, 2003.

Kleinberg-Levin, David Michael. *Modernity and the Hegemony of Vision*. Berkeley: University of California Press, 1993.

Kline, Stephen. *Out of the Garden: Toys, TV, and Children's Culture in the Age of Marketing*. London: Verso, 1993.

Kolko, Beth E., Lisa Nakamura, and Gilbert B. Rodman, eds. *Race in Cyberspace*. New York: Routledge, 2000.

Koestler, Arthur. *The Lotus and the Robot*. New York: Macmillan, 1961.

Kondo, Dorinne K. *About Face: Performing Race in Fashion and Theater*. New York: Routledge, 1997.

Kozol, Wendy. *Life's America: Family and Nation in Postwar Photojournalism*. Philadelphia: Temple University Press, 1994.

LaFleur, William R. "Between America and Japan: The Case of Daisetsu Teitaro Suzuki." In *Zen in American Life and Letters*, edited by Robert S. Ellwood, 67–87. Malibu, CA: Undena, 1987.

Lau, Kimberly J. *New Age Capitalism: Making Money East of Eden*. Philadelphia: University of Pennsylvania Press, 2000.

Lawrence, Bruce B. *New Faiths, Old Fears: Muslims and Other Asian Immigrants in American Religious Life*. New York: Columbia University Press, 2002.

Lee, Robert G. *Orientals: Asian Americans in Popular Culture*. Philadelphia: Temple University Press, 1999.

Lefebure, Leo D. "200 Years in Tibet: Glimpses in Fact and Film—Spiritual Mysteries, Political Conflicts." *Christian Century* 115, no. 8 (1998): 5.

Lentz, Harris M. *Television Westerns Episode Guide*. Jefferson, NC: McFarland, 1997.

Leong, Karen J. *The China Mystique: Pearl S. Buck, Anna May Wong, Mayling Soong, and the Transformation of American Orientalism*. Berkeley: University of California Press, 2005.

Lewis, Reina. *Gendering Orientalism: Race, Femininity, and Representation, Gender, Racism, Ethnicity*. New York: Routledge, 1996.

Lipsitz, George. *The Possessive Investment in Whiteness: How White People Profit from Identity Politics*. Philadelphia: Temple University Press, 1998.

———. *Time Passages: Collective Memory and American Popular Culture*. Minneapolis: University of Minnesota Press, 1990.

Little, Douglas. *American Orientalism: The United States and the Middle East since 1945*. 3rd ed. Chapel Hill: University of North Carolina Press, 2008.

Littlewood, Ian. *The Idea of Japan: Western Images, Western Myths*. London: Secker & Warburg, 1996.

Lopez, Donald, Jr. *Prisoners of Shangri-La: Tibetan Buddhism and the West*. Chicago: University of Chicago Press, 1998.

———, ed. *Curators of the Buddha: The Study of Buddhism under Colonialism*. Chicago: University of Chicago Press, 1995.

Lowe, Donald M. *The Body in Late-Capitalist USA*. Durham, NC: Duke University Press, 1995.

Lowe, Lisa. *Critical Terrains: French and British Orientalisms*. Ithaca, NY: Cornell University Press, 1991.

———. *Immigrant Acts: On Asian American Cultural Politics*. Durham, NC: Duke University Press, 1996.

Lutz, Catherine, and Jane Lou Collins. *Reading National Geographic*. Chicago: University of Chicago Press, 1993.

Lye, Colleen. *America's Asia: Racial Form and American Literature, 1893–1945*. Princeton, NJ: Princeton University Press, 2005.

MacDonald, J. Fred. *Who Shot the Sheriff? The Rise and Fall of the Television Western*. New York: Praeger, 1987.

Maffly-Kipp, Laurie. "Engaging Habits and Besotted Idolatry: Viewing Chinese Religions in the American West." *Material Religion* 1, no. 1 (2005): 72–97.

Mahesh, Maharishi Yogi. *Love and God*. Washington, DC: Age of Enlightenment, 1973.

———. *Meditations of Maharishi Mahesh Yogi*. New York: Bantam, 1968.

———. *The Science of Being and Art of Living*. New York: New American Library, 1963.

———. *Thirty Years around the World: Dawn of the Age of Enlightenment*. Vlodrop, Limburg, Netherlands: Stichting Drukkerij en Uitgeverij MVU, 1986.

Marchetti, Gina. *Romance and the "Yellow Peril": Race, Sex, and Discursive Strategies in Hollywood Fiction*. Berkeley: University of California Press, 1993.

Marks, Laura U. *The Skin of the Film: Intercultural Cinema, Embodiment, and the Senses*. Durham, NC: Duke University Press, 2000.

Marshall, P. David. *Celebrity and Power, Fame in Contemporary Culture*. Minneapolis: University of Minnesota Press, 1997.

Marty, Martin E. *Modern American Religion*. Chicago: University of Chicago Press, 1986.

Marwick, Arthur. *The Sixties: Cultural Revolution in Britain, France, Italy, and the United States, c. 1958–1974*. Oxford: Oxford University Press, 1998.

Masatsugu, Michael K. "'Beyond This World of Transiency and Impermanence': Japanese Americans, Dharma Bums, and the Making of American Buddhism in the Early Cold War Years." *Pacific Historical Review* 77, no. 3 (2008): 423–451.

Mason, Paul. *The Maharishi*. Rockport, MA: Element, 1994.

Masuzawa, Tomoko. "From Empire to Utopia: The Effacement of Colonial Markings in Lost Horizon." *positions: east asia cultures critique* 7, no. 2 (1999): 541–572.

———. *The Invention of World Religions, or, How European Universalism Was Preserved in the Language of Pluralism*. Chicago: University of Chicago Press, 2005.

McAlister, Melani. *Epic Encounters: Culture, Media, and U.S. Interests in the Middle East since 1945*. Updated ed. Berkeley: University of California Press, 2005.

McLagan, Meg. "Spectacles of Difference: Cultural Activism and the Mass Mediation of Tibet." In *Media Worlds: Anthropology on a New Terrain*, edited by Faye D. Ginsburg, Lila Abu-Lughod, and Brian Larkin, 90–111. Berkeley: University of California Press, 2002.

Metz, Christian. *The Imaginary Signifier: Psychoanalysis and the Cinema*. Translated by Celia Britton et al. Bloomington: Indiana University Press, 1982.

Meyrowitz, Joshua. *No Sense of Place: The Impact of Electronic Media on Social Behavior*. Oxford: Oxford University Press, 1985.

Miles, Margaret Ruth. *Carnal Knowing: Female Nakedness and Religious Meaning in the Christian West*. Boston: Beacon, 1989.

———. *Image as Insight: Visual Understanding in Western Christianity and Secular Culture*. Boston: Beacon, 1985.

———. *Seeing and Believing: Religion and Values in the Movies*. Boston: Beacon, 1996.

Miller, Toby. *Global Hollywood*. London: British Film Institute, 2001.

Miller, Vincent Jude. *Consuming Religion: Christian Faith and Practice in a Consumer Culture*. New York: Continuum, 2004.

Mohanty, Chandra Talpade. "Under Western Eyes: Feminist Scholarship and Colonial Discourses." In *Third World Women and the Politics of Feminism*, edited by

Chandra Talpade Mohanty, Ann Russo, and Lourdes Torres, 51–80. Bloomington: University of Indiana Press, 1991.

Moon, Krystyn R. *Yellowface: Creating the Chinese in American Popular Music and Performance, 1850s–1920s.* New Brunswick, NJ: Rutgers University Press, 2005.

Morgan, David. *The Lure of Images: A History of Religion and Visual Media in America, Religion, Media, and Culture Series.* London: Routledge, 2007.

———. *Visual Piety: A History and Theory of Popular Religious Images.* Berkeley: University of California Press, 1998.

Mullen, Eve L. "Orientalist Commercializations: Tibetan Buddhism in American Popular Film." *Journal of Religion and Film* 2, no. 2 (1998).

Mulvey, Laura. *Visual and Other Pleasures.* Bloomington: Indiana University Press, 1981.

———. "Visual Pleasure and Narrative Cinema." *Screen* 16, no. 3 (1975): 6–18.

Naik, M. K., S. K. Desai, and S. T. Kallapur, eds. *The Image of India in Western Creative Writing.* London: Macmillan, 1971.

Nakamura, Lisa. *Cybertypes: Race, Ethnicity, and Identity on the Internet.* New York: Routledge, 2002.

———. *Digitizing Race: Visual Cultures of the Internet.* Minneapolis: University of Minnesota Press, 2008.

O'Neill, William L. *American High: The Years of Confidence, 1945–1960.* New York: Free Press, 1986.

———, ed. *American Society since 1945.* Chicago: Quadrangle, 1969.

Pack, Sam. "The Best of Both Worlds: Otherness, Appropriation, and Identity in Thunderheart." *Wicazo Sa Review* 16, no. 2 (2001): 97.

Parks, Rita. *The Western Hero in Film and Television: Mass Media Mythology.* Ann Arbor: UMI Research Press, 1982.

Pember, Don R. *Mass Media in America.* 3rd ed. Chicago: Science Research Associates, 1981.

Peter, Nithila P. "Sacred Vocabularies for World Cinema: Transfiguring Ancient Aural and Visual Modalities To Express Sacredness for the Contemporary Age." PhD diss., University of Southern California, 2007.

Peterson, Theodore. *Magazines in the Twentieth Century.* 2nd ed. Urbana: University of Illinois Press, 1964.

Pilato, Herbie J. *The Kung Fu Book of Caine.* Boston: Charles E. Tuttle, 1993.

Poster, Mark, ed. *Jean Baudrillard: Selected Writings.* Stanford, CA: Stanford University Press, 1988.

Prashad, Vijay. *The Karma of Brown Folk.* Minneapolis: University of Minnesota Press, 2000.

———. *Everybody was Kung Fu Fighting: Afro-Asian Connections and the Myth of Cultural Purity.* Boston: Beacon Press, 2001.

Prothero, Stephen R. *American Jesus: How the Son of God Became a National Icon.* New York: Farrar, Straus, and Giroux, 2003.

Pye, Michael. *Suzuki Daisetsu: Zen Fur Den Westen.* Frankfurt: Campus Verlag, 1990.

Reed, T. V. "Old Cowboys, New Indians: Hollywood Frames the American Indian." *Wicazo Sa Review* 16, no. 2 (2001): 75.

Rony, Fatimah Tobing. *The Third Eye: Race, Cinema, and Ethnographic Spectacle.* Durham, NC: Duke University Press, 1996.

Roof, Wade Clark. *A Generation of Seekers: The Spiritual Journeys of the Baby Boom Generation.* San Francisco: Harper San Francisco, 1993.

———. *Spiritual Marketplace: Baby Boomers and the Remaking of American Religion.* Princeton, NJ: Princeton University Press, 1999.

Ross, Nancy Wilson. *The World of Zen: An East-West Anthology.* New York: Random House, 1960.

Rubin, David. *After the Raj: British Novels of India since 1947.* Hanover, NH: University Press of New England, 1986.

Said, Edward. *Covering Islam: How the Media and the Experts Determine How We See the Rest of the World.* New York: Vintage, 1997.

———. *Culture and Imperialism.* New York: Vintage, 1993.

———. *Orientalism.* New York: Vintage, 1979.

———. *The World, the Text, and the Critic.* Cambridge, MA: Harvard University Press, 1983.

Saltzman, Paul. *The Beatles in Rishikesh.* New York: Viking Studio, 2000.

Sasaki, Ruth Fuller. *Zen, a Method for Religious Awakening.* Kyoto: First Zen Institute of America in Japan, 1959.

———. *Zen: A Religion.* New York: First Institute of America, 1958.

Sato, Kemmyo Taira. "D.T. Suzuki and the Question of War," trans. by Thomas Kirchner, *The Eastern Buddhist* 39, no. 1 (2008): 61–120

Schell, Orville. *Virtual Tibet: Searching for Shangri-La from the Himalayas to Hollywood.* New York: Metropolitan, 2000.

Scofield, Aislinn. "Tibet: Projections and Perceptions." *East-West Film Journal* 7, no. 1 (1993): 106.

Seager, Richard Hughes. *Buddhism in America.* New York: University of Columbia Press, 1999.

———. *The World's Parliament of Religions: The East/West Encounter, 1893.* Bloomington: Indiana University Press, 2009.

Shin, Mina. "Yellow Hollywood: Asian Martial Arts in U.S. Global Cinema." PhD diss., University of Southern California, 2008.

Shohat, Ella, and Robert Stam. *Unthinking Eurocentrism: Multiculturalism and the Media.* London: Routledge, 1994.

Simpson, Caroline Chung. *An Absent Presence: Japanese Americans in Postwar American Culture, 1945–1960, New Americanists.* Durham, NC: Duke University Press, 2001.

Skidmore, M. J. "Oriental Contributions to Western Popular Culture." *Journal of Popular Culture* 25 (1991): 129–148.

Snodgrass, Judith. *Presenting Japanese Buddhism to the West: Orientalism, Occidentalism, and the Columbian Exposition.* Chapel Hill: University of North Carolina Press, 2003.

Spigel, Lynn. *Make Room for TV: Television and the Family Ideal in Postwar America.* Chicago: University of Chicago Press, 1992.

Steet, Linda. *Veils and Daggers: A Century of National Geographic's Representation of the Arab World.* Philadelphia: Temple University Press, 2000.

Stone, Bryan P. "Religion and Violence in Popular Film." *Journal of Religion and Film* 3, no. 1 (1999), http://www.unomaha.edu/jrf/Violence.htm.

Storhoff, Gary, and John Whalen-Bridge, eds. *American Buddhism as a Way of Life*. Albany: State University of New York Press, 2010.

Suzuki, Daisetz Teitaro. *Zen and Japanese Culture*. 2nd ed. New York: Pantheon, 1959.

———. "Zen in the Modern World." *Japan Quarterly* 5, no. 4 (1958): 452–461.

Suzuki, Daisetz Teitaro, and Zenchåu Satåo. *The Training of the Zen Buddhist Monk*. New York: Cosimo Classics, 2004.

Switzer, A. Irwin, III. *D. T. Suzuki*. London: Buddhist Society, 1985.

Szalay, Michael F. "The White Oriental." *Modern Language Quarterly* 5 (2006): 363–396.

Takaki, Ronald. *Strangers from a Different Shore: A History of Asian Americans*. New York: Penguin, 1989.

Tambiah, Stanley Jeyaraj. *Magic, Science, Religion, and the Scope of Rationality*. Cambridge: Cambridge University Press, 1990.

Tchen, John Kuo Wei. "Modernizing White Patriarchy: Re-Viewing D. W. Griffith's *Broken Blossoms*." In *Moving the Image: Independent Asian Pacific American Media Arts*, edited by Russell Leong, 133–143. Los Angeles: UCLA Asian American Studies Center, 1991.

———. *New York before Chinatown: Orientalism and the Shaping of American Culture, 1776–1882*. Baltimore: Johns Hopkins University Press, 1999.

Tebbel, John William, and Mary Ellen Zuckerman. *The Magazine in America, 1741–1990*. New York: Oxford University Press, 1991.

Thompson, John B. *The Media and Modernity: A Social Theory of the Media*. Stanford, CA: Stanford University Press, 1995.

Tipton, Steven M. *Getting Saved from the Sixties*. Berkeley: University of California Press, 1976.

Tonkinson, Carole, ed. *Big Sky Mind: Buddhism and the Beat Generation*. New York: Riverhead, 1995.

Torres, Sasha. *Living Color: Race and Television in the United States, Console-Ing Passions*. Durham, NC: Duke University Press, 1998.

Trivedi, Harish. *Colonial Transactions: English Literature and India*. Manchester, England: Manchester University Press, 1995.

Turner, Bryan S. *Orientalism, Postmodernism, and Globalism*. London: Routledge, 1994.

Tweed, Thomas A. *The American Encounter with Buddhism, 1844–1912: Victorian Culture and the Limits of Dissent*. Bloomington: Indiana University Press, 1992.

Tweed, Thomas A., and Stephen Prothero, eds. *Asian Religions in America: A Documentary History*. New York: Oxford University Press, 1999.

Victoria, Brian. *Zen at War*. New York: Weatherhill, 1997.

Vining, Elizabeth Gray. *Return to Japan*. Philadelphia: Lippincott, 1960.

———. *Windows for the Crown Prince*. Philadelphia: Lippincott, 1952.

Waldman, Anne, and Laura Wright, eds. *Beats at Naropa: An Anthology*. Minneapolis, MN: Coffee House, 2009.

Watts, Alan. *In My Own Way: An Autobiography 1915–1965*. New York: Pantheon, 1972.

———. *Nature, Man, and Woman: A New Approach to Sexual Experience*. London: Thames and Hudson, 1958.

———. *Zen and the Beat Way*. Boston: Charles E. Tuttle, 1997.

Wei, William. *The Asian American Movement*. Philadelphia: Temple University Press, 1993.

West, Richard. *Television Westerns; Major and Minor Series, 1946–1978*. Jefferson, NC: McFarland, 1987.

Westgeest, Helen. *Zen in the Fifties: Interaction in Art between East and West*. Zwolle, Netherlands: Waanders Publishers, 1996.

White, Hayden. *Tropics of Discourse, Essays in Cultural Criticism*. Baltimore: Johns Hopkins University Press, 1978.

Whitfield, Stephen. *The Culture of the Cold War*. 2nd ed. Baltimore: Johns Hopkins University Press, 1996.

Williams, Patrick. "Kim and *Orientalism*." In *Colonial Discourse and Post-Colonial Theory: A Reader*, edited by Patrick Williams and Laura Chrisman, 484–485. New York: Columbia University Press, 1994.

Williams, Raymond, and Ederyn Williams. *Television: Technology and Cultural Form*. 3rd ed. London: Routledge, 2003.

Wong, Sau-ling C. "Diverted Mothering: Representations of Caregivers of Color in the Age of 'Multiculturalism.'" In *Mothering: Ideology, Experience, and Agency*, edited by Evelyn Nakano Glenn, Grace Chang, and Linda Rennie Forcie, 67–91. New York: Routledge, 1994.

———. "'Sugar Sisterhood': Situating the Amy Tan Phenomenon." In *The Ethnic Canon: Histories, Institutions, and Interventions*, edited by David Palumbo-Liu, 174–210. Minneapolis: University of Minnesota Press, 1995.

Wuthnow, Robert. *After Heaven: Spirituality in America since the 1950s*. Berkeley: University of California Press, 1998.

———. *After the Baby Boomers: How Twenty- and Thirty-Somethings Are Shaping the Future of American Religion*. Princeton, NJ: Princeton University Press, 2007.

———. *America and the Challenges of Religious Diversity*. Princeton, NJ: Princeton University Press, 2005.

———. *Experimentation in American Religion: The New Mysticisms and Their Implications for the Churches*. Berkeley: University of California Press, 1978.

———. *The Restructuring of American Religion: Society and Faith since World War II, Studies in Church and State*. Princeton, NJ: Princeton University Press, 1988.

Yoggy, Gary A. *Riding the Video Range: The Rise and Fall of the Western on Television*. Jefferson, NC: McFarland, 1995.

Yoshihara, Mari. *Embracing the East: White Women and American Orientalism*. Oxford: Oxford University Press, 2003.

A Zen Life – D.T. Suzuki. Produced by Michael Goldberg, 2006.

Index

Note: Page numbers followed by "n" indicate endnotes.

CPSIA information can be obtained at www.ICGtesting.com
Printed in the USA
BVOW010921270912

301311BV00008B/1/P

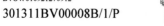

9 780199 738618